£5

THE PARSON AND JACK RUSSELL TERRIERS

JEAN AND FRANK JACKSON

POPULAR DOGS
London Sydney Auckland Johannesburg

Popular Dogs Publishing Co. Ltd

An imprint of the Random Century Group
20 Vauxhall Bridge Road, London SW1V 2SA

Random Century Australia (Pty) Ltd
20 Alfred Street, Milsons Point, Sydney, NSW 2061

Random Century New Zealand Limited
191 Archers Road, PO Box 40–086, Auckland 10

Random Century South Africa (Pty) Ltd
PO Box 337, Bergvlei 2012, South Africa

First published 1991

Photoset in Baskerville by Speedset Ltd, Ellesmere Port
Printed and bound in Great Britain by
Mackays of Chatham PLC, Chatham, Kent

A catalogue record for this book is available upon
request from the British Library

ISBN 0 09 174924 7

CONTENTS

INTRODUCTION

Over one hundred years have passed since Parson Jack Russell died. During this time the breed of terrier he developed has been joined by others which are, for all their outstanding qualities, very different from the terriers that were to be found in his kennels and the kennels of those who shared his passion for foxhunting. Jack Russell Terriers, of various types, have become very popular throughout the world. However, the absence of official recognition meant that they were denied access to the activities, services, assistance and protection that kennel clubs exist to provide. Their owners operated in a situation very different from that encountered by the owners of recognized breeds. The situation began to change at the beginning of 1990 when the Kennel Club recognized the Parson Jack Russell Terrier.

Not all the supporters of Parson and Jack Russell Terriers were, or are, convinced that official recognition would be in their or the breed's best interests. It was possible to cite a number of breeds from all over the world which, following official recognition, had lost contact with their original purpose in life. Some had been changed into what were virtually quite different breeds, incapable of carrying out the purpose for which the breed was originally developed. None of the supporters, whether pro- or anti-recognition, of Parson or Jack Russell Terriers wanted such a fate to overtake their terriers.

Recognition meant that the first steps had been taken which would enable the breed to take part in all the activities controlled by the world's official canine organizations. At the same time their traditional unofficial activities remained available. The breed's supporters had a far wider range of opportunity and service available to them than ever before. They could make use of or ignore the new opportunities according to their own preferences.

This book examines the origins and development of the terriers which carry the Parson's name. It looks at the effect the activities which gave rise to the various types have had on their development and tries to weigh how activities which recognition has made available may influence future development. The book also offers some guidance to those who may not be familiar with traditional or new activities, as well as to those who may, for the first time, have been attracted to these fine terrier breeds.

Apart from some surviving letters, extracts from diaries and contemporary references by sporting and canine authors much of what is known about Parson John Russell's life is derived from a biography, or memoir, written during the Parson's lifetime, by his friend, hunting companion and sometimes curate, the Rev. E.W.L. Davies, MA. First published in 1878, with a new edition appearing in 1883 and a further, limited edition, with somewhat imaginative illustrations by N.H.J. Baird, appearing in 1902. Davies was at Oxford in the late 1820s. He coxed the Oxford boat in the first University Boat Race in 1829 and, after coming down from university, extended his interest into water sports by hunting a pack of otterhounds from kennels at Kingsbridge in the southernmost part of Devon, earning in the process the soubriquet 'Otter' Davies. From Kingsbridge Davies went to Swimbridge as the Parson's curate before being called to better livings in Buckinghamshire and then Yorkshire. After a hunting accident, which left him confined to a wheelchair, he retired to Bath. The Parson often visited him.

The memoir has the immense advantage 'that before a line of the first edition of this Memoir was published, the proof sheets of every chapter were duly submitted to Mr. Russell himself, in order that any statement, affecting directly or indirectly the authenticity of his personal history, might be corrected, refuted, or substantiated by his own hand'. What Davies tells us is the truth, if not the whole truth. Several aspects of the Parson's life are treated with extreme discretion. Others are totally ignored and probably for good reason. Davies's choice of title appears to recognize that the biography is far from complete. This is not a book about the Parson's family life or even about his career in the church. It is the story of his exploits in the field. Unfortunately while Davies recounts a few yarns about the prowess of the Parson's terriers in the field he tells us little of the details of their life at home and nothing about their breeding. We are told nothing of the Parson's long career as a breeder of both terriers and hounds. The Parson's career as a judge, at West country agricultural shows and later at shows run under Kennel Club rules, is almost entirely ignored.

Another important source is Eleanor Kerr's excellent biography *Hunting Parson*. The book, published in 1963 and lacking the benefit of the Parson's approval, is less reliable than Davies's. It contains a number of factual errors but these should not in any way detract from the important contribution Eleanor Kerr made to our knowledge of the Parson.

We do not subscribe to Henry Ford's view of history. History is certainly not 'bunk'. History is of interest in its own right. In the context of dogs it also enables us to see how a breed arrived at its present situation and to assess this position against a valid measure. If we knew nothing of what the Parson's terriers were used for, how they were used, the characteristics he and his successors regarded as important, how could we possibly assess the terriers which today carry his name? We need to learn all we can, not only about the Parson's own terriers but about how they fitted into the contemporary scene. Equally we need to know about the developments which have taken place since the Parson's death over a hundred years ago if we are to fully understand and appreciate the breeds which nowadays carry his name.

Jean and Frank Jackson
Ashworth Moor
Lancashire

1
Origins

Although the desire is great in many dog owners to discover or even to invent an ancient lineage for their breed, even the most enthusiastic supporter of terriers would be hard pressed to find, on Stone Age cave paintings, Egyptian tombs or ancient Greek manuscripts, evidence of their existence. Unfortunately for such people the best evidence for the ancient lineage of terriers is circumstantial, problematical and imaginative.

It has been pointed out that there would have been little point in Noah saving foxes from the Flood if he had not also saved foxhounds and terriers. Those who have no enthusiasm for foxhunting would dispute this suggestion, perhaps, but it does, however, serve to introduce the fact that the history of terriers, their origins, their size and shape, even their temperaments, are inextricably bound up with hunting and, in particular, with foxhunting. Shem and Ham may have acted as whips for Noah, MFH, with Jepheth acting as his terrierman, but there is no evidence for it and it does not help in the search for real evidence for the early existence of terriers.

All that can be said on this subject is that it is probable that ever since the unique relationship between human and dog was first established man has been using small dogs to drive animals out of places in which they have taken refuge. Initially man's only interest would be in animals which he could use as food. Because of the difficulty in retrieving them, he would probably have had little interest in animals which sought refuge below ground. Only animals which lived above ground would be of interest. (Man did not arrive at his present peculiar level of sophistication, in which he regards going out in the winter weather to dig holes in the ground as fun, until fairly recent times.) Once these had been driven into the open by small, tough dogs they could be taken by larger, faster dogs or brought down by well-directed arrows or stones. Nets were eventually added to the equipment used by hunters. Finally, firearms came into use.

It can reasonably be surmised that from earliest times dogs were used to disturb and frighten the quarry so that it would leave its secure place in dense cover. Moreover it is likely that these dogs would be small, courageous enough to get into and out of restricted spaces and willing to do so. They would probably have harsh coats and thick skins to offer some protection against rough use. It is not likely that they were white. There is little to suggest what these dogs may have looked like until *De Venatione* was published in about A.D. 207. *De Venatione* was written by Oppianos of Apamea – Oppian – and describes a small breed of sporting dog then to be found in Britain. A translation was made by John Whitaker and appears in his *The History of Manchester*, published in 1771.

> A small bold breed and steady to the game,
> Next claims the tribute of peculiar fame!
> Trained by the tribes on Britain's wildest shore,
> Thence they their title of Agasses bore.
>
> Small as the race that useless to their lord,
> Bask on the hearth and beg about the board,
> Work-limbed and black-eyed, all their fame appears,
> Flanked with no flesh and bristled rough with hairs:
>
> But shod each foot with hardest claws is seen,
> The sole's kind armour on the beaten green:
> But fenced each jaw with closest teeth is found,
> And death sits instant on th' inflicted wound.
>
> Far o'er the rest he quests the secret prey,
> And sees each track wind opening to his say:
> Far o'er the rest he feels each scent that flows,
> Count the live nerve and thrill along the nose.

Here, surely, is perhaps the earliest description of terriers. Small, strong, tough, black-eyed, rough-coated, crook-limbed and lean-bodied dogs with good noses used to find 'the secret prey' and with strong jaws to drive it into the open. Oppian called them *agasses*. The word is suggestive of a dog which was regarded as a lowly servant. Much the same word, *agaso*, was used by Livius Patavinus to describe a donkey boy. Horatius Flaccus used it to refer to an awkward servant. Whatever sort of dog agasses were they had certainly not ascended far up the canine social scale.

Oppian fails to provide anything more positive than a vague reference to 'secret prey' to suggest what quarry agasses were intended to hunt, but it is likely that it was only well after when the badger, fox and otter came to be regarded as quarry that these small dogs were expected to work regularly below ground. By then a long process of selection based on functional demands would have meant that the basic type was well established. There is no indication that badger, foxes or otters were regularly hunted when Oppian was writing. Foxes, in particular, then and for long afterwards, were regarded as cowardly beasts unworthy of the attention of hounds or huntsmen. They were of interest as a quarry only because they provided the fur used to enrich gentlemen's clothing. Thus foxes were first hunted not for food or even for sport but in the name of high fashion. It is probably not without significance that in 1299 King Edward I's 'huntsman to the king's foxhounds', one William d'Blathwyck, was paid by the comptroller of the wardrobe.

It is not until the middle of the fourteenth century that there is any reliable indication that dogs were regularly used to drive animals from underground places of refuge. That this coincides with the earliest use of the word 'terrier' may not be of great significance.

> Le va querir dedans terre
> Avec ses bons chiens terriers
> Que on met dedans les terriers.

This reference occurs in Gace de la Vigne's *Poeme sur la Chasse*, first published in 1359. During the next two centuries other references to terriers do no more than confirm their existence. They reveal nothing about the dogs themselves and little about the uses to which they were put. Caxton's invention of the printing press at the end of the fifteenth century increased the publication of books. By the middle of the sixteenth century these included a number which dealt in detail with dogs and

hunting. Some of them provide information about early terriers.
As late as 1607 Topsell still did not differentiate between
'terriars' and beagles. Both he and other writers, relying
heavily on the same French originals, were happy to translate
'bassett' as either beagle or terrier. Bassett refers specifically to
a short-legged dog. The word contains no reference to or even
implication of underground employment such as is often
associated with the word 'terrier' and in which the word's
origins are usually sought.

It should not be assumed that because the word 'terrier'
seems to have first appeared in a French document that we
must look for the origins of terriers in France. French, as Latin
had previously been, was the language of literature. The
language of the common people of Britain seldom appeared in
print, and certainly not in treatises which dealt with aristocratic sports and pastimes. The forerunners of our modern
terriers may have been popularly referred to by some name
which never appeared in print and is now lost.

We might regard the early years of the fifteenth century as
the time when terriers, used to drive animals out of underground retreats, made their début. From the beginning of the
century there are an increasing number of references to terriers
which not only tell us how these dogs were used and much of
what they looked like but also give detailed advice about their
training. Terriers had well and truly arrived on the scene.

In 1409, for example, the oldest book in English devoted
entirely to sport, written by Edward, Duke of York, grandson of
Edward III, provides a list of breeds – alaunts, butcher hounds,
greyhounds, harriers, limers, mastiffs, raches, setters, spaniels,
terriers, teazers and kenettes – and gives advice on the
treatment of sick dogs, on the character of hounds and on
kennel management. Dame Juliana Berners, in 1486, refers to
'terroures' and in 1570 Bishop Still wrote a prayer in which he
asked that 'God send terroures so bold, so bold, heart will
harbour no care.'

Pride of place was then taken by Abraham Fleming's
imaginative translation of Johannes Caius's original, which he
published in 1576 under the title *Of Englishe Dogges*. Fleming
divides the various breeds of what he regards as English dogs
into various categories and it is interesting that terriers are

placed in the same category as a motley collection of hounds, including harriers, bloodhounds, gasehounds, greyhounds, lyemmers, tumblers and stealers and not with the breeds used for fowling. As Fleming explains, 'We Englishe men make a difference betweene hunting and fowleing, for that they are called by these seuerall wordes, *Venatio & Aucupium*, so they tearme the Dogges whom they vse in these sundry games by diuers names, as those which seue for the best, are called *Venatici*, the other which are vsed for the fowl are called *Aucupatorij*.' Fleming makes it apparent that terriers were by now exclusively used to hunt fur and not feather.

In spite of this development of specialist uses for different breeds the hounds used to hunt fox remained relatively unspecialized.

Of the Dogge called a Harrier, in Latine *Leverarius*.

That kinde of dogge whom nature hath indued with the vertue of smeeling, whose property it is to vse a lustines, a readines, and a courageousnes in hunting, and draweth into his nostrells the ayre or sent of the beast pursued and followed, we call by this word *Sagax* . . . This sort of Dogges we call *Levararios* Hariers, that I may comprise the whole number of them in certaine specialities, and apply to them their proper and peculier names, for so much as they cannot all be reduced and brought vnder one sorte, considereing both the sundrye uses of them, and difference of their seruice whereto they be appointed.

	The Hare	
	The Foxe	
	The Wolfe	
	The Harte	
	The Bucke	
Some for	The Badger	Some for one thing and
	The Otter	some for another.
	The Polcat	
	The Lobster	
	The Weasell	
	The Conny, & c.	

As for the Conny, whom we haue lastly set downe, wee use
not to hunt, but rather to take it, somtime with the nette
sometime with the ferret, and thus euery seuerall sort is
notable and excellent in his naturall qualities and appointed
practice. Among these sundry sortes, there be some which
are apt to hunt two diuers beastes, as the Foxe otherwhiles,
and the other whiles the Hare, but they hunt not with such
towardnes and good lucke after them, as they doe that
whereunto nature hath formed and framed them, not onely
in externall composition & making, but also inward faculties
and conditions, for they swarue sometimes, and doo otherwise then they should.

Of the Dogge called Terrar, in
Latine *Terrarius*.

Another sorte there is which hunteth the Foxe and the
Badger or Greye onely, whom we call Terrars, because they
(after the manner and custome of ferrets in searching for
Connyes) creepe into the grounde, and by that meanes make
afrayde, nyppe, and byte the Foxe and the Badger in such
sort, that eyther they teare them in pieces with theyr teeth
beyng in the bosome of the earth, or else hayle and pull them
perforce out of their lurking angles, darke dongeons, and
close caues, or at least through coceued feare, driue them out
of their hollow harbours, in so much that they are compeled
to prepare speedy flight, and being desirous of the next
(albeit not the safest) refuge, are otherwise taken and
intrapped with snares and nettes layde ouer holes to the
same purpose. But these be the least in that kynde called
Sagax.

Sagax is simply a reference to dogs which have keen senses
and includes, in Fleming's terms, both hounds and terriers but
not, surprisingly perhaps, other sporting breeds which 'findeth
game on the land' or 'findeth game on the water' and 'serve the
Hauke . . . the net, or, traine'.

Fleming makes it clear that gasehounds were also used to
hunt both fox and hare but since the relationship between
harriers and terriers is precisely the same as that between
foxhounds and terriers this might repay closer study.

Up to and beyond the sixteenth century the word 'harrier' was in general use to describe any pack hound used for harrying or driving its quarry. Only in later years did the word come to refer specifically to pack hounds used principally, though even today not exclusively, for hunting the hare before mounted followers. Even so Fleming's associated use of the word *Levararius* as well as the place which the hare occupies in the list of quarry suggests that harriers were principally used to hunt hare though the fox, still despised by many hunters, was elevated to the second place in Fleming's list. Of course, no hound could possibly be expected to hunt such a diverse list of quarry and this Fleming recognizes when he mentions the likelihood of riot when too much is expected of them.

The list of quarry offers a number of puzzles. Why, for example, should the wolf be in third place when wolves, according to some authorities, were already extinct in England? (In fact they survived in Ireland and Scotland until the early 1700s.) After the wolf comes the hart or fallow deer, then the buck or roe deer but, surprisingly, there is no mention of the red deer. Then come various members of the Musselidae family with only the pine marten, the despised foulmart, being omitted.

But how can the appearance, amid the various Musselidae, of lobsters be explained? The 1788 *East Yorkshire Glossary* offers 'clubstart' or 'clubster' as local names for the stoat, and the *English Dialect Dictionary* offers 'lobstert' as an East Anglian word for stoat. Colonel George Hanger's *To All Sportsmen* adds further information. 'There is an animal, which in Norfolk and Suffolk, is called a lobster: I know not why, for he is certainly of the same species as the weazle and stoat, but much larger: no vermin which run are so fatally destructive to all game as these animals; they will absolutely hunt a hare down which is above half grown.' Perhaps the name was applied to these animals, as it was to soldiers, because of their red coats.

Interestingly, Fleming does not expect terriers to tackle such a varied list of quarry. He made it clear that their business is confined exclusively to fox and badger. The point remains significant.

Fifteen years later, in 1591, Sir Thomas Cockaine's *A Short Treatise on Hunting – Compiled for the Delight of Noblemen and*

Gentlemen, offered advice about training terriers while the same author's *Sir Tristram's Measures of Blowing* tells us how the terrierman should be summoned.

Where the Foxe is earthed, blowe for the Terriars after this manner. One long and two short, the second winde one long, and two short. Note this, for it is the chieftest and principalest poynt to be noted. Every long conteineth in blowing seaven quavers, one minome and one quatter.

In 1600 Nicholas Cox described two sorts of terriers which go to ground and in 1718, in his *Compleate Sportsman* described both their appearance and their colour. In 1760 Daniel's *Rural Sports* also dealt with colour. The descriptions continue through Thomas Bewick's *History of Quadrupeds* of 1790 which also has a good illustration of a typical terrier of the period.

As a consequence of all this published material a lot is known about the terriers to be found in Britain at the end of the eighteenth century. At least two types existed, one with long legs, one with short. Some had rough coats, some smooth but, as yet, there is no mention of predominantly white terriers.

All the terriers which now exist throughout the world and which are used for work underground have their origins in Britain or were developed from breeds which came from Britain. The reason is simple and straightforward. They were developed in order to facilitate foxhunting and only in Britain was foxhunting a popular sport.

Only when foxhunting had become a fashionable pastime in which people with more enthusiasm than knowledge or discretion became involved did the appearance of terriers, and particularly their colour, begin to be important.

Masters who saw themselves as leaders of fashion and arbiters of taste discarded their traditional green and grey uniforms in favour of brightly coloured hunt uniforms. The fashionable foxhunter wore a scarlet or orange jacket trimmed with gold buttons and embodying all the currently fashionable details. The development was one which their more conservative colleagues must have regarded with alarm and even distaste. It was, and remains, a development which was confined to the more fashion conscious hunt countries. The more traditional countries still prefer green or grey uniforms.

Most of these are in countries which remained true to the old coloured terrier breeds. John Peel's coat was grey not gay!

Colonel Thomas Thornton, an unlikable and highly competitive Yorkshireman with a passion for all forms of field sports and much given to ostentatious displays of his great wealth, went even further. He mounted himself and his hunt servants on horses of matching colour. He even went so far as to breed terriers which matched the colours of his predominantly white hounds. He may not have been the first to do so and he was certainly not the last.

White or predominantly white terriers were a product of fashion. They first appeared in the most fashion-conscious countries whose Masters of Hounds were anxious that their establishments should present a harmonious and pleasing picture. They bred terriers which were the same colour as their hounds. Only subsequently did they feel the need to try to justify this on functional grounds.

In his classic *Thoughts on Hunting* published in 1781, Peter Beckford advises his readers that 'your country requires a good terrier. I should prefer the black or white terrier; some there are so like a fox, that awkward people frequently mistake one for the other.' Beckford does not refer to a black *and* white terrier. He writes of black *or* white terriers. He was saying that the old English terrier, which somehow turned into the Welsh terrier but which nowadays probably survives in its purest form in the Fell terrier, had its equal in the newly-fashionable white terriers. He was saying that the red and tan terriers which were used by the packs which hunted in and around his Morpeth constituency had disadvantages when they were used in the more fashionable hunting countries in the Shires. There 'awkward people', attracted to the fashionable sport of foxhunting but having little knowledge of what was involved, might, in their enthusiasm, mistake a coloured terrier for the fox. He was not saying, as is sometimes said today, that hounds might mistake other than a black or white terrier for a fox. Hounds know better. If hounds were not better able than awkward people to discriminate between one and the other foxhunting would not be possible.

By 1781 white terriers were available for work with foxhounds. Colonel Thornton had a terrier called Pitch which

appears in an engraving by Scott published in 1790. Pitch was a
racy creature, more hound than terrier. In 1796 John Sartor-
ious painted Viper, another white terrier. Sydenham
Edwards's 1800 *Cynographia Britannica* contained a picture
showing four terriers, one of which was predominantly white,
and in 1803 Reinagle engraved three terriers, two of which were
largely white. We can safely say, therefore, that by the end of
the eighteenth century, white terriers had arrived on the scene.

These four pictures provide some idea of what the white
terriers of two hundred years ago were like. Pitch, Viper and
Reinagle's terriers were on the leg, with fashionably cropped
ears, Viper and Reinagle terriers seem also to be docked.
Viper and Pitch were smooth coated, Reinagle's two white
terriers both had rough coats. Viper was quite heavily marked
but the other three had colour confined to head and the root of
the tail.

It is difficult to find anything good to say of Edwards's
terrier. It has a long head, cropped ears, long stern curled over
its rough-coated, heavily marked back, a wide front and short,
heavily boned bow legs. It is not a terrier which could be
expected to run with hounds or even work a narrow fox earth. It
might have been of use working badger, particularly if the
badger had been conveniently placed in a capacious barrel.

In spite of the growing literature about foxhunting relatively
few books exclusively devoted to hounds were published before
the middle of the nineteenth century. Of these only a handful
had anything of significance to say about terriers. From the
middle of the century the number of books which dealt
exclusively with canine matters began to increase at an
accelerating rate, which seems not yet to have abated, but
terriers continued to be largely ignored.

William Youatt's *The Dog*, first published in 1845, had much
to say about gundogs and foxhounds but all it had to say about
terriers was confined to a few paragraphs sandwiched between
descriptions of Iceland and shock dogs. The terrier was said to
be

> usually a deep-black colour ... an exceedingly useful
> animal; but not so indispensible an accompaniment to a
> pack of fox-hounds as it used to be accounted. Foxes are not

so often unearthed as they formerly were, yet many a day's sport would be lost without a terrier. Some sportsmen used to have two terriers accompanying in the pack, one being smaller than the other. This was a very proper provision; a large terrier might be incapable of penetrating into the earth, and a small one might permit the escape of the prey.

Youatt was, like others who wrote about terriers at the time, looking back on a former period of popularity which had disappeared because of the changing pattern of foxhunting. The principal enjoyment which foxhunting offered no longer stemmed from the appreciation of the way in which hounds patiently unravelled the puzzle set by their quarry. Foxhunting had become an excuse for a breakneck mounted charge across country. Waiting for terriers to move a fox was anathema to followers mounted on highly charged blood horses whose principal interest was in displaying their courage by refusing to deviate from a straight line across country no matter what obstacles they might encounter.

The way in which terrier popularity was restored during the next few years is perhaps best illustrated by the various editions of 'Stonehenge's' book *The Dog in Health and Disease*. Stonehenge was the pseudonym of John Walsh, editor of *The Field*. He was a prolific writer on canine and sporting matters. He was one of the judges at the 1859 show in Newcastle, which is often, though erroneously, regarded as the first dog show. *The Dog in Health and Disease* first appeared in 1859, went into a second edition in 1872, a third in 1879 and a fourth in 1887. Its popularity reflected the growing interest in dogs. The attention which each edition devoted to terriers traced the development of renewed interest in them.

In the first, 1859, edition there is, within the chapter on crossed breeds, an engraving of a fox-terrier. It is a prick or crop-eared, foxy headed, smooth-coated dog, with colour apparently confined to a patch on the head and over one ear. The engraving is supported by a single dismissive sentence which refers to 'the field fox-terrier, used for bolting the fox when gone to ground'. Stonehenge's use of the past tense is significant. Earlier in the book he had explained that 'terriers are now usually divided into four kinds: – 1st, The old English terrier; 2nd, The Scotch (including the Dandie Dinmont); 3rd, The Skye; and 4th, The modern toy dog.' There was no mention of fox terriers, still less of any white fox terriers. He explained that

> formerly it was the custom to add a couple of terriers to every pack of foxhounds, so as to be ready to aid in bolting the fox when he runs into a drain, or goes to ground in any easily accessible earth; the stoutness of the terrier enabling him, by steadily following on the track, to reach the scene of operations before it would be possible to obtain any other assistance. This aid, however, in consequence of the increased speed of our hounds, is now dispensed with, and the old fox-terrier is out of date, or is only kept for the purpose of destroying ground vermin.

By the time the second edition of Stonehenge's book came along his classification of terriers contained eight kinds. The old English terrier, The Scotch, The Dandie Dinmont, The Skye, The Fox Terrier, The Bedlington, The Halifax Blue Tan and The Modern Toy Terrier of various kinds. The text still referred to fox-terriers in the past tense but they had now been given a division of their own. There was also a new paragraph which repeated the reason for their loss of popularity and explained that 'in proportion as he ceased to be used in the hunting-field, he has attained popularity as the most fashionable companion for young men, and of late years the classes of fox terriers at our dog shows have been the most numerous and generally interesting'. Stonehenge was giving credit to dog shows for the revived interest in fox terriers. An engraving shows a smooth-coated terrier with colour confined to the head, now with uncropped drop ears.

The fourth edition provides evidence of further increased interest in terriers generally. Instead of a few paragraphs there is a substantial chapter in which the Fox-Terrier (Rough and Smooth) is given pride of place followed by the Hard-haired Scotch Terrier, the Irish Terrier, the Welsh Terrier, the Skye Terrier, the Dandie Dinmont, the Black and Tan or Manchester Terrier, the White English Terrier, the Bedlington Terrier, the Halifax, Blue Fawn, or Yorkshire Terrier and the Airedale Terrier. The order in which Stonehenge presented the terrier breeds and the attention he devoted to them reflected their popularity at the time. It is apparent that, by 1887, fox-terriers were very much back in the present tense.

It was largely the smooth variety which was responsible for this resurgence. The rough fox-terrier was only just beginning to gain popularity as a show dog but already the leading breeders were recognized by Stonehenge. 'The Rev. John Russell in the West of England was long famous for his strain of rough terriers, so closely resembling the modern dogs exhibited by Mr Sanderson, Mr Carrick, and Mr Lyndsay Hogg as to be inseparable by any ordinary test.'

Gordon Sanderson's were at Cottingham, near Hull. He was the owner of Venture, Lindsay, or Lyndsay. Hogg's kennels were in Middlesex. He owned Topper. William Carrick, whose kennels were in Carlisle, was the owner of Carlisle Tack, bred out of a Parson Jack Russell bitch, and Carlisle Tyro.

Stonehenge's statement is important because it shows that the Parson, who had died in 1883, was recognized as having a distinct strain of terriers. It also shows that terriers 'inseparable by any ordinary test' from his strain were to be found in a number of other kennels. We have pictures of some of these terriers. Some were bred from the Parson's own blood-lines. There is ample evidence, which cannot reasonably be refuted, of precisely the type of terrier which the Parson had developed during his extraordinary long career as a breeder. Those who nowadays attempt to preserve the type are not without exemplars.

2

School and Student Days

Parson John Russell, throughout his life, was known to his friends, from the Prince of Wales downwards, as Jack Russell. He was born in 1795 and died in 1884.

He was born during the reign of George III when William Pitt was Prime Minister. He was ordained a year before George IV came to the throne. His first son was born in the year in which William IV came to the throne and he died towards the end of Queen Victoria's reign. His life spanned the years of the Industrial Revolution. He saw a remarkable transition in public and official attitudes towards animals. He was forty years old before bull and bear baiting, as well as dog fighting, were made illegal, though only then in the face of opposition from both state and church. Less than fifty years later dog shows had taken the place of these brutal old pastimes. The Parson played his part in their burgeoning popularity.

Marie Antoinette had gone to the guillotine a year before his birth and England was living in fear that the revolution which then raged in France would cross the Channel. The slave trade was abolished when he was twelve years old, though he was nearly forty before slavery itself was abolished. In 1838 Isambard Kingdom Brunel's *Great Western* made the first steam-powered Transatlantic crossing. He probably attended the Great Exhibition in 1851 and marvelled at the Crystal Palace and the exhibits it contained. He saw the publication of Charles Darwin's *On the Origin of Species by Means of Natural Selection* in 1859.

The Parson lived through several wars, but was not called upon to take an active part in any. The Napoleonic Wars, the American Civil War, the Crimean War, the Zulu War all occurred during his lifetime. When he died William Gladstone was Prime Minister and Britain was fighting the Boer War.

Most of these major international events probably had little or no effect on the Parson's life. It was touched more strongly by some of the legendary figures of foxhunting who were his contemporaries. He knew Hugo Meynell, John Warde, Squire Osbaldeston, Dick Christian, Will Long and many others whose names are part of foxhunting history. The Parson lived through what many regard as the greatest days of foxhunting.

When he was born the horse was the most rapid means of transport. When he died the railway system was even more extensive than it is today. Man had already begun to flirt with flight, albeit only in balloons. The development of the railway system revolutionized foxhunting. It made it possible to breakfast in London, spend a day hunting in the shires and return to London to dine. Railways also made it possible for dog shows, which hitherto had been entirely local events, to attract support from all over the country. They extended the geographical boundaries of social contact. The Parson made full use of railways to hunt, to attend dog shows and to enjoy an extensive social life.

It is impossible to discuss the origins of any terrier which carries Parson Jack Russell's name without also giving some consideration to the Parson himself. His terriers were bred to satisfy his tastes and fulfil his needs. By understanding more about the man we will be better able to understand his terriers.

John Russell was born into a family which had been established in Devon since the middle of the sixteenth century. Perhaps even long enough for native Devonians to regard it as a Devon family. In 1549 Lord John Russell was sent to Devon by the nine-year-old King Edward VI's Protector of the Realm, Admiral Lord Seymour, to quell the riots which had followed the introduction of the new Prayer Book in what was still a staunchly Roman Catholic county. Russell carried out his task with brutal efficiency. Throughout the summer of 1549 the West was in flames. Pomeroy and Arundel, under Russell, led 10,000 men, including a body of German mercenaries, to besiege Exeter and fight battles at St Mary Clyst and Sampford Courtney. Thousands lost their lives and the leaders of the insurrection were taken to be hanged at Tyburn. Order was painfully restored and to ensure that the new Prayer Book received proper respect from Devon churchgoers Russell established various members of his family in the county to act as his representatives. Parson Jack Russell's family cannot be said to have had an auspicious start in their new county.

The Russell family's early antipathy to Rome was not shared by the Parson. He was quite prepared to take people as he found them whatever their creed. Though his reluctance to wear ornate, decorated religious vestments, which, he said, might cause his parishioners to drive him from his church, could be regarded as a relic of his family's earlier priorities.

Jack Russell's grandfather, Michael, was born in 1718 in Bideford. He was educated at Oxford and married Grace Allen, a well-connected widow. Their son, John, born in 1760, was also educated at Oxford. He subsequently married Miss Honor Terell. Though by now well respected throughout the West country the family was not a wealthy one. John's father was the Rector of Iddesleigh in North Devon. He was a fine classical scholar, an impressive preacher, a dedicated sportsman and an independent spirit, the last three qualities, but not the first, being inherited by his eldest son. The cost of raising a family and keeping a small pack of hounds meant that he had to supplement his meagre stipend by running a small school. This was accommodated in his home at Belmont House, Dartmouth, where he not only instructed his pupils 'in the rudiments of Greek and Latin, but in those of the "noble science"'. A former pupil recalled that 'he was one of the best classics, one of the best preachers and readers, and by far the boldest hunter in the county of Devon. Not unfrequently, too, have I seen the fine old fellow's top-boots peeping out from under his cassock.'

John senior was a kindly man who encouraged his pupils to work instead of, as was the usual custom, trying to beat knowledge into them. Hard working pupils were rewarded by being given access to a pony on which they could hunt.

Jack Russell was one of four children. Nora, the eldest was born in 1793, Jack in 1795 and two younger brothers, Michael and William, followed. Nora and Jack were born at Belmont House. The youngest children were born at Southhill Rectory near Callington in Cornwall where the family had moved when Jack was fourteen months old.

The Southhill Rectory was known locally as 'the big house'. It was an imposing Georgian mansion set in extensive parkland, with well-stocked fish ponds and walled gardens, and was approached along a wooded drive. The big house was looked up to by the local community and its incumbent was the man to whom they turned for advice on matters temporal as well as spiritual.

The move to Southhill, or rather the loss of the income from the school, meant that the hounds could no longer be kept but it did not mean that hunting was also impossible. Jack's father continued to hunt as often as he could. Young Jack cannot have failed to have been influenced by his father's pastoral duties. Nor could he have been immune to the delight his father took in hunting. Jack Russell was as much reared to be the sportsman. he eventually became as he was to follow his father's footsteps into the church.

Jack Russell became a pupil at Plympton Grammar School, an old-established school with a fine tradition of scholarship. It was here he met John Crocker Bulteel, son of another old established Devonshire family. The two became lifelong friends but their friendship did not begin at school. The Rev. E.W.L. Davies depicts young Bulteel in his memoir as a bully and Jack Russell as a doughty fighter against injustice. He is represented as waging valiant battles on behalf of younger and weaker pupils. In fact, as his subsequent career shows, Jack Russell rather enjoyed a good fight. He was confident of his ability to come out on top in most battles and seems, even after his ordination, never to have gone out of his way to avoid a fight. Jack Russell was headstrong and given to outbursts which he would later regret. His schoolboy battle with Bulteel began with Russell's pointless destruction of one of Bulteel's books. Bulteel was provoked into a fight from which, according to Davies's uncritical account, Russell, the younger boy, emerged as victor thereby ending Bulteel's career as a bully. From alleged school bully John Bulteel rose to become Master of the Dartmoor from 1827 to 1843.

Russell stayed at Plympton Grammar School until, early in 1809, he was sent to Blundell's, a minor West country public school, in Tiverton. Here he would need and would develop the physical toughness which was to become one of his outstanding characteristics. The headmaster, the Reverend William Richards, imposed a regime on his pupils which was harsh to the point of sadism. He beat them mercilessly and indiscriminately. When his cane was not at hand he used his fists. Jack Russell later claimed that Richards punched harder than many of the skilled boxers he had faced. Food was sparse and often of a quality which would be inedible except to a half-starved growing boy. Unheated buildings were dilapidated. Boys slept, two to a bed, in damp dormitories. They washed under an outdoor pump. Taking their lead from their headmaster older boys bullied younger ones without mercy. Ritual tortures were commonplace. They were only modified after a boy, who had been 'roasted', died from his burns.

Again Davies offers an example of the way in which Russell got the better of a school bully. Again the facts invite an interpretation which differs from that put forward by the Parson's loyal friend. After the headmaster had banned pets from school premises Russell discovered that Hunter, a monitor, and according to Davies a particularly obnoxious school bully, kept exotic and valuable rabbits. These could not immediately be returned to the boy's home. He had failed to comply with the headmaster's edict. Russell, too, had defied the edict. He still had his ferrets. He chose to dispose of them by introducing them to the bully's defenceless, captive rabbits with inevitable, gory results. Hunter did not respond as Bulteel had done but reported the matter to the headmaster.

'Now, sir, what right have you to kill Hunter's rabbits, and what reason can you give for committing so gross an outrage on your schoolfellow's property?'

'It was your own order, sir, that all the rabbits should be killed; and as Hunter did not seem inclined to kill his, I did it for him.'

The feeble defence failed to placate the headmaster. Russell was flogged unmercifully for an inexcusable action which Davies sought to present as a legitimate and effective way of attacking a school bully.

Not long afterwards Jack Russell and Robert Bovey, with the co-operation of local farmers, acquired four and a half couple of hounds. They were kennelled by a Tiverton blacksmith. The youthful joint masters provided good sport until, through an anonymous informer, the headmaster learned of their extramural activities. Robert Bovey admitted the offence and was expelled forthwith. He took the hounds to his home at Peartree. This enabled Russell to claim that he did not keep hounds and so escape being expelled with his friend.

Russell left Blundell's with a medal for elocution and a scholarship for £30 tenable for four years. He spent the first instalment of his scholarship buying a horse from the Reverend John Froude of Knowstone. If Russell was aware that Froude was the horse's owner he was either acting out of sheer bravado or had already developed an admiration for this notorious character. The horse was offered for sale at Tiverton Fair by a dealer called Rookes. It was said to be a five-year-old brown mare. It was well-boned, with a lean and honest head and moved well. Russell bought her 'after a few words' for £30, and was comprehensively swindled, as was inevitable for anyone who had dealings with Froude. The mare turned out to be only two years old and nowhere near old enough to be hunted. This did not deter Russell. He appears to have had no compunction in giving her a gruelling day out with the Devon and Somerset Staghounds. The master at the time was Lord Fortescue but the pack was often hunted by Stucley Lucas, who became Master in 1818 until 1824. Lucas was riding a high-spirited thoroughbred called Erebus. Russell's intense excitement was doubtless transmitted to his inexperienced two-year-old. Russell failed to keep his mount away from Erebus who lashed out and unseated the young rider.

In spite of this early mishap the young mare carried her youthful rider through a long and demanding day. She grew to become an excellent mount but we must assume that wiser heads than young Jack's ensured that for some time she was protected from any further tests. Certainly Jack appears to have been without his own horse while he was at Oxford. He had to rely on livery animals when he went hunting.

Having completed his studies at Blundell's with some distinction Russell went up to Exeter College, Oxford, as a commoner. 'In 1814, when he had just completed his nineteenth year, he was admitted as a commoner at Exeter College.'

Davies's simple and unequivocal statement does much to refute a number of stories which have since been widely circulated and almost as widely accepted. Jack Russell became a student at Oxford University at the beginning of the Hilary term. This was towards the end of January, about a month after his nineteenth birthday. In order to attain a degree it was necessary for a student to be in residence for a minimum number of terms. Davies records that he had completed fourteen terms in residence by May 1819. Had he been in continuous residence he would, by that time, have completed sixteen terms. Typically Davies offers no explanation for the discrepancy; nor does he explain why it was necessary for Jack Russell to remain at Exeter College beyond the tenure of his scholarship.

Students, then as now, enjoyed food and drink. Jack Russell certainly enjoyed his food. His large frame and boundless energy were sustained by a healthy appetite but he was not a man who loved food for its own sake. Drink held little interest for him, though in later life he developed a liking for strong port. This lack of interest did not stem from any religious puritanism. It was simply the product of a desire not to spoil the following day's hunting by rising with a headache.

Eating and drinking apart the principal student recreations were, in descending order of cost, coaching, steeplechasing, hunting, shooting, cock-fighting and boxing. Coaching was well beyond Russell's means. Steeplechasing would reach its early peak of popularity about ten years later. In any case Jack Russell was probably too big to become a successful steeplechase jockey even if he could have afforded the necessary quality horses. Shooting and cock-fighting were considered unseemly for anyone intended for a career in the church. He was left with hunting, which stretched his means uncomfortably but for which he had already developed a strong liking, and with boxing. Boxing was not a costly sport. It was one for which his physique and natural aggression were ideally suited.

At the end of Russell's second term at Oxford he was joined at Exeter by a gentleman-commoner from Kent, Denne of Lydd, who had a particular interest in pugilism. Denne had been at Eton where he had been a contemporary of Arthur Harris, a West country man whom Russell probably already knew and with whom he would establish a close friendship in

later life. Sir Harry Goodricke, whose exploits in the shires
would later earn him the title of the 'King of Melton', was also
at Eton at the same time. Denne introduced Jack Russell to
Professor Rowlands, a retired pugilist of no particular accomp-
lishment, who had learned his trade at the school run by Jack
Broughton and the Duke of Cumberland, 'Butcher' Cumberland of Culloden. Oxford was as well-positioned to indulge an
interest in pugilism as it was for hunting. Moulsey Hurst,
nearby Coombe Wood and Coombe Warren were then
becoming important centres for pugilism. All were accessible
from Oxford and were patronized by the students. They were
there in force when Bill Nosworthy beat Dutch Sam, when
Nosworthy was beaten by Jack Scroggins and they saw Tom
Spring's accession to the throne when he beat Ned Painter.
Spring was the same age as Russell and a fellow West
country man. Russell, however, was not among the spectators
who saw him become champion.

'If I do get on a horse, it shall be to see a hound with his
natural enemy, a fox, before him – a cross-country fight, not
one in the ring.'

There would have been nothing at all incongruous in
Russell's interest in pugilism, though prize fights were illegal.
At that time prize fighting enjoyed aristocratic patronage and
appears to have been regarded as complementary to an interest
in hunting. Dick Christian, the Meynell's legendary huntsman,
who had the temerity to describe Hugo Meynell as 'a regular
little dumpling on horseback', was present at the second Cribb
and Molyneux fight. He recalled that 'all the magistrates in the
county of Rutland were there. It was the Saturday magistrates'
meeting at Oakham, and they all came off to the fight when
they'd done – the whole kit on 'em.' Christian had ridden
Clinker in an epic match for 1500 guineas a side against Squire
Osbaldeston mounted on Clasher. Osbaldeston was a close
friend of John Gully, another West country pugilist who rose,
after being rescued from a debtor's jail, to be a wealthy
Member of Parliament.

Russell may have been unwilling to travel to watch a fight
but he was not unwilling to take part in one.

A fellow Exeter student, Gordon, was rash enough to
compare the pugilistic prowess of Christ Church students with

Exeter's in a way which disparaged his own college. The arrogance of the comparison, coupled with its disloyalty, was enough to provoke a challenge from Denne. Three Christ Church men would fight three from Exeter. The fights would take place in Denne's college rooms. The challenge was readily accepted by Gordon. News of the forthcoming contest rapidly spread throughout the university.

According to Davies Jack Russell was eager to take part in the contest. He was given the honour of fighting first. Having quickly dispatched his man he promptly claimed the right to fight another. The claim was denied by Denne, who reserved for himself the honour of dispatching the other two members of the Christ Church team. Having done so he and Russell then demonstrated what a fight should be. They then sat down to enjoy a sumptuous champagne breakfast at Denne's expense.

Six students fighting in college rooms cannot have escaped the notice of the authorities. They might well have taken some disciplinary action which Davies omits to mention. A period of rustication would explain Russell's prolonged student career.

A £30 scholarship severely curtailed Jack Russell's ability to hunt regularly. His transparent excuse was that he was prevented from hunting by doctor's orders. 'I am suffering just now from tightness of the chest. It's the old complaint and my doctor won't let me hunt at any price.'

There would never be a time during Russell's life when he would have the funds required to hunt on a lavish scale. Throughout his life he experienced 'tightness of the chest' but in later years this did not prevent him from keeping his own modest but very successful hunting establishment. He had inherited a love of outdoor pursuits from his father. His enthusiasm had been kindled before he went to Oxford. While he was a student there his enthusiasm grew into a passion which remained with him throughout his long life.

Within reach of Oxford were countries hunted by some of the finest packs in the country. The sixth Duke of Beaufort was hunting a huge country which included much of that now hunted by the Heythrop and South Oxfordshire. The Bicester country was hunted by Sir Thomas Mostyn. John Codrington hunted the Old Berkshire pack. Jack Russell certainly did not want for excellent hunting tutors though on at least one occasion his impetuosity can have done nothing to endear him to them.

He had gone to some trouble and, for him, appreciable expense to ensure that he had a mount for a particular meet of the Duke of Beaufort's hounds at Sandford Brake. On arriving at the appointed place he was dismayed to find Will Long there to offer 'His Grace's compliments to the field and begs to say the frost is too hard to take the hounds out of kennel.'

Russell's response was immediate, unthinking and unforgivable. He expressed the hope that 'when you get back that you'll find them all dead on their benches'. The outburst was not forgotten and years later the Parson asked Will Long if he remembered the occasion.

'Yes, sir, and I'm not likely to forget it. . . . But there, I didn't think you meant it.'

'Quite right, Will; in two minutes afterwards I could have bitten my tongue out for having made such a speech.'

Will Long, whom the Parson regarded as giving place as a huntsman only to Philip Payne and the Duke himself, became a firm friend of the Russell family. Michael Russell provided Will's son Nimrod, whose fame as a huntsman would eventually rival his father's, with his first mount.

Russell's career as a student was coming to an end. He should have been devoting all his concentration to his neglected studies when 'on a glorious afternoon towards the end of May', 1819 he bought his first terrier. That terrier was Trump.

3

A Very Sporting
Parson

It is debatable as to which aspect of the Parson's student days had the greatest subsequent significance. He got the degree which enabled him to enter the priesthood. He became actively involved in foxhunting and he bought his first terrier.

He sat his degree examinations and bought his first terrier in the summer of 1819. Of the two the purchase of Trump seems to have been the more successful. In Russell's examinations 'his ambition did not prompt him to go up for honours, nor did his name appear in the class list; but having satisfied the examiners and obtained his pass paper, he turned his back on the Bodleian Library with a grateful and joyous heart'. He had scraped through after being 'in residence some fourteen terms'. He sat his examinations at the beginning of Trinity term 1819. His twenty-fourth birthday had been celebrated, doubtless with some vigour, in December 1818. He was ready to be ordained and take up his calling in his native Devon.

Soon after receiving his Bachelor's degree he was

nominated by the Rev. W.B. Stawell to the curacy of George Nympton – a rural parish, with a sparse population, near South Molton. He was ordained a Deacon in 1819, and a priest in the following year. George Pelham, then Bishop of Exeter, performed the ceremony, in the Chapel Royal, London, where, notwithstanding the long double journeys by coach, and the expenses incidental thereto – a serious tax on a salary of £60 a year – the young candidate was summoned to attend on each occasion.

Having been nominated to his first living by a close family friend the Parson found himself in a parish which was both poor and sparsely populated. Its inhabitants were more in need of relief of their existing miseries than of promises of joys to come. The parish of George Nympton contained about 50 houses and 240 people. About one-quarter were employed in agriculture. Soon afterwards Russell was invited to extend his duties to the neighbouring parish of South Molton, though without any increase in his £60 stipend. Nevertheless he was happy to accept and so added another 2700 people to his flock. Compared with George Nympton the new parish was huge. Four-fifths of his parishioners were employed in various manufacturing processes connected with the production of duroys, serges and other light cloths.

From the outset the Parson made it apparent that he fully intended to maintain and even to extend his interest in hunting. There is no evidence, however, to suggest that he did so at the expense of the service he provided for his parishioners. Throughout his life he was never less than a conscientious parish priest. Even so Davies found it necessary to devote a few pages of his biography to defending the Parson's passionate interest in field sports.

Although an unusually active sporting life did not in any way interfere with Russell's pastoral work it undoubtedly did prevent the sort of advancement within the church which his social contacts suggest might have been well within the bounds of reasonable expectations.

The Reverend John Russell was far from unique among his colleagues in his passion for field sports. The era offers a number of sporting parsons. The Rev. John Loder hunted what is now the Old Berkshire country from 1760 to 1805. The Rev. Joseph Arkwright hunted the Essex from 1857 to 1864. The Rev. C.A. Williams hunted the Llangibby from 1854 to 1857. The Rev. Davers hunted the Newmarket and Thurlow from 1804 to 1827. Even within his own bishopric there were the examples provided by the Rev. Harry Farr Yeatman who hunted hare, fox and roe deer with the Blackmore Vale from 1826, having purchased the pack from George Templer of Stover; and the Rev. John Froude of the nearby parish of Knowstone, who became a close friend. Nor should we forget that all the Parson's curates, including Davies, were expected to act as whips and, perhaps most often, as hunt secretaries.

Other priests hunted modest private packs, as did the Parson himself. Still more remain hidden behind the anonymous title of Mister. There was nothing unusual about a hunting parson, nor about the Parson's ready acceptance that hunting would reduce his chances of being called to a better living.

In spite of what must have been a busy life as a parish priest it was not long before the Reverend Jack Russell again became master of his own small pack of hounds. He kennelled five or six couple at the home of one of his parishioners and with these unsuccessfully hunted otter.

He said, 'I walked three thousand miles without finding an otter and although I must have passed over scores, I might as well have searched for a moose-deer.' He eventually acquired a mute draft, Racer, from John Woolcombe, whose country was near Hatherleigh. In spite of his failings Racer had been entered to otter and knew what was expected of him. From then on the Parson was able to show such good sport that he even attracted the notice of the sporting journalist Nimrod, who, following his 1820s tour of the West country, wrote that the Parson has 'killed the almost incredible number of twenty-five otters in the last two summers, for which he should receive the thanks of the fish'.

Hunting otter provided Jack Russell with sport during the summer months but foxhunting remained his main interest. The vicar of the neighbouring parish of Knowstone was the Reverend Jack Froude. It was to him that Jack Russell turned for his foxhunting and for the completion of his hunting education.

'My head-quarters at that time were at South Molton,' he wrote some years later, 'and I hunted as many days in every week as my duties would permit with John Froude, the well-known Vicar of Knowstone, with whom I was then on very intimate terms.

His hounds were something out of the common; bred from the old staghounds – light in their colour, and sharp as needles – plenty of tongue, but would drive like furies, I have never seen a better or more killing pack in all my long life. He couldn't bear to see a hound put his nose on the ground and 'twiddle his tail'. Hang the brute,' he would say to the owner

of the hounds, 'and get those that can wind their game when
they are thrown off.'

It is interesting that Russell should notice the colour of
Froude's hounds before he mentioned their hunting qualities.
Colour was evidently a matter of some importance to the
Parson.

Froude's personal life provided his parish with an unsavoury
example which some parishioners were quite prepared to
follow. A local paper even took to running a regular column
entitled *Knowstone Again* which recounted the many and varied
indiscretions which took place in both parish and rectory. The
bishop, of course, got to hear of this worrying state of affairs but
whenever he visited Knowstone to demand an explanation and
a greater concern for duty Froude would ensure that he was not
at home or would feign illness. On one occasion he even went so
far as to convince the bishop that typhus was in the house.

Davies plainly states that

> there can be little doubt that the friendship and example of a
> man like the vicar of Knowstone did not only influence
> Russell at the very outset of his professional career, but, in all
> likelihood, biased the whole course of his life.
>
> Froude was himself a first-rate sportsman; but always
> acted on the principle of 'kill un, if you can; you'll never see
> un again!' . . . You could hear his view-halloa for miles; and
> his hounds absolutely flew to him when they heard it. Let me
> add, his hospitality knew no bounds.

The Reverend Jack Froude, the very same man who had
swindled Jack Russell when he purchased his first horse, was,
from all accounts, a villain with few admirable qualities. He
was a cheat, violent, a drunkard, a liar and, at a time when
standards were not high, an exceptionally poor parish priest.
Yet he turns up regularly in Jack Russell's life. It seems that
Jack Russell was able to find some mitigating qualities in the
man, though there were also times when the two came to
unseemly and un-Christian blows. In spite of his friendship
with Froude the Parson was not entirely blind to his faults. In
March 1883, at the end of a letter to John Hawker he remarked
that 'Lord Poltimore returns next week – but not to hunt, for I

fear there are no foxes in N. Molton, nor will there ever be until Froude ceases to receive cubs from the keepers.'

Perhaps Jack Russell simply admired Froude's knowledge of hunting, his devotion to it and the extraordinary hold he exerted not just over hounds but also over other dogs. He was prepared to forgive the rest. Froude appears to have been one of those rare people, the Parson himself was another, who had an almost magic affinity with dogs. This enabled him to understand them and to control them without apparent effort. Doubtless the Parson learned a great deal about hunting from Jack Froude but it could not have been wise for a young curate to associate himself so closely with such a notorious character. But Jack Russell, man or boy, seldom gave thought to the immediate consequences of his actions.

The Parson remained at South Molton for the next six years, tending to the needs of his vast parish, hunting as often as he possibly could with Froude and even finding time to become involved in the formation of a cricket club at Teignmouth. The cricket club had the Rev. Henry Taylor of West Ogwell, a formidable rider across country, as its president. George Templer of Stover, who from 1845 to 1849 was master of the South Devon Staghounds, was its vice-president. His younger brother, the Rev. John Templer, was also a member. George Templer was a man who shared the Parson's passion for hunting and was, in his own way, every bit as extraordinary as was Froude. His pack of dwarf foxhounds, averaging 19 inches at the shoulder, were out of the ordinary but it was his method of hunting which really set him apart from the rest.

When, some years later, the snobbish sporting journalist Nimrod deigned to spend a few days with the South Devon Staghounds Templer's establishment demanded his notice.

There is one gentleman who is a constant attendant on Mr Templer's hounds, a very fine horseman over a country, and, report says, quite the clipper of the West. This is the Rev. Henry Taylor. There is another gentleman of the same cloth, the Rev. John Russell (but much better known by the name of 'Jack Russell'), who, though he resides about thirty miles from him, hunts a good deal with Mr Templer, and who also stands high among the Devonshire bruisers. This gentleman finds hunting so conducive to his health, that with stag-hounds, fox-hounds, harriers, and otter-hounds, he contrives to enjoy it all the year round. . . .

The most curious part of Mr Templer's establishment is his method of keeping foxes. He has nearly thirty brace of cubs and old ones, many of the latter of which he has had for some time; and strange to say, there is one called 'The Bold Dragon' which has been hunted six-and-thirty times – often affording most excellent runs. What is also most extraordinary, when he comes home at night after the sport of the day, he never goes into his kennel without taking his supper with him. . . . Mr Templer's old foxes are kept in two large yards, in which their kennels are placed, and they are confined by collars and chains, the latter six feet long.

In spite of the scarcity of native foxes, due either to a strong vulpicidal tendency among farmers or to a natural scarcity, Templer's methods were too artificial to be widely condoned. They were of interest because of their peculiar nature but they had one more important significance. Templer's knowledge of hounds, his ability to control them and his tendency to leave them to puzzle out their own course without assistance, which earned the pack the name of 'The Let 'em Alones', meant that he was able to get quality drafts from the top packs. There was a strong dash of Beaufort blood in his kennel. His drafts were even welcome at the Belvoir. If the Parson's apprenticeship required anything further Templer was well able to provide it. During the time when the Rev. Henry Taylor of Ogwell near Newton Abbot and the Parson whipped in to the Stover hounds both cannot have failed to learn a great deal about hunting.

In many ways the Parson was an old-fashioned man. His religious beliefs, his social attitudes and even the cut of his clothing were all rooted in times which had passed. In the hunting field the Parson was not one of the old school. He was bang up to date. He did not potter along while hounds slowly and meticulously unravelled even the most fitful scent. Though he lacked the means to live alongside the thrusters of the shires whose stables might contain forty horses, many of them thoroughbreds, and a day's hunting might employ half a dozen, he did the best his limited means would allow. The Parson's income meant that his covert hack might also be his hunter. On one occasion he exchanged a fat pig and a five pound note for a promising mount. Some were bought privately. Others at local sales. The majority had some fault which made them unattractive to richer buyers. Some the Parson bred himself. Even so his reputation across country was a formidable one. When he was well-mounted he could match the best. When his ambition was not matched by the quality of his mount he accepted the risk of a fall.

In 1826 the *Sporting Magazine* records that while out with his own hounds,

> Mr Russell handled them, and did his best to show us sport; most unfortunately he got a rattling fall, over a terrible fence; two ribs were smashed and he was otherwise much damaged. We carried him to Tetcott, where he was bled, bedded, bolstered, bandaged, physicked, gruelled and otherwise learnedly treated or doctored.

Even though the cure sounds more dangerous than the damage it was intended to rectify the Parson was hunting again within a week.

Jack Russell's social life was full of variety as well as contradictions. His intimate friendship with the notorious Froude coincided with him becoming friendly with Admiral and Mrs Bury and their two daughters, of Dennington House, Swimbridge. The family was one of the most respected in Devon. Like Russell's the family was of old Devonian stock. Unlike his own it was relatively wealthy. The youngest daughter, Penelope Incledon, shared Russell's passion for hunting. A close friendship rapidly blossomed between the two and just a few months after their first meeting, at the end of 1825, they were married. On 1 June 1826 among the announcements of marriage published by the *Exeter Flying Post* was one which said, 'Yesterday at Swymbridge the Rev. John Russell, junior, to Penelope, youngest daughter of the late Admiral Bury of Dennington.'

The entry in the Parson's hunting diary for Tuesday 30 May 1826 records, 'Took Penelope Incledon Bury to Wife, adjourned with Ditto in a chariot & four greys, furnished by ???

and Old London Exeter, to So. Molton & Tiverton, & slept at the George Inn, Bridgewater!!!'

The formal wording of the diary entry contrasts sharply with the final row of exclamation marks and their likely significance!

Penelope Russell was, within the constraints imposed on Victorian ladies, every bit as keen on hunting as was her husband. She had a reputation for straight and fearless riding across country. When funds became even more than usually scarce she was quite prepared to use her money to support her husband's hounds. She was also independent enough to contrive to do so without his knowledge.

It was not long after his marriage that the Parson became his father's curate. The couple went to live with his parents at the Rectory at Iddesleigh where they were to remain for the next six years. After the veritable metropolis of South Molton Iddesleigh must have provided a life much more to Jack Russell's tastes. The parish contained just 62 houses and about 450 people. All but a few were employed in agriculture. The rector was well provided for by 'Rectorial Tithes of about 3000 acres of very fertile and productive land, the greater part of which is annually in tillage, and in the hands of very respectable farmers'.

The only possible impediment to the couple's complete happiness was that the otter hounds had now been dispersed to other packs and the nearest pack, which belonged to the Rev. W.H. Karslake of Dolton, were harriers. The adjacent packs of foxhounds being those of the Rev. Peter Glubb and of Mr Newton Fellowes, which afterwards became the Eggesford. However, with his wife's willing help, the Parson solved the problem by again setting up his own modest pack of foxhounds. Newton Fellowes generously provided room in his country for Jack Russell to hunt.

The Parson, initially at least, received less co-operation from the local farmers. They were confirmed fox killers whom former masters had failed to convert to a more amenable attitude. Typically Russell adopted a direct method of tackling the problem. Out one day with his hounds he came across a group of parishioners whose intention was to shoot the Parson's fox. During the ensuing discussion someone committed the unforgivable sin of kicking a hound. The Parson was quickly off his horse and threatened to horsewhip the culprit. The culprit wisely chose not to reveal himself. From that day on the Parson enjoyed the co-operation of his parishioners. Very sensibly they decided that shooting foxes or interfering with the Parson's sport was not worth the risk of being horsewhipped.

The hounds, though probably of a far better quality than anything Jack Russell had previously owned, were a very mixed bunch. Some were drafts from the Stover pack which had been disbanded after the death of its owner, Russell's old friend George Templer. Others were drafts from the packs of various other friends. For a couple of seasons the motley collection, which would have been flattered to be referred to as a pack, indiscriminately harassed both fox and hare.

George Templer was an extremely hospitable man and it was at parties at Stover that the Parson developed the friendships with other local masters. These included his old school adversary John Bulteel and John King of Corhampton, who earned the title of 'John King of the West' during the period 1829–41, when he was master of the Hambledon. They also included Arthur Harris with whom the Parson became firm friends. Harris was a man of about Jack Russell's age but had the advantage of having his own money. During the 1827 season the two decided to amalgamate their packs. When the resultant seventy couple had been whittled down to a more manageable thirty or thirty-five couples they had a pack to be reckoned with. Russell kept all the big hounds. He further strengthened his pack with drafts from the Meynell, still being hunted by its founder Hugo Charles Meynell Ingram.

On 29 May 1827 Penelope Russell had given birth to a son, John Bury. The 1828 season was, however, overshadowed by his death. The birth of their second son, Richard Bury, some three months later, provided some much needed solace.

Under Russell's excellent tutelage the two packs, supplemented by some first-class drafts from famous packs, were quickly welded together into a single very efficient unit. During the 1828 season they found thirty-two foxes of which twenty-eight were killed and a brace run to earth. In addition the pack killed seventy-three brace of hares. The disparity in numbers is a better indication of the scarcity of foxes than of the Parson's hunting priorities. During the nineteenth century the British fox population was much more sparse than it is today. In contrast hares were much more plentiful.

Russell and Harris decided against adopting what were then the customary methods of ensuring sport – stealing foxes from adjacent countries, or buying them from local gamekeepers, as did Froude, or buying imported French foxes from Leadenhall Market, in London. Nor did they adopt George Templer's eccentric system of hunting. Instead Russell and Harris decided on a system of conservation. In various places on Harris's Hayne estate they built artificial earths. When a vixen took up residence and gave birth food was provided twice a week until the cubs were fully grown and henceforth every Saturday. A population of resident foxes was created and they were encouraged to stay in the area. The design of the earth made it possible to entrap a fox at any time. As a consequence there were few blank days on the Hayne estate. This, however, proved to be a mixed blessing. Neighbouring masters, unable to explain such consistent success, invented their own explanations.

During this period of his life the Parson, thanks to the generosity of adjacent hunts, had access to a vast country. It stretched from Broadbury to Bodmin

> with many great rivers between them; and a country abounding in wild open moors, fairly undulated, and holding a grand scent, over which a hound and a horse could travel at tip-top pace, while every passage of a run might be seen by the rider; a country, in fact, such as Meynell and Warde never saw in their happiest dreams.

This was the country for which the Parson bred his terriers. Hounds might cover vast distances at a considerable pace. Terriers were expected to keep in touch as best they could and be at hand when they were needed.

After six years at Iddesleigh the annual cycle of his life changed. In 1832, the perpetual curacy of Swimbridge and Landkey became vacant. The living was in the gift of the Dean of Exeter, Whittington Landon. He was Penelope Bury's cousin and offered it to the Parson. Swimbridge had a population of just over 1000. Most were employed in agriculture. Nearby Landkey contained another 600 people. Almost all were employed on the land.

The Rev. Davies stresses the inadequacy of the Parson's stipend in his memoir. It was £180 a year. From it had to be deducted the cost of a curate for Landkey as well as obligatory charities to support the needy in a very poor parish. It fell a long way short of providing a 'living'. The Parson was not an ambitious man or, hunting apart, an extravagant one. The prospect of having his own parish for the first time must have been irresistible even if it meant moving away from his idyllic hunting country and into a less affluent living. For Penelope the move meant that she would no longer have to live with her in-laws. It also took her nearer to her widowed mother's home at Dennington. The inhabitants of Swimbridge and Landkey already knew their new parson and his wife and many already had considerable respect for them. 'There was,' said a local newspaper, 'general satisfaction in the neighbourhood over the nomination of the new vicar.'

The couple rented Tordown, a long low house built on the side of a hill and approached by a steep drive. They stayed there until the death of Mrs Bury, when they became the owners of Dennington House. The Rev. Jack Russell was to remain the rector of Swimbridge and Landkey for the next forty-five years, in effect for the whole of his working life. He never showed any inclination to leave the parish or to better himself in the church. He was happy at Swimbridge, and was surrounded by people, of both high and low degree, he loved and who loved him. During those forty-five years the Rev. Jack Russell proved himself to be a conscientious parish priest. He raised money to build village schools and a chapel in a distant hamlet. He restored the parish church. He increased the number of services from one to four each Sunday and he did his utmost to protect his parishioners from want and need.

In spite of his obvious devotion to his duties there were stories of the way in which hunting interfered with his pastoral work. From time to time these reached his bishop's ears and, unfounded though each was proved to be, cannot have improved any chance he may have had for advancement in the church.

The Parson was not only a good parish priest but also played his part in the secular life not just of the area but of much of Devon. He was active in raising funds for hospitals and for schools. He was interested in and especially enjoyed an association with the local county agricultural societies. These had begun to be formed towards the end of the eighteenth century. They were, as the Parson doubtless saw, instrumental in helping to improve agricultural prosperity and, so, the prosperity of all his parishioners.

John Warde had begun to run hound shows during the 1770s when he was hunting a pack of hounds from his home at Squerries in Kent. These informal summer events allowed him to display his new entry for the admiration of his supporters and his neighbours. They provided an opportunity for masters to get together to compare one another's hounds. One of these masters was Thomas Coke of Holkham in Suffolk. Warde's hound shows may have given him the idea for his Sheep Shearings. These were what inspired the growth of the agricultural societies and shows that rapidly became such an important part of British rural life. Before the eighteenth century had run its course a number of agricultural societies were already in existence. When Jack Russell moved back to Devon after his time at Oxford it would have been expected that he would play his part. He did so with typical enthusiasm and energy.

Throughout his life the Parson was a man of boundless energy, ever prepared to put some of that energy into fostering worthwhile secular West country activities. As already mentioned, he helped form the Teignmouth Cricket Club. He was an active freemason and supported hospital and other charities, but it was to the burgeoning local agricultural societies he devoted most energy.

In 1831 he had become a founder member of the Devon Agricultural Society and in 1840 of the North Devon Agricultural Association. He was on the committee of the North Molton and Twitchen Agricultural Society, and was President of the Bishop's Tawton, Swimbridge and Landkey Agricultural Society. He was active in the Devon Agricultural Association, the Torrington Agricultural Association, the Devon Wool Fair and the North Molton and Twitchen Agricultural Society, as well as other organizations both local and further afield. It was at the shows which these societies organized each summer that Jack Russell served his apprenticeship first as an exhibitor of dogs, hounds as well as terriers, and then as a judge.

For two years after leaving Iddesleigh the Parson kept no hounds, though we may be sure that his kennels were not devoid of terriers. Perhaps the demands of a new and large parish made it impossible to keep hounds. Perhaps he regarded the cost as beyond him. Whatever the reason it was not a situation his hunting friends were prepared to see continue.

In 1834 Harry Fellowes, whose brother was Master of what would become the Eggesford country, and who was himself Master of the Vine, arranged for six and a half couple of his drafts, 'which had all passed the distemper, and that no better blood had ever tackled a Devonshire fox,' to be presented to the Parson. The Parson was overjoyed.

> There they stood alone in my kennel – the greatest beauties my eye had ever rested on – looking up in my face so winningly, as much as to say, 'Only give us a trial, and we'll not disappoint you,' that I mentally determined to keep the lot and go to work again.

The way in which the Parson laid emphasis on the hounds' appearance again demonstrates the importance he attached to beauty, though, of course, to beauty allied to and arising out of functional qualities. He applied precisely the same attitude to his hunters and to his terriers.

In spite of his decision to keep the hounds Jack Russell knew that he could not afford to do so. He knew that his beauties would have to follow his previous pack to Restmorel. Penelope Russell saw her husband's distress. It was she who persuaded him to keep the hounds. No matter what financial difficulties they might face Jack Russell would again hunt his own modest pack.

The pack remained in existence for thirty-seven years, until 1871. During this time, by careful breeding and judicious selection, the Parson produced hounds of a quality which would have been welcome in any pack. He bred his hounds just as carefully as he bred his hunters and his terriers. When old age eventually forced him to give them up they went to Henry Villebois of Marham Hall, Norfolk. Villebois's father had been

Master of the Hampshire. He had been Master of the Norfolk and Suffolk from 1837 to 1841. In 1871 he was Master of the West Norfolk, hunting one side of the country while Henry Henley of Sandringham hunted the other. No hound which was not of absolute top quality would have been welcome in Henry Villebois's kennels, yet he was happy to take Jack Russell's entire pack. It is apparent that the Parson's reputation as a hound breeder was on a par with his reputation as a breeder of Fox Terriers.

Having finally and reluctantly parted with his foxhounds he replaced them with a small scratch of pack harriers and these he continued to hunt until 1882. By this time he was in his eighty-seventh year. Even so he finally parted with his hounds with extreme reluctance and then only to his old friend Arthur Harris on condition that 'you give an especial account in Bailey's of my dear hounds'.

Harris and Russell corresponded regularly. As a result far more is known about the Parson than might otherwise have been the case. At one stage Harris even appears to have come close to suggesting that he should write the Parson's biography. The tentative idea, however, received short shrift.

> What are you driving at? Are you writing my life? You won't get anyone to read it! For I am getting into the sere and yellow leaf, and shall soon be forgotten. Few, very few, alas! of my old companions of the chase are left to greet me, as of yore at the covert side, though, thank goodness, I am still welcomed wherever I go, and that, too, by those who look in vain for the deer old horn and couples. I wish you had seen my last run, just before Christmas, with ten couple of hounds, over Exmoor, twenty-five miles on the map, eighteen as the crow flies at least. The natives say more.

It was as a consequence of the Parson's involvement with agricultural societies, allied to his position as a freemason, that he first came to the attention of the Prince of Wales. It was through Henry Villebois that the acquaintance grew into friendship.

Russell was presented to the Prince during a visit to the Royal Agricultural Society's Show at Plymouth in 1865. The two had a number of mutual friends so the Prince probably already knew something of the old man's reputation. The Parson was subsequently invited to spend Christmas 1873 at Sandringham, which the Prince and Princess had built some years earlier. It remains one of the royal family's favourite retreats. An invitation to a very informal gathering of close friends would not have been issued on the basis of a single meeting, especially one which had taken place eight years previously. The Prince and the Parson must have met in the meantime.

Parson Jack Russell was a lifelong freemason who took the craft seriously. In 1835, at the age of only forty, he was invested as Provincial Grand Chaplain. Freemasonry opened many doors to the Parson and may well have opened the door to Sandringham. After all the Prince himself was also a committed freemason. Previous meetings may have gone unrecorded because they took place under the cloak of masonic secrecy, but they may also have taken place in the hunting field.

Evidence of some prior mutual involvement and even of a developing friendship is provided by an incident that took place during the Parson's first visit to Sandringham. During dinner the Prince read out a spoof telegram, supposed to have come from a notorious London dog dealer. 'Bill George, Canine Castle, Kensal Green, to Anthony Hammond Esq., at Sandringham, Wolferton. The Rev. John Russell having disappointed me in not calling for a bagman as he passed through London this afternoon, shall send him down tomorrow by first train to Wolferton. Hope he'll arrive fresh.'

Such a telegram, joke though it was, would nowadays, when attitudes to hunting released foxes are ostensibly so very different, provoke more anger than laughter. Even in 1874 such a telegram would be only likely to be regarded as funny among good friends.

It was not the first time that the Parson's name had been associated with the practice of hunting bagged foxes. John Bulteel used to tell a story of how one of the Parson's and Harris's kennelmen, Blatchford, had complained of having developed a sore stomach as a result of 'lying so long, wi' the fox in a bag, on the cold ground, awaiting for Parson Rissell to bring up they hounds!' Perhaps Bulteel was merely extracting revenge for a schoolboy beating. Perhaps he was jealous of the regular sport Russell and Harris could show, which, not knowing of their artificial earths, he could explain in no other way. In any case if the Parson did make occasional use of bagged foxes he was doing nothing more than many other, far more famous, masters.

The weekend parties at Sandringham were relaxed. The Prince was an exceptionally good host. He went to great lengths to ensure that the individual likes of his guests were fully satisfied. In the Parson's case this meant a second helping of fish and a supply of good port. In a letter to Margery Stucley the Parson captured the atmosphere of his first visit.

I have been staying here with the Prince and Princess of Wales, and a happy time I have had of it and so has every one who comes here. So, dear, I have taken the greatest part of the duty in the Church, and they both thanked me for my sermon here. There never was a happier family in the world, there never can be, their children climb about their father and mother as the Collyns children do in our part of the world, and as to their dogs, the Prince told me they have six in their room. The Princess is very beautiful, and so is the second girl, but all, boys and girls, are very good looking.

The letter ends with his itinerary for the next few days which included a trip to Yorkshire, perhaps to see Tom Wootton and his terriers. This was followed by a week with Mark Rolle at Stevenstone.

The Parson was one of a very select band who attended the Prince's masonic installation in 1875. He was again a guest at Sandringham in December 1876. In August 1879 the two enjoyed a day out with the Devon Staghounds and again in February 1882. In 1882 the visit preceded a visit to the Smithfield cattle show after which Russell went to see his old friend Davies, by now crippled and living in Bath. From Bath he went home for a day and then on to Eggesford to perform a wedding prior to a day's hunting.

In August 1873 the Parson lost Will Rawle, an old friend and colleague. He had been the Parson's kennelman for more than forty years. It must have been a sad blow, but worse was to come.

Penelope Russell's failing health had prevented her from

accompanying her husband on his first visit to Sandringham. He, unable to refuse what was virtually a royal command, did his best to recompense her by writing what, in a letter to Margery Riccard his favourite niece, daughter of his sister Nora, he described as 'full accounts every day to the Missus'. Penelope's health failed to improve and she died at the end of 1874. The Parson and she had been married for forty-eight years.

Fate had not finished with the Parson, however. He and his son Bury became involved in unwise speculations in the Devon and Somerset Railway Company and were well-nigh ruined, particularly the Parson who helped his son out of his financial straits. The Parson was now in his eighty-fifth year, widowed and impoverished.

Efforts were made to persuade Mr Palmer Acland to offer the Parson the living at High Bray but, with a notable want of Christian charity, he had refused on the grounds that he had no wish to be hunted to death by the 85-year-old.

Lord Poltimore had known the Parson for many years both as a fellow Master of Hounds and as a man who had worked with great energy and dedication for the improvement of conditions in Devon. In all probability he had also known the Parson as a fellow mason. He sought some way to alleviate the old man's poverty. In 1879 he invited the Parson to accept the living at Black Torrington. The parish contained just 700 people about half of whom were employed in agriculture. It would be much less demanding than Swimbridge. More importantly, the living was worth £500 a year, over twice what the Parson received at Swimbridge. Although the Parson had no wish to leave the parish he had looked after for nearly half a century and for which he had done so much, he really had no choice. He wrote to his old friend, Davies,

'Tell me, my dear old friend, what shall I do about Black Torrington? I cannot live on £200 a year which is all I shall have after I have paid a certain annuity for another three or four years. Black Torrington is a clear £500 a year and there is a good house; but then it is neither Tordown nor Exmoor; and by the time I am settled in there, I shall perhaps be called upon to leave it again for Swimbridge churchyard! What shall I do? How can I leave my own people, with whom I have lived in peace and happiness for half a century? It will be a bitter pill to swallow, if it must be taken; but it will be my poverty and not my will that will consent to it.'

The Parson moved into the rectory at Black Torrington in July 1879. He had new stables built to house his two hunters, Simon and a valuable Irish mare. The stables were also intended to accommodate the terriers which did not live in the house. Unfortunately the stables were destroyed by fire, along with their occupants, soon after the Parson had moved into his new home. He never replaced his hunters. Henceforth he relied on being mounted by his willing hosts.

Mary Cocking, his maid ever since he and his wife rescued her from a stark life in a charity school at eight years old, had moved with him to Black Torrington and continued to care for him. Bury also did what he could to help his father. The old man turned to his niece Margery for solace, and addressed to her the letters which recorded his many trips away from the new home into which he had moved with such reluctance.

He also expressed his misery to his close friends. When he was too weak to hunt, all appetite gone and feeling miserable, he wrote to John Hawker to tell him that 'Calmady's Hounds, George tells me, have not found today – and no wonder – one fox was found poisoned about a mile from here, and another caught in a gin outside one of his friend's [?] abode about a week since. In short, I am living among backbiters, poisoners and Fox trappers . . .'

He continued to hunt with all his old enthusiasm and to breed terriers, but even his tough old frame was not immune to the passage of time. During the winter of 1882 the Parson became very weak and depressed. The Prince of Wales, hearing of the old man's illness dispatched Henry Villebois from Norfolk to express his concern and to gather first-hand information. Later in the year the Prince expressed his own concern.

Sandringham

My dear Jack Russell,

I hope you will not object to my addressing you by your old familiar name. It gave me more pleasure than I can describe to get your letter yesterday written in such a firm hand. Most sincerely do I hope that you are now in a fair way towards recovering, but you have indeed suffered severely, I fear, and most deeply have we felt for you.

With God's blessing I hope you will recover your customary health and then we may see you at the covert-side.

With the Princess's regards and hoping that I may continue to get a good account of your recovery.

Believe me.

Yours very sincerely,
Albert Edward

Although he was becoming increasingly frail and at times was depressed the Parson stoically refused to accept the inevitable. In January 1883 he wrote to William Turner of West Molland and though bemoaning the fact that 'it is now four months since I heard the tongue of hounds' and that 'I am very weak and can't walk across my room without assistance' was still sufficiently interested to ask 'is "Mercury" the puppy I gave you, living?' and sufficiently optimistic to say, 'I kept back a couple of little bitches. I should like to breed from these in time.'

It was not to be. During the spring of 1883 his condition declined and on 28 April he passed peacefully away.

Parson Jack Russell was buried in his beloved Swimbridge, the place in which he spent most of his long life. His coffin was followed to the grave by over 2000 mourners and countless others of both high and low station sent their tributes.

One of the best tributes appeared in the *Kennel Gazette*. The Parson had become a member of the Kennel Club on 13 March 1874, within a year of the Club's formation, and was still a member when he died. He was proposed for membership by George Lowe, the Club's Secretary, and seconded by Evelyn Shirley, its Founder and Chairman, who had the added distinction of owning at least one of the Parson's terriers. The May 1883 issue of the *Gazette* contained the Parson's obituary. It was probably written by John Murchison, one of the foremost Fox Terrier breeders and an old friend of Jack Russell's. The terms and the tone of the obituary make it abundantly clear that Fox Terrier breeders had nothing but respect for the Parson's aims and achievements. There is absolutely no evidence to show that the Parson did not reciprocate this respect.

IN MEMORIAM – THE REV. JOHN RUSSELL

Though fiction in a past generation gave us a Parson Adams, there is no likelihood of a nearer prototype of that worthy than the kind old clergyman who passed quietly away just ten days ago. The resemblance between the country parson of the novelist and the Rev. John Russell ends, however, at the point where both are seen to exercise an influence upon all those with whom they came into contact, and an honesty of purpose to be constantly helping others out of scrapes or troubles. This was the character of John Russell, but he was a greater gentleman than Parson Adams, and his journey through life may be looked upon as an odd mixture between the old-fashioned parson, the country gentleman, and the courtier. In his parish he was the adviser and friend of his flock, at cover side or at the agricultural meeting he was hearty and well met with every one, and in the hall or the palace he was polished and affable to a degree. It is no wonder, therefore, that he was a universal favourite, from the prince to the peasant, and it is possible that no one has ever surpassed him as an arbitrator and peace-maker in every sort of circle. He would travel third-class from Devonshire to Yorkshire for no other purpose, and whether bringing together broken ties, or preaching a charity sermon, he had a way of his own of reaching the heart that few could equal and no one could surpass. Born a sportsman, he never thought it incompatible with duty to join in every sort of legitimate sport and pastime; and besides being the most genuine foxhunter in the country, it was by no means unusual to see his well-known figure at Ascot or Stockbridge, or on the box of a friend's drag in the coaching season. There was no cant or humbug about John Russell; he performed the duties of his religious profession better than the majority of clergymen, and he was ever ready to join in any thing to promote sport or fellowship amongst sportsmen. The writer of these lines asked him, when the Kennel Club was established, to join as a member, and he was quite delighted with the idea, and has been a member ever since. It will be remembered that Mr Russell judged the Fox Terriers at the Crystal Palace for the club in 1875, and although the old gentleman was not altogether at home with all the requirements of the modern fox terrier, he was greatly pleased with all he saw at the show, and expressed to us the very strong admiration he had for Rattler. Mr Russell's own breed of fox terriers were wire-haired, and his greatest aversion were those that had in them any signs of a bull cross. A real fox terrier, he would say, is not meant to murder, and his intelligence should always keep him from such a crime. Thus, he boasted that the best he ever had never tasted blood to his knowledge, but that they could not lose their way, and that their eye to country and memory was so great that, as soon as hounds were out of cover, some of his terriers have gone ten miles, and reached well-known earths in time to stop a fox from entering a destination that he had been making for. This Mr Russell thought was the highest character that could be found in a terrier, and he would have none that hesitated to go to ground, but he liked them to teaze or worry a fox rather than to kill him or fight him. He said his terriers worked for the pack, and knew as well as he did what they were wanted for.

The Jack Russell terrier was hardly as big as the modern show terrier; in working condition the dogs would not be more than 15lb., and many of them barely that, and five-and-twenty years ago they formed a very distinct type. Since that time they have been crossed on to other strains, and their uniformity has been probably lost, though they live in all descendants of Foiler. Mr. Russell started his breed at Oxford when he was eighteen, so something like seventy years ago, and he had his pedigrees that he could trace to from the time he started them. As the oldest fox terrier breeder in England Mr. Russell's connection with the Kennel Club was an honour to that body, and we personally regret the loss of a very old friend in the fine old English gentleman who has been recently gathered to his fathers, and that a thousand followed him to his grave that were nearly all of them sportsmen shows that our slight contribution, as well as many others written by staunch friends and admirers, is largely shared in sentiment to the memory of the Rev. John Russell.

4

The Parson's Terriers

A fellow churchman and sportsman, the Rev. Thomas Pearce, the Vicar of Morden, near Blandford in Dorset, was one of that band of terrier enthusiasts, which included Thomas Wootton, the Honourable Thomas W. Fitzwilliam and John Henry Murchison and William Carrick, who were among the Parson's many friends and admirers. He provides one of the earliest and most reliable sources of evidence about the Parson's terriers. In 1872 he wrote *The Dog* under the name 'Idstone'. It contains a number of valuable references to the Parson's terriers.

I have always had a good one myself hanging about the place, and with all the qualities required, or he would not stay with me. I prefer a white one. I believe fox or otter would bolt from a white dog best, and I can see him in the dark nooks and angles of a barn, and so can the lads and helpers who let and hinder on a wet day at his rat-killing vocation. I like a small Terrier; in fact, I am no advocate for lumber in Foxhound, Harrier, Setter, Retriever, or Spaniel. I don't admire a Deerhound for his size, unless his muscle and bone and formation warrant him agile and speedy as well as stout; size belongs to St. Bernards, Mastiffs, and Newfoundlands. A dog should be able to make up for his want of size, like the coachman to whom the lord objected for his want of stature: 'My lord,' he replied, 'what the big ones does by strength I does by hartifice.'

I don't mean to say that I have anything to compare with Mr Wootton's old 'Jock' or 'Tartar', or such beauties as have appeared from time to time upon show benches; but I have generally one or two which can trace back to Jack Russell's Devonshire's, and maintain an average with any vermin-dogs in courage and intelligence.

So little were these dogs known amongst so-called breeders in 1860 that only four Terriers were shown at Birmingham that year except black-and-tans. Three years later, in an exhibition of 1,678 dogs, there was no class for Fox Terriers in May, whilst in the November of the same year Birmingham had two classes and thirty-seven entries. In 1867 these had almost doubled; and in 1871, at the Crystal Palace, Fox Terriers numbered more than an eighth of the whole number exhibited, the total being 828!

Pearce was here talking about the Fox Terrier, by which he meant the Smooth Fox Terrier. It is interesting that he should choose both Jock and Tartar to represent perfection because these were two of the dogs which the Parson used on his bitches. It is interesting, too, that he expressed a preference for a white terrier, and not, it must be noted, a white and tan or white and black. Here Pearce's preferences are the same as the Parson's, and he also shared the Parson's attitude towards size and the use of '*hartifice*' rather than force and brute strength. Pearce's evidence will be called upon later.

Little is known of Parson Jack Russell's early career as an owner and breeder of terriers, but it began when he was at university. As a 24-year-old student with his final bachelor degree examinations at Exeter College, Oxford, beginning to loom over the horizon Russell should have had little on his mind other than those examinations, particularly so since he had, during the previous three years, 'spent much of his time shooting, fishing, hunting, rowing, boxing and driving tandem, finishing each day with heavy drinking and convivial songs'. Not an orthodox preparation for life as a parish priest. He certainly should not have been entertaining thoughts of buying a terrier. The loyal Davies makes the event look like a lucky accident. Perhaps it was. On balance, however, it seems far more likely that Russell knew where a quality terrier was to be found and may even have arranged to meet the terrier's owner. Jack Russell had been resident in Oxford for four years when he bought Trump and had had plenty of time and doubtless plenty of opportunity to discover where good terriers were to be found in the area. It is less surprising that Russell bought a terrier than that he didn't do so until his student days were nearly at an end. Whatever the explanation for the timing of the purchase there is no doubt but that Davies's introduction of the element of lucky chance, a suggestion that Russell was guided by the hand of destiny, improves his version of the story.

At the end of May, when strolling round Magdalen meadow with Horace in hand, but Beckford in his head, he emerged from the classic shade of Addison's Walk, crossed the Cherwell in a punt, and passed over in the direction of Marston, hoping to devote an hour or two to study in the quiet meads of that hamlet, near the charming slopes of Elsfield, or in the deeper and more secluded haunts of Shotover Wood. Before he had reached Marston, a milkman met him with a terrier – such an animal as Russell had yet only seen in his dreams; he halted, as Actaeon might have done when he caught sight of Diana desporting in her bath; but, unlike that ill-fated hunter, he never budged from the spot till he had won the prize and secured it for his own. She was called Trump, and became the progenitress of that famous race of terriers which, from that day to the present, have been associated with Russell's name at home and abroad.

Trump has gone down in history as the Parson's first terrier, but one wonders whether she really deserves this distinction. If the Parson's father owned terriers, which is likely, the Parson himself would surely have had his own favourite. Davies claimed that Trump 'became the progenitress of that famous race of terriers' and not that the Parson had never previously owned a terrier. Anyway the Parson must have bred from Trump, but what she was mated to, what she produced and where her descendants went are probably things we will never know.

What do we know about Trump? She too has subsequently been woven into the legends which, for want of hard facts, surround the Parson's early career as a breeder. It has been said that she was bought by the elder John Russell as an eighteenth birthday present for his son and that she subsequently had her first litter to one of his Devonshire terriers. No evidence is available to support the tale. Surely it is unlikely that the Parson would still be waiting for his eighteenth

birthday present when he was twenty-four years old? Perhaps
she was bought to mark a later birthday or even to mark the end
of his student days?

It is, of course, entirely possible that Trump was mated to a
Devonshire terrier. It is far less likely that, as some accounts
have suggested, she was mated to a black and tan terrier. Why
would anyone buy a fashionable white terrier, especially
someone whose subsequent career demonstrated a dislike of
coloured or even heavily marked terriers, and then mate her to
a black and tan dog?

We know that Trump was owned by a milkman who
probably lived bear Marston in Oxfordshire. We don't know
his name or anything else about him. We might suppose that
Russell had seen Trump at work with one of the local packs or,
at the very least, knew from a reliable source, of her reputation.
Surely Russell, of all people, would not buy any terrier, let
alone a foundation bitch, on the basis of her appearance alone.
We might even go so far as to suppose that he knew something
of Trump's ancestry.

Fortunately we have no need for supposition when it comes
to Trump's appearance. There is a painting of Trump, dated 18
January 1820, just eight months after she came into Russell's
possession, and signed by the artist, Mary Palmer. The
painting may have been commissioned by the Parson himself
but it would be nice to think that it might have been a singularly
happy present given to him when he left Oxford. What is
certain is that he saw the portrait and approved of it as a true
likeness of his first terrier. By 1878 the painting had come into
the possession of the Prince of Wales, perhaps as a gift from the
Parson to his friend, but the important thing is that the portrait
gives a good idea of what Trump looked like. It is not the only
source of information about Trump's appearance, for we have
Davies's description of her. Jack Russell saw and approved of
the description.

In the first place the colour is white with just a patch of dark
tan over each eye and ear, while a similar dot, no larger than
a penny piece, marks the root of the tail. The coat, which is
thick, close, and a trifle wiry, is well calculated to protect the
body from wet and cold, but has no affinity with the long,

rough jacket of a Scotch Terrier. The legs are straight as arrows, the feet perfect; the loins and conformation of the whole frame indicative of hardihood and endurance; while the size and height of the animal may be compared to that of a full-grown vixen fox.

The portrait of Trump shows a smart terrier, perhaps very slightly longer in the back than would please some modern tastes and perhaps with stifles with more angulation than is desirable in a dog intended to gallop across country. Her ears too leave something to be desired. They are either half-pricked or had been fashionably cropped. Her tail also looks like it had been docked, both operations complying with what was then the current fashion for both terriers and foxhounds. It is significant that what Davies left out of his description, colour apart, were largely cosmetic or fashionable points which had little or no effect on Trump's ability to work. Maybe he mentioned colour because it was something to which the Parson himself attached some importance. Davies stressed the weather-resisting qualities of the coat, the straightness of the legs, the feet, the impression of hardihood and stamina and, last but by no means least, the size. Trump was about the size of a full grown vixen. In other words about 13 or 14 lb in weight and about 14 in. at the shoulder.

So Russell the student had got himself a typical example of one of the relatively newly fashionable type of terrier. Typical? Certainly her markings were exactly like those of Pitch. Her entire make and shape resembled Reinagle's white terriers. Furthermore we have a portrait of yet another terrier which is also very similar to Trump. That terrier was Vixen, described as a pied terrier and appearing in an engraving dated 1818, the year before Russell bought Trump. She is a mature bitch who has known maternal duties and has a somewhat matronly look about her. Her colouring is exactly like Trump's, her coat perhaps a little smoother but very dense. Perhaps she is a little heavier boned than was Trump but she is undoubtedly of the very same type. She is of the very same type as the best of today's Parson Jack Russell Terriers and could certainly take her place in the ring with every expectation of success. Few other breeds have managed to retain a consistent type for over

170 years. To have done so without the benefit of a reliable system of registration or a breed standard really is a remarkable achievement. Type has been maintained because throughout that period the breed has never lost contact with its original purpose in life. Breeders have bred for working qualities. Only if they continue to do so will type remain consistent.

Forty years after the young Russell had acquired one of the fashionable white fox terriers, Stonehenge wrote about them in the past tense. The desire for speed had changed hunting from a careful and deliberate resolution of the puzzle provided by the fox into little more than an excuse for a headlong mounted dash across country. Speed was of the essence. Only in the less fashion-conscious countries in the north and the west did the old type of hunting retain its hold. They continued to need good terriers. The northern hunting countries had their own coloured terriers. It was only in the west that the white terrier retained its faithful supporters.

Then in 1872 the Rev. Thomas Pearce included a chapter in *The Dog* called 'The Broken-haired Fox Terrier' and created a mystery which remains unsolved, by writing that

> the broken-haired or Wiry Scotch Terrier used to be the favourite vermin-dog. White was the fashionable colour, and he was in perfection about thirty years ago.
>
> For general work, vermin-killing, or the otter, he had no superior, and one or two – perhaps with an undistinguishable or unknown Bulldog cross – were celebrated for their ferocity and fighting. . . . The breed would have died out, I am persuaded, but for the Rev. John Russell, of Dennington, near Barnstaple, North Devon, who has always declared them to be the best of good Terriers, and his opinion carries great weight.

Pearce obviously supported Walsh's view that the fox-terrier's days had come and gone, except that is for the Parson, but why he should refer to the breed as wiry Scotch Terriers we cannot say. No other author of the period did so. Nor did he mention their value as fox terriers, though he made amends later. However, Pearce had not yet finished creating mysteries which remain unsolved. He went on to describe Russell's terriers.

The best breed are wire-haired. The peculiar texture does not interfere with the profile of the body, though there is a shaggy eyebrow and pronounced moustache. The eyebrow is the great mark, giving the dog the look of a Bristol merchant. Mr. Russell's have a keen jaw; narrow, but strong; short, well-set limbs; a long back; small ears; and white is the prevailing colour; but the best-looking and most serviceable bred by him, and belonging to Lord Poltimore's capital huntsman, Evans, was a pale tortoiseshell, mixed with white and grey, a hard-coated, enduring dog, fit for any work, however hard, with a rough jacket, defiant of all weather and resolution (combined with sense enough) to serve him in all difficulties.

Devonshire rejoices in this Fox Terrier, and stands almost alone in its admiration of the rough breed, as a county; but the huntsmen of England know them well, and generally produce a few specimens at the Yarm Hound Show, whether they win or no.

The old sort was a blunt-headed dog; how Mr. Russell has refined them I cannot tell, but refined they are, and easily educated, especially when in the hands of their breeder, whose power over Hound and Terrier has been equalled by few and surpassed by none.

White is the useful as well as the fashionable colour, but a coloured ear or head is not objectionable. The eye is generally small and black, the neck long, the shoulders deep, the form long and low; the tail, about as brushy as a Hound's, is carried higher than that of Terrier's in general. In other respects the points are those of the Foxhound as to body and legs.

How do we resolve Pearce's apparent contradiction of referring to the breed as having short limbs and a long back with his later statement that 'the points are those of the Foxhound as to body?' Are we to believe that foxhounds were short-legged and long-backed? If Pearce had been writing towards the end of the century we might have been inclined to suggest that there was no contradiction. His reference to short legs and long backs could be explained as a comparison with the leggy, ultra-short backed Smooth Fox Terrier which, even today, is compared with the outline of a hunter rather than a hound. When Pearce was writing the process that would produce the modern Fox Terrier had scarcely begun.

Some confusion also seems to exist about whether or not the Parson ever developed his own strain. The Rev. Rosslyn Bruce expressed the view that

> in one strain of Wires the name of "Juddy of Rev. J. Russell's strain" catches the eye; but his famous Juddy was called after his college friend, Mr Judd; this Juddy whelped Whitebrine in 1891, when Parson Jack, who certainly never 'had a strain' in the modern sense, had been dead some ten years. The marvellous old Padre had little faith in pedigrees, and was known to have said that any Fox Terrier that can kill an adult Tomcat is well bred. It is an ancient fable that he ever bred a strain of Terriers.

Without producing any evidence Bruce contradicts that which had been said by the Parson's contemporaries. The few facts which Bruce does offer are easily checked. The Parson died in 1883 so that by 1891 he had been dead six not 'some ten years'. Juddy was mentioned by Davies who wrote while the Parson was still alive. There may have been more than one Juddy but if there wasn't she must have been very old when she whelped Whitebrine.

Bruce mentions Juddy in his book *Fox Terrier Breeding*. He says that 'records of systematic breeding of modern Fox-terriers can only be traced to about 1862, in which year the Rev. W. Handley bred a bitch called Sting who became the dam of Grove Nettle. . . . Parson Jack Russell produced a little later the rough coated Juddy, who was the dam of Moss I.' Bruce goes on to give Juddy's date of birth as 1868. This Juddy he says was commonly called Judy. Whitebrine's dam must have been a different animal of the same name.

Compare then Bruce's statement that 'it is an ancient fable that he ever bred a strain of Terriers' with his comment that 'the question of "Jack Russell" terriers seems to have a peculiar interest, and it is worthy of note that, though all smooth fox-terrier descend from the old sporting parson's strain, only certain ones descend from it in direct female succession'. Bruce contradicts the Parson's contemporaries about the existence of the Jack Russell strain. He also contrives to contradict himself.

Every contemporary account written by those who knew the Parson and who knew his terriers is categoric that he was a careful breeder who took immense pride in his terriers and in their breeding. Nevertheless rumours to the contrary proved remarkably resistant to the facts. The debate about the Parson's role as a breeder surfaced once more in 1956. Published correspondence which took place in 1956, largely in the pages of *Horse and Hound* and *The Field* seems to have made a concerted effort to discredit the Parson as a breeder. None of the protagonists had any first-hand knowledge of the Parson or his terriers. Each claimed to have some second- or third-hand evidence. This they tried to use to discredit any claim the Parson might have to being a breeder of terriers, let alone any claim to having produced a distinctive strain.

Captain G. Percival Williams was master of the Four Burrow from 1922 to 1955. He claimed that the Parson

> used to ride or drive down every year to stay with my grandfather George Williams at Scorrier House, when he had these hounds. He was a *terrier* dealer, and always on leaving asked by grandfather if he had any terriers to spare. He would say: 'If there are any at kennel they don't want, you can have them.' He would then collect terriers on his drive back to Exeter off anyone who had any to spare.

A similar view was expressed by Lord Poltimore when he wrote,

> with regard to his terriers, my father-in-law, the late Hon. Gerald Lascalles, C.B. (for thirty-five years Deputy Surveyor of the New Forest), who also knew Mr. Russell, told me that Mr. Russell always used to tell him that he had no particular breed or sort of terrier, but if he chanced to come across a likely looking dog and it proved to be a game 'un he would buy it and breed from it, if he so thought, with the result that he always had a good kennel of working terriers.

The two accounts not only conflict with what the Parson himself wrote and with what contemporary writers have written but disagree between themselves. The case they offer, based entirely on hearsay, is unconvincing in the extreme. It can confidently be dismissed.

One of the most famous of the amateur huntsmen of the time and subsequently master of some famous packs was Colonel John Anstruther Thomson, a native of the kingdom of Fife, who met the Parson while he was stationed at Exeter. The two became firm friends. Colonel Thomson's hunting career extended until he was an octogenarian and was otherwise remarkable not just for his ability with hounds but for the way he moved from country to country. At the start of the century he had two short spells as Master of the Fife; he spent the 1847–9 seasons as Master of the Atherstone, went back to Fife for one season before returning to the Atherstone until 1855 when he had two seasons as Master of the Bicester. He then returned to Fife until 1864 before spending the 1864 to 1869 seasons as Master of the Pytchley, rounding off a remarkable career with a final season at the Atherstone.

In 1879 the Parson sent Thomson two terriers. The letter which accompanied them says,

> I will send off the two terrier puppies by train to Charleston tomorrow morning and 'hope they will arrive fresh'. Take your choice of them, and send on the other to Pat Carnegy with my best wishes to the missus and himself. . . Please put a few potatoes into the hamper and send it back – not that I want the hamper, but I do the potatoes.

Is this the sort of letter a dealer would have written? Do dealers offer terriers in exchange for a few potatoes at a time when other terriers were changing hands for their weight in silver?

The Parson may or may not have been responsible for saving the white wire-haired terrier from extinction. He certainly refined it during his long career as a breeder. He did so by careful and systematic breeding allied to careful selection. In the process he produced a distinctive strain of terrier. It is entirely just that his name should be commemorated by that breed.

Of course Russell did not act alone as a breeder, no breeder can ever do so, though many have tried and have failed. He had friends who were closely involved with foxhunting and with the increasingly popular world of dog shows and who shared his interest in Fox Terriers.

Sadly the *Kennel Club Stud Book* offers little help in tracing details of the Parson's breeding programme even during the later stages of his career. The first Stud Book was published in 1874. The Parson died ten years later. During these ten years he made use of some of the foremost Fox Terrier stud dogs but unfortunately the resulting progeny were not registered. Even so we can find and fit a few pieces of the jig-saw together.

A picture emerges which refutes much of what has subsequently come to be regarded as depicting the Parson's attitude towards breeding. All manner of claims have been made: he did not keep and was not interested in pedigrees; he never went outside Devon for breeding stock; the appearance of his terriers did not concern him; even that he did not breed all but merely bought any likely looking terrier he happened to come across. There is no documentary support for any of these claims and more than enough to refute them all absolutely. On the contrary, all the evidence suggests that the Parson was a dedicated breeder, prepared to go to considerable trouble to ensure that his bitches were mated to the dogs he regarded as most likely to produce the sort of terrier he was trying to breed.

The Parson certainly mated his bitches to well-known Fox Terriers. Most, as a result of surviving correspondence, is known about Old Jock and Tartar but we know also that the Parson's Vic was mated to Grove Willie to produce both Grip and Juddy, that Juddy was also mated to Old Hornet, that Wasp was mated to Troilus as well as Little Jim.

Both Old Jock and Tartar were well-known and highly successful show dogs – and neither was resident in Devon. The Parson passed both appreciative and critical comment on the appearance of both. We know for certain that he recognized the value of pedigree and breeding. He sought out the best dogs, no matter where they lived. His vision was not so narrow and restricted that he could not recognize the links between appearance and function.

Three terriers and a handful of people dominated the early days of the development of Fox Terriers. The three dogs were Old Jock, Tartar and Old Trap. The Parson was involved in the careers of all three. He used two of them on his bitches.

Rawdon Lee wrote that Jock was

> said to be bred by Jack Morgan, who, when the dog was
> pupped some time during 1859, was first whip to the Grove
> when Tom Day hunted them and Sir Richard Sutton was the
> master. I have also heard it stated that Jock was born at the
> Quorn Kennels. The Kennel Club Stud Book gives the
> breeder as either Captain Percy Williams, who was then
> Master of the Rufford, or Jack Morgan; Mr Wootton, the
> authority at that time, says Jack Morgan bred the dog; but
> uncertainty of the month in which the terrier was born, and
> the little thought then given to terrier pedigrees, make me
> extremely sceptical as to Jock's breeding, as I am of most of
> the early stock terriers. Anyhow, Jock, who was purchased
> from Morgan by Mr T. Wootton for £5, has left his mark
> behind him.

In the first volume of the *Fox Terrier Stud Book* Jock's breeding
is, on Luke Turner's evidence, given as Branson's Twister. The
second volume, however, says that the breeding given in the
Kennel Club Stud Book is almost certainly correct. This gives
Jock's sire as Captain Percy William's Jock. Rawdon Lee
supports this latter suggestion and stresses the fact that both
Jock's parents were 'huntsman's terriers both of them we may
be sure'. Neither provides any useful information because we
know nothing about either putative sire.

Of Jock's dam we know a little more. Thomas Wootton said
that 'Jock's dam, Grove Pepper, was left in the kennel by Will
Merry, the retiring huntsman. The bitch was given to me by
Morgan; white in colour with a slight tan mark on her face,
about 16 lb. She was a wonder, with a hunting coat, and could
go the pace and do the trick.' The Parson probably saw Pepper
either when she was at the Grove or during her time with
Thomas Wootton.

Even if we knew Old Jock's complete breeding with absolute
certainty what would still be of even greater importance is
what he looked like. It would be important because according
to the Parson himself he 'never saw a sweeter animal than Jock,
so perfect in shape, so much quality. He is as near perfection as
we poor mortals are ever allowed to feast our eyes on. His

temper is so beautiful and his pluck undeniable, for I had to choke him off a fox.'

A detailed description of Jock was provided by Rawdon Lee. He said that

> in show form Old Jock was just about 18 lb. weight, standing a little high on his legs, which gave him an appearance of freedom in galloping. His colour was white, with a dun or mixed tan mark on one ear, and a black patch on the stern at its root. He was not what one would at the present time (in 1893) call a 'varminty-looking' dog, i.e. one with an unusual appearance of go and fire and gameness in him – he was a little deficient in terrier character. His ribs were well sprung, and his shoulders and neck nicely placed. When in this condition he had the appearance of a rib short; but his hind quarters and loin were strong and in unison with the other parts of his formation. To some modern tastes he would appear a little loaded at the shoulders; his forelegs, feet and stoutness of bone were good, and his stifles strong and well turned. His ears well placed, neither too large nor too small and he had a nice, strong jaw. With increasing years he grew a little full in the cheeks. All round Jock was a symmetrical terrier, and no specimen of late years has reminded me so much of him as the dog Rattler, who did so much winning. Jock, who is said to have run seasons with the Grove Hounds, had his tail cut, but the portion left on was longer than one usually sees at the present day.

Jock seems to have lived an unsettled sort of life, as many working terriers still do. They are expected to make the best of what fate has in store for them. Thomas Wootton, who bought Jock for £5, wrote,

> I sold him upon several occasions. The first time I parted with him was to the Hon. T.W. Fitzwilliam, Wentworth, who came with Lord Aboyne to see my terriers, when I lived at Mapperly House. The price was £35. . . . I next sold him to Captain Kindersley, then quartered at Brompton Barracks, Chatham, for £100. The Captain was ordered abroad. I had Jock and eight other terriers back, which he purchased from me. Afterwards he went to Mr Cropper, of Minting House,

Horncastle, for £50, and he resold the dog to Mr Murchison, of London; the price I never knew.

Lee put these prices in perspective when he commented, 'Old Jock was sold for more than his weight in silver, which might be about £80 or a trifle more.' The equivalent price at the beginning of 1991 was about £600.

The life seems to have suited Jock. Having been born in 1859 he was still winning at shows in 1870 when, owned by Murchison, he came second to Trimmer, a more fashionable black and tan headed terrier.

Rawdon Lee also described Tartar. He had

no pedigree who was said to have been bred by Mr Stevenson, of Chester, about 1862. I think there is little doubt that he was a cross bred dog, for, as he was shown at Birmingham in 1863, had those who looked after him cared to determine his parentage (or if they possessed it to publish it), they could easily have done so.

According to Lee, Tartar

was full of go and fire, a hardy-looking, strongly built terrier . . . Tartar 17 lb. in weight, was a pure white dog, excepting for a light patch of pale tan over one eye, unusually compact in build – a pocket Hercules in fact, with a back as muscular and strong as is the neck of a mighty Cumberland and Westmoreland wrestler. A little wide in front was the old dog, but straighter perhaps on the forelegs than Jock, and with better feet. The latter, far the longer and more terrier-like in head, was beaten in size of ears, their mode of carriage, and in neatness of hind quarters. Tartar was a peculiarly elegantly moulded dog behind, notwithstanding the amount of muscle he showed, and he stood neither too high on his legs nor the contrary. . . . Both Tartar and Jock had fair coats, that of the former, the harder and smoother, and no doubt he was much the gamer of the two.

Finally there is Old Trap. His best performance in the ring came when he was second to Old Jock at Birmingham in 1862. He, too, was of uncertain pedigree. The Kennel Club Stud Book says that 'Mr J.H.D. Bayly, already mentioned, purchased him off Mr Cockayne, then kennel man to the Oakley

Hounds, and later at the Tickham. Mr Cockayne bought him
from a groom of Mr Isted's, well-known in the Pytchley Hunt.
Trap was believed to have some black and tan blood in him.' So
Trap too could lay claim to being a genuine hunt terrier bred in
the kennels which produced so many top-rate terriers.

He was a tan head dog, with a black mark on one side down
the saddle which he passed on to his offspring to the extent that
the marking became known as 'Trap marked'. Was the
Parson's dislike of black markings the reason why he chose not
to use Old Trap on his bitches? Or should we look elsewhere in
Lee's description of a dog with a head which was

> terrier-like and good in appearance, the latter improved by
> his beautifully placed and perfectly shaped eyes. He was a
> little too long in the body, and not nearly so elegantly formed
> in ribs, neck, hindquarters, shoulders, and elsewhere as
> either of the terriers previously mentioned. His forelegs and
> feet were fairly good, he had more than an inclination to be
> cow-hocked, and his coat was a trifle long and at times rather
> too open, though generally of good texture. Old Trap was
> about 17 lb in weight.

Apart from his colouring there seem to be so many things about
Old Trap which might have turned the Parson against him. He
seems not to have been well made, did not have galloping
quarters and did not have a weather-resistant coat.

So much for these three important dogs but what of the
people or, perhaps more importantly, the hunts involved?

When Old Jock was born the 6th Viscount Galway was
master of the Grove and not, as Lee says, Sir Richard Sutton.
Sutton never was master of the Grove but, from 1847 to 1856,
was master of the Quorn. Lee, however, is right about Captain
Percy Williams being master of the Rufford at the time. He
succeeded the 6th Viscount Galway as master in 1841 and
remained until 1861. Then Major Welfitt was succeeded in
1867 by Mr Harvey D. Bayly. Harvey Bayly has been
mentioned as one of Old Trap's owners. He was a guest at the
Parson's wedding and went hunting with the happy couple on
the following day.

A number of these people were personal friends of the
Parson's. He was probably acquainted with almost all of them.
When he made his début as a Kennel Club judge it was

alongside his old friend and more experienced judge the Hon.
T.W. Fitzwilliam. It was Murchison who introduced the
Parson to the Kennel Club and, ten years later, he had the task
of writing his obituary. He knew Tom Wootton well enough to
ask him for the loan of both Old Jock and Tartar so that they
could be mated to his bitches.

It is likely that his friendship with the people who bred,
owned and worked these two terriers meant that he knew more
about them and, quite possibly, their breeding than has been
handed down. Indeed it is entirely possible and quite likely that
one or both carried some of the Parson's own breeding.
However, the temptation to venture too far into speculation
must be resisted.

Tom Wootton, the owner of both Old Jock and Tartar,
loaned both dogs to the Parson for use on his bitches. In a letter
to Wootton the Parson said,

> I have put one bitch to Jock and shall put another – although
> she is only nine months old – a rather precocious young you
> will say – tomorrow or next day; and Lord Portsmouth's
> huntsman will send her on Saturday. I have never seen this
> bitch – she is seven years old and of my purest blood, and I
> hope she may not miss.

The Parson's reference to a bitch of his 'purest blood' refutes
any suggestion that he was not interested in pedigree. Another,
though slightly oblique, comment by Davies also supports the
view that the Parson had a very high regard for the value of
pedigree. Speaking of the Parson's marriage he said, 'If Russell,
then, had an eye to a "lass wi' a lang pedigree" – a point he
would have considered of the first importance in selecting a
horse or a hound – he could scarcely have made a better choice'
than Miss Penelope Incledon Bury. So the pedigrees of his
horses and hounds was a matter of some importance to the
Parson. Can it be doubted but that he attached just the same
importance to the pedigrees of his terriers?

It seems also that the Parson retained breeding rights over
terriers, even terriers which he hadn't seen, which were in the
hands of neighbouring hunts. Lord Portsmouth hunted the
Eggesford from 1858. The Parson's friends were very much
involved with the pack, Robert Luxton, Lord Poltimore,

Froude Bellew and Mark Rolle all having, at one time or another, hunted hounds over the Eggesford country.

The Parson then went on to discuss a problem he had had with his two famous guests:

> Since they came here I have kept both Tartar and Jock chained up in two separate loose boxes, because they are warmer than kennels. Yesterday morning I gave Jock a run before I went to meet hounds and after my return from hunting I did the same for Tartar. He went with me very kindly, as he had frequently done before; indeed they both recognised my voice and were mad to come to me whenever they heard it; when suddenly without the least provocation, he started back and ran full tilt back to the stable, the door of which was open, and in one moment fastened upon Jock. I caught hold of him immediately, put his foot in my mouth, and bit it with all my force, choking him with my left hand at the same time; and no harm – or very little – would have happened had not Jock resented the insult and had him across the nose. This enabled Tartar, when I freed him from Jock's foreleg, to seize his hindleg. But I soon released him and took Jock in my arms. The whole thing annoyed me dreadfully, and I am sure you will believe jealousy is the cause of the mischief.

In fact, as the Parson probably knew, Tartar had a reputation as a fiery sort of individual. He was an inveterate fighter, confirmed cat killer and had been used in both rat and badger pits. Giving him an opportunity to fight with Old Jock was the result of just the sort of carelessness which, from time to regrettable time, happens in every kennel.

In January 1883 the Parson wrote to his old friend William Turner of West Molland. He concluded the letter by asking 'is "Mercury", the puppy I gave you, living? I kept back a couple of little bitches, I should like to breed from these in time.' A report written for the Temple Bar magazine in 1885 by one of the Parson's locums, the Rev. Cowan, mentions the terriers which were in the Parson's home shortly before his death. There was Rags, a bitch with a blind eye, which was probably the result of a more legitimate pursuit. There were Sly, Fuss and Tinker, all terriers, as well as a collie, Laddie, and two fearsome cats. Unfortunately the Rev. Cowan did not share the Parson's interest in terriers and so their names are all he tells us of them.

Within three months of writing to Turner the Parson was dead. He could not have bred from his two little bitches. There can be no doubt but that his interest in his terriers and in breeding remained with him right up to his final days.

The Parson's influence over Fox Terriers, of both coats, had been profound. He was credited with saving the rough-coated variety from extinction though this may not have been strictly true for he was not the only breeder interested in rough-coated fox terriers. Some of the most successful show kennels were founded on bitches he had supplied. Shirley, Wootton, Fitzwilliam, Murchison and Carrick all had bitches which the Parson had bred, in their kennels. People such as Sanderson and Lyndsay Hogg were flattered to be told that their terriers resembled the Parson's. No one but a very talented breeder could possibly have established such a reputation or exerted such influence.

Perhaps the scale of his influence can best be illustrated by examining the pedigrees of Old Foiler, of the great champion Brockenhurst Rally and of Carlisle Tack.

Old Foiler started life as Willie but had his name changed to Foiler. In old age he became Old Foiler in order to differentiate him from his imitators. He was bred in 1870 by George Whitemore, huntsman to the Atherstone. His pedigree will raise the eyebrows and probably the hair of anyone who is suspicious of the value of inbreeding. It is included here, partly for that reason, partly because it shows to what extent the Parson's breeding was valued by those who were intent on producing show terriers and partly also because it shows three generations of the Parson's breeding. Better still, in this last respect, is the pedigree of the great champion Brockenhurst Rally, which embodies even more of the Parson's breeding, going back through at least six generations. Carlisle Tack also had at least six generations of the Parson's breeding behind him. The bitch Twile, the dam of Alys Serrell's Sharper, through Wasp, Moss II, Moss I, Juddy, Vic and Nettle also has six generations of the Parson's breeding.

It would not be difficult to find still more examples which show how highly the Parson's breeding was valued.

Pedigree of Foiler (Old Foiler), born 1870

Parents	Grandparents	GG-parents	GGG-parents
			Unknown
		Grove Tartar	Unknown
	Grove Willie		Grove Tartar
		Grove Nettle (1862)	Handley's Sting
Sire Grip (Old Grip)			Unknown
		Grove Tartar	Unknown
	Russell's Vixen		Grove Tartar
		Grove Nettle	Handley's Sting
			Unknown
		Grove Tartar	Unknown
	Grove Willie		Grove Tartar
		Grove Nettle	Handley's Sting
Dam Russell's Juddy (1868)			Unknown
		Grove Tartar	Unknown
	Russell's Vixen (1860)		Grove Tartar
		Grove Nettle	Handley's Sting

Pedigree of Brockenhurst Rally, born 8 March 1878

Parents	Grandparents	GG-parents	GGG-parents
		Belvoir Joe	Cooper's Trimmer
			Cooper's Trinket
	Belgrave Joe (1880)	White Vic	Tartar
			Russell's Vic
Sire Brockenhurst Joe (1874)		Chance	Tyrant
			Lady
	Tricksey	Russell's Ruby	Old Jock
			Russell's Grip
		Tyrant (Old Tyrant)	Trap (Old Trap)
			Lady
	Gibson's Bitters	Unknown	Unknown
			Unknown
Dam Russell's Moss II		Hornet (Old Hornet)	Fitzwilliam's Trap
			Grove Nettle
	Russell's Moss I (1869)	Russell's Juddy (1868)	Grove Willie
			Russell's Vic

Pedigree of Carlisle Tack (Tack), born 5 May 1884

Parents	Grandparents	GG-parents	GGG-parents
			Old Tip
		Pincher	
			Lord Faversham's bitch
	Old Jester		
			Unknown
		Fan	
			Unknown
Sire Swainson's Trick (1882)			
			Buffer
		Gibson's Buffet	
			Frolic
	Patch		
			Unknown
		Millie	
			Unknown
			Grip
		Foiler (Old Foiler)	
			Russell's Juddy
	Troilus (Young Foiler)		
			Jock (Old Jock)
		Cropper's Nectar	
			Grove Nettle
Dam Wootton's Lill Foiler (1883)			
			Russell's Tip I
		Russell's Tip II	
			Russell's Fuss
	Russell's Wasp		
			Gibson's Bitters
		Russell's Moss II	
			Russell's Moss I

5

The Parson and
Dog Show

Perhaps one of the strongest of the objections voiced against recognition is that the breed's ability to work will be eroded by Kennel Club demands and by show ring fashions. The objection is not unreasonable but is both exaggerated and misdirected.

It cannot be denied that there are a number of breeds, including terrier breeds, which can no longer carry out the job for which they were originally intended. To list them would be invidious. However, it must be said that the present state of these breeds is not the result of Kennel Club dictat or even of show ring demands. Breeds change over time partly because change, without a conscious effort to prevent it, is inevitable, and partly because, in some breeds, breeders have themselves opted for change. This has happened to Jack Russell Terriers. What happens in the show ring follows what breeders themselves want and the Kennel Club does no more than reflect what breeders themselves want. Only when what breeders want comes into conflict with the welfare of their breed is the Kennel Club likely to oppose their wishes.

When the Kennel Club was going through the task of revising breed standards in order to put them into a common format the opportunity was taken to remove or modify any clause which called for exaggerated characteristics. These exaggerations often went a long way toward making dogs unsuitable for the purpose for which they were originally intended, and it was the breeders themselves who had introduced them. More might have been achieved had the Kennel Club chosen to override the views expressed by breed clubs but only in extreme circumstances was such a course adopted. In the main the Kennel Club accepted the views of the clubs and, as a consequence, a number of breed standards may still contain requirements which militate against working ability or which are the cause of health problems.

What is often supposed to be the Parson's attitude towards show dogs and dog shows rests largely on one particular passage in Davies's biography and on subsequent interpretations of it. The passage suggests that the Parson was opposed to the baleful influence of the show ring, had little or no regard for show dogs and, by implication, was equally distrustful of the Kennel Club and all its works.

Davies quotes the Parson as telling a friend,

'seldom or ever see a real fox-terrier nowadays, they have so intermingled strange blood with the real article, that, if he were not informed, it would puzzle Professor Bell himself to discover what race the so-called fox-terrier belongs to.'

'And pray, how is it managed?' inquired the friend, eager to profit by Russell's long experience in such matters. 'I can well remember Rubie's and Tom French's Dartmoor terriers, and have myself owned some of that sort worth their weight in gold. True terriers they were, but certainly differing as much from the present show dogs as the wild eglantine differs from a garden rose.'

'The process,' replied Russell, 'is simply as follows: they begin with a smooth bitch terrier; then, to obtain a finer skin, an Italian greyhound is selected for her mate. But as the ears of the produce are an eyesore to the connoisseur, a beagle is resorted to, and then little is seen of that unsightly defect in the next generation. Lastly, to complete the mixture, the bulldog is now called on to give the necessary courage; and the composite animals thus elaborated, become, after due selection, the sires and dams of the modern fox-terriers. This version of their origin,' continued he, 'I received from a man well qualified to speak on the subject.'

The bulldog blood thus infused imparts courage, it is true, to the so-called terrier; he is matchless at killing any number of rats in a given time; will fight any dog of his weight in a Westminster pit; draw a badger heavier than himself out of his long box; and turn up a tom-cat possessed even of ten lives, before poor pussy can utter a wail. But the ferocity of that blood is in reality ill suited – nay, is fatal – to fox-hunting purposes; for a terrier that goes to ground and fastens on his foe, as one so bred will do, is far more likely to spoil sport than promote it, he goes in to kill, not to bolt, the object of his attack.

Besides, such animals, if more than one slip into a fox-earth, are too apt to forget the game, and fight each other, the death of one being occasionally the result of such encounters. Hence, Russell may well have been proud of the pure pedigree he had so long possessed and so carefully watched over. Tartars they were, and ever have been, beyond all doubt; going up to their fox in any earth, facing him alternately with hard words and harder nips, until at length he is forced to quit his stronghold, and trust to the open for better security.

A fox thus bolted is rarely a pin the worse for the skirmish; he has had fair play given him, and instead of being half strangled, is fit to flee for his life.

Davies did not claim that the Parson was expressing his own opinion. It was the opinion of 'a man well qualified to speak on the subject'. Qualified or not what he said was nonsense. The process described would not achieve the result claimed for it. Even if it could possibly have done so, it would have introduced qualities of which show terriers had no need. What need had fox terriers, intended only for the show ring, for the sort of courage to be got from an infusion of bulldog blood, itself a breed whose courage was said to have been already ruined by a career in the show ring?

If this represented the Parson's view why did he support dog shows? Why did he become a member of the Kennel Club? Could it be that Parson Jack Russell was a hypocrite? Is it not more likely that Davies was here expressing his own ill-informed opinion and that the Parson, out of kindness to his old friend, let the comments remain in the manuscript?

If the Parson did make such a silly statement it is as well to remember that it was not unknown for him to act rashly or make statements which he would afterwards regret. The incidents which involved Bovey, Bulteel and Will Long provide examples. Threatening to horsewhip his parishioners and a very unecclesiastical brawl with his good friend Froude provide others. There are several instances which show that the Parson's actions and words were not always well considered, and that when the heat of the moment had passed he would regret them. In this case he was probably doing no more than allowing Davies to express his own opinion.

The simple fact is that if breeders want to change any breed they can do so with or without Kennel Club recognition, and with or without any involvement with dog shows.

Foxhounds have from time to time suffered from the demands of changing fashions. For instance, white terriers came into being simply in order to satisfy the demands of a fashion which dictated that the colour of hounds and terriers should create a pleasing picture in the field. There is no basis for any suggestion that breeds not connected with dog shows avoid the influence of fashion.

There is, however, evidence which suggests that the Parson was, at least from the early 1860s, involved with shows of one sort or another. His links with and energetic support for agricultural societies meant that he must have been deeply involved in their annual shows, most of which would have included a few classes for dogs. From the outset many, among the classes for sheep, cattle and poultry and the exhibitions of new machinery and new methods, provided a few classes in which the owners of working or sporting dogs could compete. As a master of hounds and a well-known breeder of terriers these classes could not have failed to attract the Parson's interest. It is likely that it was his close involvement with and active support for early shows as well as his reputation as a breeder of both Fox Terriers and hounds which led to the Parson becoming the Kennel Club's thirtieth member on 13 March 1874.

Throughout his life the Parson was ready to give his support to endeavours he regarded as worthy, ranging from cricket clubs to agricultural societies. He must have regarded the Kennel Club and its aims as worthy of his support. Its founder members regarded the Parson as a very desirable member who would support the Club's aims.

On the basis of critical remarks made by Davies, and,

surprisingly, not refuted by the Parson, and as a result of misinterpretation of a remark in the Parson's obituary, it has become generally accepted that the Parson disliked dog shows and show dogs, and that his career as a judge lasted for only one show. Why a man who disliked dog shows should ever become a member of a club founded with the sole purpose of promoting dog shows is conveniently ignored.

It is odd and not a little sad how often efforts are made to misrepresent the Parson's views and attitudes. The evidence used to support these efforts is often spurious or inaccurate.

In Herbert Compton's *The Twentieth Century Dog*, published in 1904, is a reference to the Parson's terriers which is also typical of many of its successors and which have formed the basis for subsequent comment.

> Where shall you find any terrier strain, or for that matter any strain of dogs, so honoured and renowned as that of the Devonshire Parson, whose distaste for show dogs was almost as profound as his admiration for working ones? I suppose he is the only terrier fancier who has achieved a world-wide reputation for his stock without the aid of red tickets and championship certificates. Mr Russell has been called the father of the breed; he started his strain in Waterloo Year and he died in the nineties, and his experience comprehended the whole gamut of type from the chaotic to the completed. He was as particular about the pedigrees of his own dogs as the most expert and successful of modern exhibitors, and only once admitted an outcross when he imported a dash of old blood from Old Jock.
>
> Parson Russell's terriers were on the small side, the dogs seldom exceeding eighteen pounds and the bitches running two or three pounds less.

Because these comments, as well as others of a like nature, have tended to form the basis for much subsequent comment it is well worth examining them in some detail.

Compton treats easily verified facts with disdain. Russell did not acquire Trump until 1819, four years after Waterloo. He died in 1883, not in the nineties. He used not one but at least six well-known show terriers on his bitches.

His terriers appeared in the ring at the Bath and West in

1863, where forty classes were judged by Mr Blyth from London and the Parson had the satisfaction of dividing the Hon. Mark Rolle's exhibits in the terrier class. He showed his Harriers, and took second place, at the Second International Show held at the Agricultural Hall, Islington, London, in May 1864. The show attracted 1047 entries. It was notable also as the show at which the Prince of Wales made his début as a winning exhibitor in the classes for harriers. The show also included classes for 'Kennel- or Fox-terriers' in which the Parson would have been interested to see his friend Tom Wootton take first and second place with Jock and Venom. Davenport's Tartar came third.

During 1868 and 1869 he appeared regularly in the ring as an exhibitor of both Fox Terriers and hounds and it is interesting to note the way, during the early years of national dog shows, so many of the Parson's friends appear as both judges and exhibitors. The Hon. T.W. Fitzwilliam, the Rev. Thomas Pearce, the Rev. Cumming Macdona, the Prince of Wales, Thomas Wootton, Sewellis Shirley, John Carrick, John Murchison, even A. George of bag-fox notoriety, all appeared regularly in the ring. Classes in which Fox Terriers could compete were not provided at every show and, quite often, when they were provided the classification was, to say the least, eccentric with genuine hunt and working terriers being expected to appear among non-sporting breeds. But the perseverance of Fox Terrier exhibitors was slowly repaid as entries began to increase and classification became more acceptable.

By the time the 2nd Annual Scottish National Exhibition of Sporting and Fancy Dogs in Glasgow came along in 1872 Fox Terrier classes were divided into smooth and rough or wiry-haired from which John Murchison emerged with most of the prizes as he did a few weeks later when a show took place at Edinburgh, with William Carrick carrying off all the prizes in Otterhounds.

Shows continued to increase in size and number and to attract their own band of supporters. People like Murchison and Shirley, who had terriers from the Parson, branched out into other breeds but there was no sign that the sporting fraternity had developed any sort of antipathy to shows.

Masters of Hounds appeared regularly as both judges and exhibitors and at the 1872 Nottingham show T.W. Fitzwilliam, Captain Shipworth and Frank Gillard made an impressive panel of judges for Foxhounds and Fox Terriers.

When the Parson judged at the National Dog Show, held at the Crystal Palace, Sydenham, London, in June 1874 most of the judges were fellow-members of the Kennel Club and the Parson's co-judge for Fox Terriers and Wire-haired Fox Terriers was also his hunting companion the Hon. T.W. Fitzwilliam. He was joined by Lieut.-Colonel Barlow to judge Harriers. It is interesting that Charles Lowe, in his *Dog Shows and Doggy People*, in listing the show's judges diverted to record that the Rev. Jack Russell's was 'quite a name to conjure with in the West of England, and a dear friend of one of my clerical brothers.' Lane also comments that 'there were large entries of Harriers from Messrs Lewis, Chesshyres, Saxby, Steyning, Lionel Patton, and Everett; and a good lot of Fox-terriers, with J. Fletcher, H. Gibson, J.H. Shaw, J. Shepherd (with Buffet), and other in front rank. Mr T. Wootton took all the prizes in Wire-haired Terriers.' The Parson himself appears not to have made any remarks, critical or otherwise, about the quality of the exhibits. Others described the terriers as 'a good lot'.

The Parson's awards at the Crystal Palace speak for themselves. They make it quite clear that he was very impressed by the dogs which appeared before him. Not only did he go to the unusual extent of awarding two championships in dogs but he also did the same in bitches. If he had not been impressed he might have considered withholding the championships, as was his right. He certainly wouldn't have awarded two to each sex. The winners were J. Fletcher's Rattler and F.J. Ashbury's Tyke. Rattler was said to have been very like Old Jock in appearance. How could the Parson have failed to like him? He liked Tyke just as much. Rattler was a great-grandson of Tartar. Tyke was bred by Fitzwilliam. He was not only a son of Tartar but also a grandson of Old Jock. It is not surprising that the Parson liked them both.

The Parson also found it impossible to divide his winners in bitches. J. Shepherd's Lillie and S. Dixon's Myrtle were equal first. Once more the Parson had found the sort of breeding which he had used in the past. Lillie was by Tartar and went back to Old Jock on her dam's side. Myrtle was a great-granddaughter of Old Jock on her sire's side and his grand-daughter on her dam's side.

In his two open classes the Parson again found the breeding he liked. Gibson's Rivet, a white dog with an evenly marked head, and another great-grandson of Old Jock, won the dog class. Third was the same owner's Flasher, yet another Old Jock great-grandson. The same owner's Spiteful won the Open bitch class. She was a granddaughter of the Parson's own Moss I. Another granddaughter of Tartar was second, Horsefall's Giddy, and third was Shore's Fury, another white terrier with a small spot over the left eye. She was also a granddaughter of Tartar.

There can be very little doubt but that the Parson not only knew precisely what he was looking for in the terrier ring but also that he managed to find it. How can we possibly accept Irving Ackerman's suggestion, made in his *The Complete Fox Terrier*, that 'the terriers he saw failed to impress him', when one of his winners was so like Old Jock and even then he could not beat Tyke?

Rattler was a dog whose breeding Rawdon Lee regarded as having few if any pretensions to quality. He had a pheno-menally successful show career, earning the soubriquet of 'The Dreaded Rattler'. He was bred in 1871 by Sam Turner in Nottingham. The litter contained five pups, two black and white dogs, an all-white bitch and two nearly all-white dogs, Rattler and Ripple. They were by W. Hulse's Fox, a heavily tan marked dog out of Fan, a white bitch with a cherry nose and a liver ear. Rattler was sold at five weeks of age for 5 shillings and a canary and his breeder later declined an opportunity to buy him back for £25. At a year old he was sold for £1 to Ingleby who showed him at Manchester to get a VHC. Rattler was then sold to Jack Terry for £17 and in 1873 won a first prize at the Free Trade Hall, Manchester, under the Hon. T.W. Fitzwilliam. He was then sold to Messrs. J. Douglas and S. Handley for £50 and then for £100 to Mr Fletcher. While in Fletcher's ownership Rattler was cared for by George Helliwell of Sheffield and, between 1873 and 1879, went on to win over 250 prizes.

At stud the dog was a failure, about which Rawdon Lee expresses no surprise.

The appearance of Trimmer II in any pedigree being quite
sufficient to condemn it. Oh, what ears that dog had! Big
even during an era when such were rather the rule than the
exception. Rattler, in appearance just an enlarged edition of
Old Jock, was about 19 lb. weight, in fair show condition;
good all round, the more one looked at him the better he
suited.

Ratler (The Dreaded Rattler), born 1871, bred by Mr Sam Turner, Chesterfield Street, Nottingham

Parents	*Grandparents*
Sire Hulse's Fox	Trimmer II by Old Tartar
	Old Tartar
Dam Fan	Underwood's Spot
	Cowlister's Dutch

So Rattler was 'just a larger edition of Old Jock'. Is it likely
that the Parson was 'unimpressed' by a terrier which was so like
one which he had described as 'the nearest thing to perfection
we poor mortals are ever likely to be allowed to set our eyes
upon.'?

The pedigrees of the four principal winners are revealing.
Both Tyke and Lillie were by Tartar. Tyke was also a grandson
of Old Jock, who appeared one generation further back in
Lillie's pedigree. Rattler was a great-grandson of Tartar and
Myrtle was a granddaughter of Old Jock. Perhaps of even more
significance is that both Myrtle and Lillie went back to Old
Jock through Vic, a bitch which the Parson himself had bred.

Whatever the Parson actually thought he was prepared to
make the arduous journey from Devon to Darlington to judge
fox terriers at the South Durham and North Yorkshire Show in
July. Charles Lane records that 'Fox-terriers had a good entry,
Messrs Astbury, G.K. Proctor, W. Allison, Thackray, and
Denham being amongst the most successful.'

In October he was in Nottingham to judge Foxhounds,
Harriers, Beagles and Wire-haired Terriers at the 5th Annual
Exhibition of the National Canine Society held at Haymarket
Place. On this occasion the judging panel also included

Captain Skipwith, Peter Pilgrim, and Frank Gillard, huntsman to the Duke of Rutland's hounds at Belvoir Castle. Lane tells us that 'Blood-hounds, Fox-hounds, Harriers and Otter-hounds were poorly supported but Fox-terriers had large and good classes, with many well-known names as winners.'

In Nottingham the Parson had entries of Otterhounds, Harriers and Beagles from packs and individuals all over the country. The Carlisle pack, whose Master owned terriers bred by the Parson, was represented by Stanley, a 5½-year-old Otterhound which had taken a first prize at the Crystal Palace and which was for sale at £500. He had attracted a huge entry of Fox Terriers which contained most of the current winners, including several which carried his bloodlines or were closely related to dogs which he had used on his bitches.

The Parson had attracted a huge entry of 267 Fox Terriers, one of the highest up to that date, and among these were a number which represented various hunts, including the Grove, the Belvoir and the Fitzwilliam, as well as the major individual Fox Terrier breeders, Gibson, Bassett, Fitzwilliam, Redmond, Wootton, Turner, Cropper and Astbury among them. It was evident that the Parson's opinion of show Fox Terriers was highly respected and that the destructive split between show and working fox terriers which would eventually take place was still in the future.

Of even more interest are the terriers themselves. Old Jock, Tartar, Rattler, all dogs which the Parson is known to have liked enormously, were particularly well represented.

The Parson had travelled from Devon to Nottingham to be faced by well over 300 dogs in four different breeds, more than the Kennel Club would now regard as an acceptable load for any judge let alone one who was already in his eightieth year. Even such an unusually vigorous old man must have found the task daunting. Much has been made of the fact that the Parson's judging career under Kennel Club rules appears to have been ended by the Nottingham show. The Parson had given his foxhounds up some three years previously, though his enthusiasm for hunting was not diminished in any way. Surely he would have retired from judging long before his eightieth birthday if he disliked dog shows.

In fact though the Parson did not judge at any shows run

under Kennel Club rules after 1874 he didn't retire completely
from the centre of the ring. The Rev. W.H. Thornton, in his
Reminiscences and Reflections of an Old West Country Clergyman,
records that, in 1876, the Parson had ridden from Swimbridge
to Scorrier, a distance of seventy-four miles, in order to judge
hound puppies for its master George Williams.

Even though the Parson retired from active participation in
major shows, his influence on what was happening in the Fox-
Terrier ring was by no means at an end. Terriers which he had
bred were in demand by people who combined an interest in
hunting with an interest in dog shows and from his bloodlines
emerged some of the most successful Fox Terrier kennels of the
period.

The Parson described Old Jock as the nearest thing to
perfection we poor mortals are ever likely to be allowed to set
our eyes upon. He used him, on at least two occasions, on at
least three of his bitches. Was Old Jock a show dog? In 1862
Old Jock took a first prize at a show at Birmingham. In 1863 he
won at Cremorne, Halifax, Manchester and Birmingham. In
1864 at Islington, Alexandra Park, Nottingham, Birmingham
and Manchester. In 1865 he won at Islington, Brighton,
Birmingham, and Manchester. Throughout 1866 and until his
death on 18 November 1872 Old Jock remained a consistent
winner at shows all over the country. He won in Darlington in
the north, Brighton in the south, Hull in the east and Liverpool
in the west. There can be no denying that Old Jock was a show
dog of the very highest quality.

Charlie Littleworth, of Wembworthy, North Devon, knew
Fox Terriers both as workers and as show dogs. He was
huntsman to the Eggesford. His view was that

> the best strain for work has descended from George White-
> more's [of the Grove] Willie, afterwards called Foiler, and
> eventually the property of Mr Wootton, who paid £45 for
> him. A bitch I once had, named Mustard, was a really
> honest worker. She was about 18 lb weight, and after
> running all day with hounds would gamely go to ground,
> and show us and reynard what blood ran in her veins. This
> bitch was by Whitemore's Trick out of Eggesford Fury, who
> was out of the Rev. J. Russell's Fuss, a most famous one as a

worker. She was a hard coated bitch, and eventually became the property of Mr Wootton, and was stolen from his father's place in Leicestershire. Mustard, too, had taken prizes at the West of England shows, under the well-known and popular sportsman above-mentioned, including first prize at Plymouth in 1873.

Charlie Littleworth was under no illusions about whether show dogs could work and working dogs acquit themselves well in the field. He took justified pride in having taken prizes under Parson Jack Russell.

To suggest that the Parson did not like show dogs or dog shows is to fly in the face of the facts.

6

Development After
the Parson

Sir Jocelyn Lucas makes the claim that 'Jack Russell was much addicted to badger digging, and his terriers became renowned for their prowess. This was presumably how he tried his dogs for hardness.' No evidence is produced to support the claim, which is at odds with Davies's statement that the Parson's terriers were entered only to fox. All the reliable evidence which exists suggests that he had little or no time for a 'hard' terrier. In the absence of any contemporary evidence to support Lucas's suggestion it must be refuted. The Parson was not interested in badger-digging and his terriers were not used for badger-digging.

Badger-digging, and even nocturnal hunting using hounds have been practised at least since the sixteenth century. Neither had ever achieved the status of a fashionable sport. It seems that the exquisite fun to be had from digging a hole in the ground in order to reach a creature whose escape was barred by a terrier, or from night-time hunting in Britain was appreciated only by connoisseurs of these peculiar pleasures. Badgers, because of their ready availability, their strength and their stubborn resistance to attacks were frequently baited in the pits where bear-baiting and dog-fighting took place. They continued to be tormented even after 1835, when these activities became illegal. Badger-baiting and dog-fighting were the activities which gave rise to the bull-and-terrier breeds. They produced the Staffordshire Bull Terrier and the Bull Terrier.

Towards the end of the Parson's life and well into the twentieth century, badger-digging became a fashionable, though still very much a minority, pastime. There was some semblance of regard for fair play for badgers which, having been subjected to the indignity of summary eviction, were often then released unharmed. This form of badger-digging should not be confused with the barbaric ritual of badger-baiting in which fair play has no part. Half-starved and half-grown badgers, often cruelly incapacitated, their jaws and even their backs broken, their forefeet nailed to boards, are set upon by a succession of terriers. These are urged on by their brave owners. Sadly badger-baiting involving cruelties which would have nauseated even the hardened denizens of Paris Gardens and the Westminster Pit has reappeared and is practised by some people who profess support for legitimate field sports but are, in effect, its worst enemies.

Badger-digging in the form which became popular towards the end of Victoria's reign, gave rise to the Sealyham Terrier, produced on the Haverfordwest estate of Captain Edwardes. It also produced the Cowley Terrier, produced in Oxfordshire by John Cowley and, somewhat later, to the terriers bred by Sir Jocelyn Lucas. In Ireland it gave rise to the Glen of Imaal Terrier, the Kerry Blue Terrier and to the Soft Coated Wheaten Terrier. Doubtless there were also a number of other local breeds which failed to achieve national notice.

In Devon Arthur Heinemann and, later, his housekeeper Annie Harris, *née* Rawle, were busily producing large numbers of what they described as Jack Russell Terriers. These were not intended either to run with hounds or even, primarily, to work to fox. The majority were produced for sale. Annie Rawle and, to a somewhat lesser extent, Arthur Heinemann would nowadays be regarded as commercial breeders, if not as puppy farmers. Some terriers were intended for badger-digging. These were both very different from the type of terrier the Parson himself had developed and from the fox terriers which were then to be found in hunt kennels throughout the country.

Arthur Blake Heinemann must be regarded as a major character in the history of what have come to be regarded as Jack Russell Terriers. He was a sporting journalist and consequently many of his statements remain available. These must be accepted with considerable caution. Not to put too fine a point on it, though Heinemann seems nowadays to have attained something close to beatification among some Parson and Jack Russell breeders, he must be seen as a saint whose feet of clay reach at least up to his knees. He was prone to making claims which left the truth at a distance. He regularly contradicted himself. Since his death some of his statements have been further embroidered, and the embroidery accepted without question. It is necessary to try to separate the truth from what was said only to enhance a good story.

Heinemann was born of well-to-do Sussex country parents in 1871. His childhood was spent in Sussex. He was subsequently educated at Eton, then at Trinity College, Cambridge. After spending a short time in South Africa he returned to Britain and set up residence in Porlock, Somerset. There he set about establishing himself as a West country character.

It is difficult to pin down precisely when he went to live in the West country. It has been claimed that he was tutored for Eton by Jack Russell. Why anyone would choose as tutor someone who, over fifty years previously, had been no better than a mediocre scholar and whose life since had not been one which would tend to keep his store of knowledge in good repair, is not easy to understand. Heinemann himself made it clear that the Parson was not his tutor. He referred to the time 'when I came as a boy to read with the parson of Porlock'. The Parson of Porlock was Prebendary Hook. Since Heinemann refers to himself as a 'boy' it may seem most likely that he refers to a period of tutoring prior to going to Eton. He was not the sort of person who could delay his accession to man's estate. Dan Russell, in his *Jack Russell and His Terrier*, takes a different view and suggests that Heinemann lived in Porlock after he came down from Cambridge and after his return from South Africa. By this time he was no longer a boy. Dan Russell suggests that Heinemann read with Prebendary Hook during his short-lived and, in view of his subsequent career, surprising ambition to join the ministry.

There is no doubt that Prebendary Hook and not Jack Russell was his tutor. If he read with Prebendary Hook prior to going to Eton he may have been established in the West country by about 1883. If Dan Russell is right then Heinemann may not have arrived in the West country until about 1890.

His Somerset and Devon Badger Club was founded in 1894 so he must have been living in the West country by that date. In

1902 he became, briefly, Master of the Cheriton Otterhounds. In 1912 Arthur Heinemann wrote that he had 'been breeding rough and smooth terriers for over twenty years'. The actual time is more likely to have been longer than shorter. If twenty years is accepted, he began breeding terriers in about 1892. Perhaps he began to breed terriers before he arrived in the West country but since he always claimed that his original terriers were descendants of the Parson's stock this seems unlikely. He also claimed that only once had he been outside the West country in order to obtain fresh blood. We may take it, therefore, that his career as a terrier breeder began only after he had arrived in Somerset. It is likely that his vague reference to 'over twenty years' experience as a terrier breeder stretched the truth at least a little. In 1892 he was twenty-one years old, not old enough to have graduated from Trinity (though if he failed to graduate his time at Trinity may have been curtailed), lived for more than a very short period in Africa and became established in Somerset. The best that can be done is to accept that Heinemann was established in Somerset a short while prior to 1894.

Heinemann also claimed that he had spent some time as Master of the Essex Otterhounds. The pack was formed in 1898 by W.P.N. Ridley, H.H. Crozier and J.R. Vigne. Ridley was the first Master and the record of Masterships is complete from 1898 until well after Heinemann's death. Nowhere does his name appear. Perhaps Heinemann's association with the pack coincided with his time at Cambridge and before it was known as the Essex Otterhounds but is it likely that a teenage youth, with, as far as is known, no prior family associations with hunting, would have been given the privilege of acting as master?

It has been claimed that Heinemann bought or inherited all the Parson's terriers when the old man died. Heinemann was born in 1871 and the Parson died in 1883. The overlap is enough to allow the two to have met, though there is no evidence that they ever did. Even if they had done so it seems unlikely that an eleven-year-old boy and an 88-year-old man would have had much in common. It is even less likely that an eleven-year-old boy would have bought the Parson's surviving terriers or have inherited them. If, as Heinemann himself suggests, his career as a terrier breeder began about 1892 he may well have been able to acquire terriers directly descended from the Parson's but by then even the last terriers bred by the Parson would have been nearly ten years old. During his brief mastership of the Cheriton he would have had access to other terriers which carried the Parson's bloodlines.

Whatever the precise circumstances, by 1894 Heinemann had completed his education, spent some time in South Africa, abandoned his ambition to join the ministry and developed a taste for hunting. He was not, however, of the Parson's school. There is no reference of any sort to Heinemann's ability to stay with hounds on a screaming scent. His early connections with hounds were with pedestrian Otterhounds and, when these connections ended, they were replaced by an interest in badger-digging. As a sporting journalist he wrote voluminously about both fox and staghounds and doubtless he wrote from the basis of some experience. It was not the experience either of a Master or even of a mounted follower whose courage and ability were widely recognized.

Heinemann claimed to have been, at one stage in his chequered career, the owner of the Cheriton Otterhounds. He even published an account of how he replaced William Cheriton of Ellicombe, Morchard Road, North Devon, who had formed the pack in 1850, as the pack's owner.

> I shall never forget my first visit to him. For hours he refused me a glimpse of the pack and kept assuring me that he would sell and that he was not asking an exorbitant figure, though he would not name the price, and all this muggy afternoon we were imbibing hot gin. Finally he fixed the price at £50 and showed me the pack. Most of them were too old and fat as puddings, but there were some good, rough hounds among them. I agreed to Mr Cheriton's terms provided he circularised the water-owners in my favour, publicly acknowledged me as his successor, and kept the hounds until I wanted them.

The account makes a good story of the sort which Heinemann was adept at telling and which made him a very readable journalist but it isn't entirely true. Cheriton had ceased to be the owner of the pack in 1880. Heinemann was then nine years old. A succession of Masters, including Cheriton's son, hunted the pack until 1900. The Mastership fell vacant and remained so for two years before Heinemann filled the vacancy in 1902. He remained the Master until 1904 when Loraine Bell took over. During the whole of this period hounds were owned by a committee and maintained on the basis of subscriptions. Heinemann never owned the pack though he may have been, and very likely was, a member of the committee which did own the pack. His story is neither totally untrue nor entirely true. Heinemann's supposed and actual relationship both with the Essex Otterhounds and the Cheriton provide evidence of his ability to tell a good tale. The facility is at least as strongly developed in hunting men as it is in fishermen.

The Cheriton's uniform consisted of white bowler hat, dark-blue coat and waistcoat, white breeches, dark-blue stock and gold buttons engraved COH. Compare this with the uniform eventually adopted by the Somerset and Devon Badger Club. In 1922 Henry Williamson, author of *Tarka the Otter*, described a day out with Heinemann's badger club.

The field consisted of men carrying picks and shovels.

> One, with a nose once broken and re-set irregularly, carried a large basket of sandwiches and a gallon earthenware jar of whiskey. About twelve terriers, some of the rough-haired kind, were trotting on single and double leashes. In front walked a tall man in old fawn riding breeches, cloth leggings, a red waistcoat, tweed coat, white stock fastened by a pin made from a badger's penis bone. It resembled a two-inch length of quill. He wore a grey bowler hat. He was, as I soon learned, the Master of the Club. . . . The innkeeper who carried the food and drink . . . a farmer and two labourers with digging tools; three small boys; an adolescent schoolgirl with flaxen hair, ruddy face, always smiling; her father a small, nattily-dressed red-faced, long-nosed man who reminded me, vaguely, of a badger; and his wife, a brown-faced woman in tweeds.

It couldn't have been a prepossessing group and doesn't suggest that the Club enjoyed a great deal of local support.

The declared aims of Heinemann's Somerset and Devon Badger Club were 'the promotion of badger-digging and

interest in badger-digging generally' and 'the breeding of
working terriers'. It should be noted that Heinemann referred
to 'working terriers', not to Jack Russell Terriers. Though the
membership was less than a hundred the Club was said to have
been a considerable success. It organized digs as far afield as
Hereford and Northamptonshire. Heinemann ensured that its
activities were well- publicized. For most of its life the number
of terriers owned by the Club probably outnumbered its
membership. In 1910 it owned seventy-four terriers, including
three Bedlingtons and a Staffordshire Bull Terrier. The Club
didn't need so many for its digging operations. Most of the
terriers were the breeding stock from which Heinemann and,
later, Annie Harris, produced large numbers of puppies.

The presence of three Bedlingtons in the kennel might have
an entirely innocent explanation. The presence of a Staffordshire Bull Terrier seems more sinister. Photographs of
Heinemann's terriers suggest that some carried Stafford or Bull
Terrier blood.

In *The Kennel*, 1910, Heinemann wrote that

> personally speaking, if I ever failed for gameness, I would
> cross with a small Bedlington, but this is an event I don't
> anticipate. The only other cross admissible is the small old-
> fashioned bull terrier, but it takes years of breeding to cross it
> out sufficiently, and you are always getting chesty or smooth-
> coated, or under-hung, or too game dogs in your litters.

There, surely, speaks the voice of experience!

By the time Williamson wrote, Heinemann had dissipated a
substantial fortune. He was supporting himself by work as a
sporting journalist, using the name *Peep-out*, the name of the
cottage in which he lived. An important part, perhaps the
major part, of his meagre income, came from the sale of
puppies. It may well have been to improve puppy sales that he
later changed the name of his badger-digging club to the
Parson Jack Russell Terrier Club. Using the local terrier stock,
in which the blood of Russell's terriers ran strongly, he bred a
stronger, heavier and shorter-legged type of terrier. The type
was far better suited to facing badger than fox. He was fond of
referring to these terriers as Jack Russell Terriers, thus laying
the grounds for confusion which still exists. Perhaps it would be

more appropriate and more just, both to their original breeder and to the terriers themselves if terriers of the type bred by Heinemann were to be called Heinemann Terriers.

Heinemann's claim, in 1912, that he had then 'been breeding rough and smooth terriers for over twenty years', went on to say that 'they are founded on the old Devonshire stocks . . . traceable to the Rev. John Russell ("Parson Jack") and with two exceptions I have never been out of these two countries for fresh blood'. With over seventy terriers at his disposal it is not surprising that he seldom found it necessary to bring in new blood.

Heinemann did not, as has since been suggested, claim to have stock direct from the Parson. He said only that his original breeding stock was 'traceable' to the Parson's terriers. Nor did he claim that he had never used an out-cross, even an out-cross of another breed. He said only that he had only twice gone outside Somerset and Devon for fresh blood. Why this should concern him when he repeatedly expressed such disdain for pedigree it is difficult to say.

Fortunately there are several photographs of Heinemann's terriers still in existence. There need be no dispute about precisely what type of terrier Heinemann bred.

Miss Alys Serrell was a contemporary of Heinemann's and, like him, left a record which tells a great deal about her terriers. She was born in 1848 the daughter of a sporting parson, the Rev. Henry Digby Serrell. He had hunted with the Rev. Harry Farr Yeatman and through him father and daughter had got to know the Parson. The father, his son Campbell, and the two sisters, Geraldine and Alys, were all passionately fond of hunting. They learned their craft when Mr Garth himself was Master of what is now the Garth and South Berkshire. Subsequently they hunted the Blackmore Vale country. After hunting for some years Miss Serrell developed a particular interest in terriers. She subsequently recorded the development of this interest in her book *With Hound and Terrier in the Field*, first published in 1904.

Alys Serrell was lavish in her praise of fox terriers. She regrets, however, that

It is unfortunately true that we have tried hard to spoil him.

On the one hand he has been treated as a mere household pet, and thus become so soft that he has lost all taste for sport; and on the other hand he has been made an instrument of show-bench extravagance. There are fox-terriers with heads so long and narrow as to leave no room for brains; so high on the leg they cannot go into a fox or badger earth without being crippled with cramp; or again so flat-sided as to have no stamina. . . . It is on the kennel terrier, then, as I have had him, keen and eager for sport and ready to hunt the rabbit, swim after the otter, or drive the fox or badger from his earth, that I shall speak.

It is abundantly clear that Alys Serrell's terriers were not, like the Parson's, entered only to fox. Her terriers were expected to be Jacks of all trades.

Alys Serrell reveals that 'the tap-root of my own kennel was Redcap, a smooth terrier born in 1880, of whose pedigree there was sufficient doubt for me to enter it in the Stud-Book as "unascertained"'.

She went on to express pride in Redcap's show success. She described him in a way which demonstrates her appreciation of appearance.

He took first-prize at Barnstaple in 1883. Redcap has a beautiful bright tan head, with a black mark under the right ear which was constantly transmitted to his descendants, and his head was of medium length, with not a trace of the greyhound about it. His ears were small and well carried, and his jaw long and punishing, with big strong teeth, and at eleven years of age he had only lost one small front tooth. His legs were straight, and he had good feet, with a pad like leather. In size he was, I consider, perfect for underground work, his weight being 16 lb. He was short and compact everywhere, with the best coat that could be – short, hard, and dense – with plenty of undergrowth and a thick skin.

Redcap, mated to Amber by Ajax I, produced Redtop and Royal and Racer. Since Redcap's pedigree was 'unascertained' any links between Redtop and the Parson's terriers must go through Amber and Ajax I. Fortunately Alys Serrell again provides valuable additional information. Amber weighed

16 lb, had a tan head and hard, broken coat, a very keen
varminty expression, an uncertain temper and produced a
number of litters both to King Pan, a heavily marked little dog
with which Alys took a first prize at Sherborne in 1885, and a
Sealyham whose name was changed from Ranter to Tartar.
Alys Serrell tells us that Amber was 'bred from Mr Russell's
celebrated old Devonshire strain, and [was] a great-great-
daughter of his famous Old Tip'. In fact Ajax was bred by Jack
Russell out of a daughter of Tip.

Eventually Alys Serrell was obliged to find a replacement for
Redcap. She did not go to any of the hunt kennels whose terriers
she must have known well. Nor did she go to any of the breeders
who, by then, were laying claim, with various levels of
justification, to continuing the strain of terriers which the

Pedigree of Alys Serrell's Sharper, born 1885

Parents	Grandparents	GG-parents	GGG-parents
		Grip	Grove Willie
			Russell's Vic (1860)
	Old Foiler (1870)	Russell's Juddy (1868)	Grove Willie
			Russell's Vic (1860)
Sire Troilus		Old Jock	Branson's Twister
			Grove Pepper
	Fitzwilliam's Nectar (1865)	Grove Nettle	Grove Tartar
			Handley's Sting
		Ashbury's Tyke (1869) br Fitzwilliam	Grove Tartar
			Carry by Old Jock
	Macdona's Little Jim	Unknown	Unknown
			Unknown
Dam Twile		Russell's Tip II	Russell's Tip I
			Russell's Fuss
	Russell's Wasp	Russell's Moss II	Sales' Hornet
			Russell's Moss I

Parson had developed. Miss Serrell went to Tom Wootton and bought Sharper from him.

In Sharper she had found a terrier which, on both sides of his pedigree, went back to the Parson's stock. She had got a terrier with a reliable pedigree which, mated to Amber's offspring, would bring together a considerable amount of the Parson's breeding.

Miss Augusta Guest was another formidable hunting lady with a particular interest in Jack Russell Terriers. She formed her own pack in 1914 in the eastern part of the Blackmore Vale country and hunted this as the Blackmore Vale (Miss Guest) until 1954. Augusta Guest was also joint master of, and often hunted, the Blackmore Vale from 1939 to 1946, from 1954 to 1955 and again from 1959 to 1960. The pack had a long association with the Parson, hounds having originally been bought from George Templer in 1826 by the Rev. Harry Farr Yeatman. It would have been surprising if a few terriers which carried the Parson's blood were not, from time to time, to be found in kennels. Augusta Guest, however, went much further than that.

In a letter to *Horse and Hound*, November 1956, she claimed to

> have a line of terriers distinctly tracing back to his [the Parson's] by name: viz. Jack Russell 'Ajax I' and 'Ajax II' and 'Old Tip', through Miss Alys Serrell's 'Redtop' and my 'Rachael', though, as that is practically seventeen generations back, I do not suppose the Jack Russell blood is still predominant. I can also trace back my 'Pixie', the dam of which was said to be a Jack Russell dog but I cannot vouch for that, it being so long ago.
>
> I have kept my pedigrees very carefully and have only gone for an out-cross to a working strain, when necessary, that I can rely on.

In a subsequent letter she identified Jack Cobby, huntsman of the South and West Wilts whose kennel of Border Terriers, shown under the affix *Motcombe* were as well-known in the show rings as they were in the field.

The Parson's breeding was also valued by his friends who bred Fox Terriers. In particular Tom Wootton, from whom the Parson had borrowed Old Jock and Tartar, had two bitches,

The text to Scott's 1790 engraving of Pitch says that 'it would be necessary to notice Colonel Thornton's terriers if it were only on account of his justly celebrated Pitch, from whom are descended most of the white fox terriers in the kingdom'

Trump was the Parson's foundation bitch, bought from a Marston milkman in 1819. Over 170 years later she would not have looked out of place in a British ring

Old Jock, which the Parson mated to his bitches and which he described as 'the nearest thing to perfection'. Compare him with the modern smooth Jack Russells pictured on other pages

Above: The Reverend Jack Russell in old age. It was the basis for a sketch by N. H. J. Baird which appeared in later editions of Davies's Memoir and which included three terriers. Their appearance cannot be taken as a reliable guide to that of the Parson's terriers

Below: Pictured from left to right are Old Jock, Grove Nettle and Old Tartar, all of which contributed to the Parson's strain of terriers

A silver model, dating from the late 19th century, of a hunt or working terrier. The type is very different from that to be found in the Parson's kennels *Photo: Steve Parkinson*

Will Rawle, the Parson's terrier man for 40 years, bred Ellicombe Spot, who was lost underground at the age of 14. This photograph (the only one in existence) tells us that she was entirely or almost entirely white, had a thick coat and a punishing muzzle

This photograph of a young Arthur Heinemann shows him attired in the Dartmoor Otterhounds' uniform. The terrier at his feet is not one with any pretensions to quality

A brace of Heinemann's own terriers – Lorne on the left and Handycross Nestor on the right. Neither appears to be of the type bred by the Parson and both are probably more suited to badger digging than working to fox

This group of Heinemann's own terriers is probably representative of the type to be found in his kennel

William Carrick's Fox Terrier, Carlisle Tack, was regarded by contemporary judges as indistinguishable from the Parson's own terriers. Tack was out of a bitch, Lill Foiler, which was bred by the Parson

Carlisle Tyro, Tack's son, and very like his sire. It is apparent that the Parson's type was strong enough to bridge the generations

The Hawkestone Otterhounds terriers form a link between the Parson's own terriers from which they are descended and those of the David Davies which are their descendants *Photo: courtesy of Steve Ribbons*

Badger baiting in France during the 1920s appears to have been a popular spectator sport Here Sir Jocelyn Lucas tests the mettle of some terriers which are very close to the Parson' type *Photo: courtesy of Steve Ribbons*

Nancy Turrall's Jack Russell Terrier, Dick, bred in the Pytchley Kennels in 1921. His make and shape, though perhaps not his colouring, are precisely the same as modern Parson Jack Russell Terriers

The Duke of Beaufort's Terrier Show during the early 1970s. It is a salutary thought that 100 years previously the Parson would probably have been standing at the ringside *Photo: Jean Jackson*

Derek Hume's Jack Russell Grip was the Supreme Champion at the Great Yorkshire Show in 1980, winning the honour for the second time at 9 years of age *Photo: courtesy of Shooting Times*

A very typical brace of Jack Price's hard-bitten, smooth-coated Jack Russell Terriers *Photo: Anne Roslin Williams*

Pussy and Wasp, from the Parson. Pussy was later sold, for £40, to Sewellis E. Shirley, founder of the Kennel Club. In 1881 Wasp was mated to Troilus to produce Harding Cox's Ch. Timothy Foiler and again in 1883 to produce Lill Foiler. These three terriers made an appreciable impact on the world of show terriers but perhaps none more so than Lill Foiler who was owned by William Carrick, Master of the Carlisle Otterhounds. Mated to Swainson's Trick she produced Carlisle Tack, a terrier who took the show ring by storm. He was said, by people who had a right to an opinion, to be identical to the terriers the Parson had bred.

Pedigree of Master Tiger (1881), Timothy Foiler (1881) and Lill Foiler (1883)

Parents	Grandparents	GG-parents	GGG-parents
Sire Troilus	Old Foiler	Grip	Grove Willie
			Russell's Vic
		Russell's Juddy	Grove Willie
			Russell's Vic
	Fitzwilliam's Nectar	Old Jock	Branson's Twister
			Grove Pepper
		Grove Nettle	Grove Tartar
			Handley's Sting
Dam Russell's Wasp	Russell's Tip II	Russell's Tip	Unknown
			Unknown
		Russell's Fuss	Unknown
			Unknown
	Russell's Moss	Fitzwilliam's Hornet	Fitzwilliam's Trap
			Grove Nettle
		Russell's Juddy	Grove Willie
			Russell's Vic

The pedigree of Master Tiger, Timothy Foiler (1881), and Lill Foiler (1883) shows that they carried in their veins a great deal of the Parson's bloodlines. The pedigree shows the extent to which the Parson made use of well-known show Fox Terriers, the extent to which his stock was used by the top show kennels and the way in which the breeding of show stock and working stock remained closely intertwined. Only subsequently did each choose to go their separate ways.

Heinemann, Serrell and Guest all bred what they referred to as Jack Russell Terriers. Other terrier breeders also made use of the Parson's bloodlines. Foremost among these was William Carrick, whose Carlisle Tack and Carlisle Tyro have already been mentioned and which were regarded as faithful replicas of the Parson's own terriers.

One of the Parson's bitches, Moss II, mated to Brockenhurst Joe, was the mother of the famous champion Brockenhurst Rally, whelped in 1878. He was owned by the brothers A.H. and C. Clarke who used him to produce Roisterer, the sire of

Pedigree of Ch. Brockenhurst Rally, born 1878, bred by H. Peel

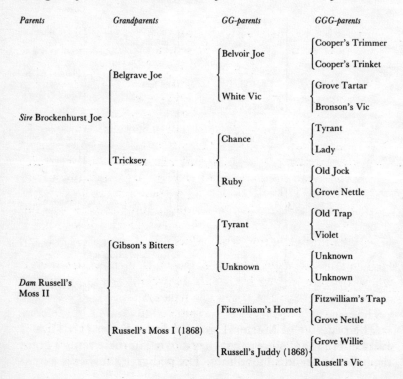

Parents	Grandparents	GG-parents	GGG-parents
Sire Brockenhurst Joe	Belgrave Joe	Belvoir Joe	Cooper's Trimmer
			Cooper's Trinket
		White Vic	Grove Tartar
			Bronson's Vic
	Tricksey	Chance	Tyrant
			Lady
		Ruby	Old Jock
			Grove Nettle
Dam Russell's Moss II	Gibson's Bitters	Tyrant	Old Trap
			Violet
		Unknown	Unknown
			Unknown
	Russell's Moss I (1868)	Fitzwilliam's Hornet	Fitzwilliam's Trap
			Grove Nettle
		Russell's Juddy (1868)	Grove Willie
			Russell's Vic

Result, one of the most successful Smooth Fox Terriers. Rally not only proved to be an excellent sire of top-class show terriers but, used extensively by the Belvoir, among others, also produced some top-class working terriers.

Heinemann was fond of denouncing what he claimed to regard as the pernicious influence of the show ring on dogs in general and on terriers in particular. In this he was not alone. Some of his journalist descendants are still writing much the same stories. Heinemann's aversion to the show ring was not, however, sufficiently strong to prevent him from accepting an invitation to judge working terriers at Cruft's in 1909, though the invitation seems not to have been repeated in subsequent years.

Having accepted the invitation to judge at the show which must have represented the worst of all he professed to see in dog shows, Heinemann then had the effrontery to declare that it was

> impossible to judge by appearances, for a dead-game dog may bear a scar, while a more useful and cautious one with a tongue may not. I once judged a working class. Of course two ladies were among the competitors, for they dearly love dog shows, and like the late Lord Granville Gordon, I was tempted to give the first prize to the best-looking lady; but being out for business, I asked what each terrier had done. Well, one of them had killed twenty moles in one night, and the other was made to sit up and beg, when I discovered he was one I had bred and drafted as the ugly duckling of my litter! In this class the terrier I gave first prize to was utterly useless next week to badger, while an unplaced one was the best a man could wish to work. All of which shows I am a very bad judge; if not, what a farce it all is.

Heinemann was right in some respects. Dog shows are a farce when they are judged by people as prejudiced, unprincipled and inconsistent in their views as he was.

Heinemann's inconsistent attitude is illustrated in the very same article in which he dismissed appearance as an irrelevance. He then goes on to describe, in some detail, what he regarded as the ideal appearance of a working terrier.

Turn to Nature's handiwork, and you will find the badger and otter with their short, pudgy jaws give more punishing bites than the longer-jawed fox, whose brain-pan behind it is larger than a modern show terrier's. . . . Natural coats, hard as bristles on a dandy brush, with plenty of undercoat, are what you want and can get, too, if you have the right blood, and, generally speaking, a rough-coated terrier is more likely to turn a worker than a smooth one. . . . In fox hunting a smaller terrier is necessary, especially in drains, but you want one (at least in moorland countries) who can keep up with hounds all day, and run the line, casting up some few minutes after hounds have marked their fox to ground. To do this he must have a certain length of leg and be built on galloping lines.

When Arthur Heinemann died, aged 59, in 1930 his large but motley kennel of terriers went to his housekeeper and kennel-maid Annie Harris. She is said to have been a relation of Will Rawle, the Parson's kennel-man. Mrs Harris then went as housekeeper to Henry Williamson. She continued to breed large numbers of terriers from bitches which she had farmed out all over the locality. What were referred to as Jack Russell Terriers had already become a sound commercial proposition.

When did the Jack Russell Terrier become a breed in its own right and with a value which reflected that status? The question has often been debated. It was again pushed to the fore when the Kennel Club recognized the Parson Jack Russell Terrier as a separate breed. The Kennel Club chose to describe the Parson Jack Russell Terrier as a variant of the Fox Terrier. It might have been more historically accurate to have described the Fox Terrier as a variant of the Parson Jack Russell Terrier.

During the Parson's own lifetime it was widely acknowledged that his terriers were sufficiently different to be regarded as a distinct strain. Whether they were already a distinct breed is debatable.

Doubt, however, was set aside by a court judgement in 1923. A W.J. King had the misfortune to run over one of Arthur Heinemann's terriers. Heinemann, never a man slow to spot an opportunity to turn misfortune into profit, sued for damages.

These were assessed at 15 guineas, quite a hefty price at a time when terriers often changed hands for a few shillings. Heinemann accepted that the Jack Russell Terrier was not recognized by the Kennel Club and did not appear at shows. Nevertheless he argued that he could trace the pedigrees of his terriers back to 1890. He produced evidence to support his claim that his terriers had a considerable market value.

The defence argued that there was no such breed as a Jack Russell Terrier. Heinemann argued that there was and the judge pointed out that he had seen Jack Russell Terriers advertised for sale. Eventually Heinemann won his 15 guineas damages, with costs. In the process he had established, before the courts, that Jack Russell Terriers were a breed in their own right.

What he had inadvertently also done was to reveal that his pedigrees stretched back only to 1890, seven years after the Parson's death. His terriers might have, and very probably did, carry the blood of the Parson's own terriers but Heinemann could not produce pedigrees to prove the relationship.

Heinemann was principally interested in badger-digging and in hunting otter. This sort of work demanded a different type of terrier than that which the Parson had bred. It is not surprising that, during nearly forty years as a breeder, Heinemann should have evolved a terrier of a very different type from that bred by the Parson. Nor is it surprising that Annie Harris, breeding primarily for sale, would accept and even perpetuate the development.

Another force had also been at work which tended to make the type of terrier bred by the Parson and his rather old-fashioned hunting cronies even more distinctive. This had begun during the Parson's lieftime but continued and accelerated after his death.

During the middle years of the nineteenth century the craze for speed among the followers of the fashionable packs had led to the virtual extinction of the rough-coated white terriers which they predominantly used. When the craze subsided there was a reluctance to run terriers with hounds.

The more fashionable hunts began to employ runners to lead their terriers across country and to ensure that they did not get into mischief. Terriers no longer needed to be intelligent, self-reliant or resourceful. They had a runner to do their thinking for them. The OBH (West) had the famous 'Jack'; the Puckeridge had Piggott. David Swinton ran with the Belvoir's terriers; Harry Swinton and Dick Baker were at the Quorn. Lord Lonsdale described them as turning out 'in a scarlet coat of a texture not too heavy, white flannel knickerbockers, black stockings and a well groomed cap'. Sellars was at the Cottesmore, Butler at the North Cotswold and William Grant at Lord Middleton's. During the early years of this century terrier men had a status which has since been forfeited.

A runner's job was not easy. It was not long before the more enterprising terrier men, notably William Grant, began to appear mounted, with their terriers slung in a leather pouch over their backs. Now terriers not only did not need the intelligence to find their own way across country but did not need the agility, speed or stamina to do so. The way was open for a new type of terrier.

It was about this time that a further development lent even more weight to the forces for change. Terriers began to be carried about in cars. They could now recline in warm comfort in their straw-lined boxes until, chauffeured up to the very mouth of the earth at which they were needed, they were decanted and asked to interview Charley. It was not very long before this development led to the use of terriers with short legs whose use had previously been confined to badger-digging. A new fashion had begun and it was a fashion which would, along with Heinemann's and Harris's efforts, in time, form the public's image of what a typical Jack Russell Terrier should look like.

There is no point in regretting any of these developments, indeed there is no need to do so. Certainly they gave rise to terriers which were very different from the Parson's own. It might have been better if Heinemann and others had not made use of the Parson's name. The terriers they produced, though very different from the Parson's, had their own merits and attractions. They rapidly achieved popularity both as working terriers and as jaunty companions. The type produced by the Parson lived on only in the kennels of breeders who were determined that the original type should survive.

Little changed until some years after the Second World War.

Then hunts and their newly formed supporters' clubs began to look round for new ways of raising the money they needed. At the same time, much as John Warde had done over two hundred years previously, they wanted to organize activities that would interest their supporters during the summer months. They began to attach a few classes for terriers to their traditional annual hound show. By doing so they were doing no more than re-create the sort of classification which had once existed at all the principal hound shows. Nowadays terriers are excluded from these events. If hound shows exist to promote an interest in and to encourage the improvement of hounds the inference to be drawn from absence of terrier classes is obvious.

The classes were well-supported and so were increased in number. Other country organizations recognized their popularity and they too joined in the fun. Before very long about five hundred terrier shows, which, like the terriers they attracted, varied in size and quality, were being crammed into the British summer weekends each year.

Having spent years decrying the insidious influence of shows the supporters of Jack Russell Terriers now found themselves breeding stock for the show ring. They travelled the country in pursuit of show ring success. Trophies were put on prominent display. They were rightly proud of their successes and advertised them to the world. The wheel had come full circle. A terrier originally bred exclusively for work had now become one of the most popular breeds as a companion. It had also been provided with a new career as a show dog. The problem was that the uniformity in type the Parson had established had long since disappeared. The different types which Heinemann and his successors had developed were now joined by a motley collection of terriers whose owners insisted were all genuine Jack Russell Terriers.

Some of these were travesties of what a working terrier should be. They had short, crooked legs, barrel ribs, short backs, weak loins, uncertain tempers and a tendency to hop along on their three sound legs. Slipping patellas, which accounted for this characteristic movement, were not the only inherited problem to be found. Commercial exploitation had created precisely the same problems in Jack Russells as it had in other popular breeds. In the absence of a central authority, a registration system, access to schemes intended to screen for hereditary disease and even of a breed standard, little could be done to alleviate the overall problem.

The best breeders were still producing top-class terriers. It was still possible to find terriers which could do the job for which they were intended. Unfortunately thousands of puppies were also produced by commercial breeders whose only purpose was profit. They were not interested in quality or type. These puppies came in almost every conceivable shape and size but all had their sale value enhanced by being referred to as Jack Russell Terriers. The only thing they had in common was that they made use of the Parson's name. What a pity he could not have been around to get off his horse and knock some sense into their breeders.

7

Recognition

Well before his death the terriers bred by the Parson had become sufficiently differentiated from other fox terriers as to be regarded as a very distinctive strain, if not quite as a separate breed. They did not receive official recognition as a breed in their own right until 1990. During the 107 years that had passed Jack Russell Terriers had become established as one of the world's most popular breeds. They continued to be used for work of various sorts. They were popular companions. For many years they had dominated the scene at hundreds of shows outside the system over which the Kennel Club exerts control.

Inevitably there were differing attitudes towards recognition. These were sometimes expressed in ways which were not compatible with the breed's sporting background. It was not always easy to understand what motivated those who opposed recognition. It would not deprive anyone who had no wish to be involved of any of their existing freedoms and activities, and it would offer, to those who chose to become involved, a degree of protection, a range of activities and services and of opportunities previously unavailable.

If recognition achieves nothing else it will, at least, end the sort of situation from which Jack Russells seem always to have suffered. A very similar situation was described by the Rev. Thomas Pearce in 1872.

> Not many years ago, any dog under 35 lbs. in weight, provided he had his ears cut short, was called a Terrier, unless his owner preferred describing him as a Bull Terrier, a Bulldog, or a Pug. On the same principle, a dog with so much coat that he was only a sketchy notion of an animate being went by the name of a 'Skye' or a 'Dandie', the name being a matter of taste, and the breed or points one of

opinion; the owner of such animals taking for granted what the breeder said to them, and frequently knowing just as much of dogs in general as a boarding-school miss does of a horse.

The Kennel Club was formed in 1873. As its influence grew the situation Pearce described became less common. It became much more difficult to claim that a dog was of some particular breed unless it and its parents were registered with the Kennel Club. That particular benefit was not available to breeds the Kennel Club did not recognize. Over the years a great many breeds have been added to the handful that were originally given official protection. The Parson Jack Russell Terrier has now achieved recognition. The Jack Russell Terrier remains unrecognized in Britain. An Australian version of the breed was recognized by the Australian Kennel Control Council. This was called the Australian Jack Russell Terrier, thus making it abundantly clear that the breed had little or no affinity with Britain and, therefore, with the Reverend Jack Russell. Australian Hunt or Working Terrier might have been better and more diplomatic names.

Ever since the term 'Jack Russell Terrier' was coined, probably during the Parson's life, it has been possible to describe almost any small dog as a Jack Russell Terrier. Any small, nondescript mongrel could have its value enhanced by describing it as a Jack Russell Terrier. The situation Pearce described well over 100 years ago did not substantially change as far as Jack Russell Terriers were concerned. This, however, should not be taken to mean that every dog described as a Jack Russell Terrier was nothing more than a nondescript mongrel. Many were carefully bred by breeders whose standards were exemplary. The terriers they produced have well-authenticated pedigrees. Mated to their own kind they reproduced that kind, something which is beyond the capability of any mongrel. Had the types not been well established and their pedigrees well-authenticated neither the Parson Jack Russell Terrier nor the Australian Jack Russell Terrier would ever have been recognized.

A number of clubs, formed with the intention of preserving and promoting the breed, have existed for a number of years. During the 1920s the Parson Jack Russell Terrier Club, Arthur

Heinemann's old Somerset and Devon Badger Club in a new guise, existed as an offshoot of the Fox Terrier Club. It was assisted by the Fox Terrier Club in its efforts to preserve the old type of fox terrier as bred by the Parson. The Club ceased to exist towards the end of the decade. By 1938 no clubs devoted to the breed were mentioned in the Kennel Club Calendar and Stud Book. None were mentioned in the canine or sporting press, though from time to time, efforts were made to form clubs which were intended to promote the cause of all working terriers. None were devoted exclusively to Parson or Jack Russell Terriers.

The situation, as far as Jack Russell Terriers were concerned, changed in 1972 when Roma Moore formed the Jack Russell Terrier Club of Great Britain. Originally this was an offshoot of the Midland Working Terrier Club, which she had formed in 1963. Subsequently Peter Wheatland founded the South East Jack Russell Terrier Club. Both clubs existed in order to encourage the breeding of pure-bred Jack Russell Terriers of what each club regarded as the correct type. Both during their early days sought Kennel Club recognition of and assistance for their efforts.

The early moves towards recognition were often very tentatively made and cautiously received by the Kennel Club. Neither party appeared entirely convinced of the value of recognition. The half-hearted campaign continued. From its foundation until about 1983 the Jack Russell Terrier Club of Great Britain took soundings and inched forwards, and then backwards, in its negotiations with the Kennel Club. The South East Jack Russell Terrier Club went so far as to submit a formal application for recognition. The North East Region of the Club of Great Britain was also in favour of recognition. In 1983, however, the Club of Great Britain had what their minutes describe as 'a long debate about joining the Kennel Club'. They seem to have been unaware of the fact that 'joining' the Kennel Club was never a possibility. The meeting overwhelmingly resolved that it had no wish to 'join' and from that date the Club of Great Britain went to extraordinary, though ultimately and inevitably futile, lengths to prevent any other club from achieving Kennel Club recognition.

In 1983 the Parson Jack Russell Terrier Club was revived

with the expressed intention of seeking official recognition for the type of terrier the Parson himself had bred. The Club immediately took the lead in negotiations with the Kennel Club and energetically promoted the idea of recognition. The campaign was motivated by several factors. There was growing concern that the name of Jack Russell was being exploited by unscrupulous breeders to give commercial value to almost any small predominantly white mongrel. Pedigrees were falsified, often with little attempt at concealment. A growing catalogue of hereditary disease was blithely ignored by commercial breeders. People overseas, who had often paid high prices for allegedly well-bred Jack Russell Terriers, were perhaps the most important victims but many people who set out to buy a Jack Russell as a companion also suffered. Without some central disciplinary authority there was little hope of redress or even of improving the situation.

There were also fears that the growing popularity of hunt and working terrier shows and the increasing size of the prizes to be won were giving rise to abuses which, in the absence of any central authority, could not be prevented. Terriers were being shown as puppies well into their second year, pedigrees and ownerships were being falsified, judges and exhibitors were colluding to increase their successes. The situation was very similar to that which existed at nineteenth-century British shows before Kennel Club authority had been established.

Recognition would also provide a degree of insurance against the growing likelihood that hunting might be banned in Britain. At the same time it would provide affiliation to an influential organization which could be relied upon to argue strenuously against any proposed curtailment of field sports. However, if hunting was banned not only would the opportunity for terriers to be legally worked disappear but the informal system of working terrier shows, often run by hunt or hunt supporters' clubs or by other organizations which relied for their existence on the continuation of field sports, would probably also cease to exist.

In Britain the Kennel Club had acted promptly, following the banning of otterhunting, to enable Otterhounds to take part in shows. With their original purpose in life gone shows represented the only remaining activity available to the breed.

Without some purpose in life the entire future of the breed was in jeopardy.

Making Kennel Club licensed shows available to Parson Jack Russell Terriers was the most obvious effect of recognition. The opportunity to become part of the system of Kennel Club licensed events, shows, obedience, agility and other competitions, was something to which many owners eagerly looked forward. They were proud of their terriers. They relished the opportunity to extend their activities by competing at the highest level in the biggest dog shows in the world. Others found the idea daunting but it would be, as it always had been, for individuals to decide just what form their interest would take.

Recognition would have limited or possibly no effect on those who chose not to take advantage of what it had to offer. Submission to Kennel Club authority would not, as some opponents claimed, become compulsory. These opponents could continue to breed unregistered terriers and take part in events outside Kennel Club control, as many Border Terrier owners had chosen to do since their breed achieved recognition in 1920. It is true that recognition in Britain would inevitably lead to overseas recognition and therefore the opportunity to export unregistered dogs would decline. This was in the hands of overseas kennel clubs over which clubs outside the Kennel Club system could not hope to exert control. There was never any suggestion that opposition to recognition was based on a fear that lucrative overseas markets would be lost to breeders of unregistered stock. Moves towards official recognition, most notably in America, Australia and Holland, would continue independent of what happened in Britain. If they were successful before recognition had been achieved in Britain it was possible that influence over the breeds would be lost to British breeders.

In 1986 the Parson Jack Russell Terrier Club made a formal application to the Kennel Club for recognition of a 14 inch/14 lb Parson Jack Russell Terrier. The type was supported both by those who sought recognition and by those who opposed it. There was little or no disagreement about what should be regarded as the correct type of Parson or Jack Russell Terrier. Disagreement was confined to the concept of recognition.

The application was rejected in terms which suggested that the Kennel Club Committee had failed to appreciate the reasons for the application. Nevertheless the terms of the rejection gave reason for hope for the future. The Kennel Club had based their assessment on a meeting at which those who opposed recognition were far more strongly represented than those who supported it. Furthermore they failed to take the opportunity to visit any hunt or working terrier shows at which misconceptions and ill-informed prejudices might have been modified.

Without taking the trouble to visit any shows at which they could have seen the breed in force, the Kennel Club Committee had decided that the Parson Jack Russell Terrier was not sufficiently established as a breed type. They also argued that the breed was already recognized in the Smooth Fox and Wire-haired Fox Terriers. The argument ignored the precedent which had been set when the Cavalier King Charles Spaniel had been recognized as a re-creation of the old type of toy spaniel, even though the King Charles Spaniel was already recognized. Mainly, however, it seems that the Kennel Club had been impressed by vociferous opposition to recognition without giving due consideration to the real reasons for that opposition or to their own role as an organization dedicated 'to promoting in every way the general improvement of dogs'. The terms of the rejection irritated those who supported as well as those who opposed recognition.

Rejection was a disappointment but some reason for hope was found in the Kennel Club's statement that 'the General Committee decided it was not appropriate to recognise the breed at the present time'. Perhaps at some future time recognition might be regarded as appropriate.

In June 1989 W.D. Crowley, then Chairman of the Australian National Kennel Control (ANKC) Council, wrote a résumé of the negotiations which had taken place with regard to official recognition of the breed in Australia. He explained that the matter had been discussed at some length at the ANKC Conference held in Adelaide in April 1989, when a proposal to accept the breed for recognition was narrowly defeated. However it was agreed that the Jack Russell Terriers could be shown at ANKC shows, though they could not compete for championship honours. A major step towards recognition had been made.

He recorded that an ANKC observer had attended the 9th Annual Jack Russell Terrier Show held in 1986 where there were 144 dogs. Another ANKC observer had attended the 12th Annual Show of the Jack Russell Terrier Club of Australia in 1989 where he had seen 147 dogs.

The judges at the 1989 show were E.A. Boxhall and G.A.A. Lane. They reported that 'type' was excellent and matched the Breed Standard as well as or better than recognized breeds at many ANKC Breed Shows. This view was supported by the judges at the 1986 show.

W.D. Crowley then went on to record that while

> the Australian National Kennel Council has great respect for the English Kennel Club . . . unless a decision is soon made [about the question of recognition], it will have seriously to consider embracing the Jack Russell Terrier, just as it did with the Border Collie some 45 years ago.
>
> If, as well it may, the English Kennel Club decides that the Jack Russell Terrier launched by Parson Jack Russell is the 14 inch dog, we may then have to consider introducing the 'Australian Jack Russell Terrier', 10 to 12 inches high.

Following its meeting in October, 1989 the ANKC announced that it had resolved in principle to recognize the Jack Russell Terrier for registration in the pure breed registers and that the breed be identified as the 'Australian Jack Russell Terrier – the decision being subject to ratification at the April 1990 Conference, the circularizing of an acceptable Breed Standard and further discussion with the Jack Russell Terrier Club of Australia'.

The announcement passed without comment and almost without notice in the rest of the world. The breed's supporters elsewhere were either unconcerned or unaware of the implications of the Australian decision.

In Britain movement towards recognition had proceeded slowly. Supporters of recognition had established their case with care. At the same time the style and content of some of the public statements of those who opposed recognition had effectively undermined the validity of their case. In sharp contrast to what had taken place in Australia none of the members of the Kennel Club Committee which would assess any new application had accepted any invitations to visit hunt or working terrier shows. The continued debate had led some to modify their previous attitudes and they were beginning to accept the force of arguments which supported recognition. Even though they did not accept that their former attitude ran contrary to the Kennel Club's purpose, they had begun to realize that the Club might be exposed to domestic and international difficulties if the breed became recognized overseas before recognition had been achieved in Britain.

During 1989 the Parson Jack Russell Terrier Club made a second application for official Kennel Club recognition of the type of terrier bred by the Parson. The Chairman of the Club of Great Britain was at the forefront of opposition to recognition. He expressed the reasons for his club's opposition in *Our Dogs*.

The Parson Jack Russell Terrier Club have again put forward an application to the Kennel Club to recognise the Jack Russell Terrier. The Parson Jack Russell Club is a small organisation, of 60 members at most, aiming for Kennel Club recognition.

This time they have persuaded the powers in the KC into believing that all the working terriers and the terriers belonging to the members of the many other terrier clubs are inferior to the dogs they have on their register. You can't blame the Standards committee of the KC – have they ever seen a kennel of line-bred Jack Russells, bred for work and correct in conformation?

If any of these ladies and gentlemen of Clarges Street would like to contact me, I could rectify that very quickly.

But no, they have been told that everyone thinks a Jack Russell is a short, thick set little dog with bandy legs, and the correct type of Jack Russell is in danger of extinction, and now the world needs educating.

In fact, the correct Jack Russell Terrier has never been stronger, not just in this country but world-wide. The KC have allowed a group of 60 to persuade them the terrier needs recognition, while the voices of more than 6000 remains unheard – a ridiculous state of affairs.

The Kennel Club have sold the Fox Terrier down the river. As I understand it the Fox Terrier Club was formed to preserve the original and correct type of Parson Jack Russell – indeed many of his dogs' names appear in old Fox Terrier pedigrees. So, you have your dog Clarges Street, leave ours alone! The Fox Terrier has lost its popularity and its working ability and no longer resembles its original ancestors; on the other hand the Jack Russell Terrier has been kept pure by the working terrier men of this country. Leave this dog where it has been safe for 200 years, in the hands of the people who have guarded the correct type so well.

The Parson Jack Russell Terrier will not be allowed the benefit of a regular injection of working blood to keep it on the right track, because there will be no true working terriers on the KC register, simply because the true working terrier man will shun the KC shows and registration and soon there will be another Fox Terrier.

So come on Clarges Street, get your heads out of the cupboards and take a long hard look at reality. Don't believe a walk round Regent's Park takes you to the man in the street. There is a whole world of terriers out here, that so far you have been kept unaware of.

The letter cannot have failed to impress the Kennel Club but perhaps not in the way its author had intended. At the same time the Kennel Club was receiving letters of protest from all over the world. They expressed arguments very similar to those advanced by the Club of Great Britain Chairman. They were couched in much the same style. Their failure to put forward any cogent arguments in opposition to recognition probably did a great deal to ensure that recognition would be achieved sooner rather than later.

In March 1990 the *Kennel Gazette* was able to announce:

The General Committee of the Kennel Club has recognised for registration the Parson Jack Russell Terrier, a variant of the Fox Terrier.

A most important feature of this breed is the height of the animal. Dogs are ideally 35 cms (14 inches) with a minimum height of 33 cms (13 inches) at the withers and bitches ideally 33 cms (13 inches), minimum 30 cms (12 inches) at the withers. . . .

Initially the dogs eligible for registration will be those already on the register of the Parson Jack Russell Terrier Club which have at least a two generation pedigree and where the third generation is generally known in respect of either the Sire or Dam. Additionally, siblings of these dogs will also be eligible for registration. No other dogs will be accepted.

Owners of Parson Jack Russell Terriers eligible for registration and who wish to register them should apply to the Kennel Club for registration.

In the same month the New Zealand Kennel Club 'noted that the Australian National Council had approved a breed to be known as the Australian Jack Russell Terrier [and that] this breed appeared to be different from that recognized in England as the Parson Jack Russell Terrier'.

The Kennel Club in Britain had made it clear that recognition for the under 12 inch Jack Russell Terrier was not on its agenda. Indeed by the time recognition had become a real possibility the under 12 inch type had virtually disappeared from all hunt and working terrier shows in Britain. It did not satisfy the standards set by any British breed club. Its survival relied on its popularity as a companion and on the output of commercial breeders.

As early as 1973 the *Shooting Times* had written the obituary of the dwarf type: 'At long last the mini-terrier boom is over and though stunted oddities are still seen as popular pets, serious hunting folk are at last doing their best to revert to a terrier higher in the shoulder, narrower in the chest and more like the original Russell standard.'

Those who supported as well as those who opposed recognition were totally united in their support for the classic 14 inch/14 lb working terrier and in their opposition to the dwarf types. A very different attitude existed in Australia where the final step towards recognition of an Australian under 12 inch version of the breed was taken in October 1990 at the ANKC Conference. Afterwards it was announced that it had been 'unanimously decided that the Jack Russell Terrier [10–12 inches] be accepted for registration in the Pure Breed Register. It also agreed that the Parson Jack Russell Terrier, imported from England with authorised pedigrees, and their progeny, will be accepted for registration.'

The decision was an unprecedented one. In the past whenever a kennel club had recognized any breed not of native origin great care had been taken to ensure that the type recognized would be that which existed in the country of origin. Australia had chosen to recognize a type that was regarded as incorrect by all British breeders and authorities. Their reason for doing so may be contained in the final paragraph of the ANKC's announcement which said, 'there is no doubt that their inclusion will give a substantial boost to the Terrier Group'.

By the end of its first year as a recognized breed 465 Parson Jack Russell Terriers had been registered with the Kennel Club. Their owners reflected the entire spectrum of those who take an interest in the breed. The names of the Oakley and the Grove are still there, just as they were when the Parson was alive. They were joined by the Exmoor and the East Devon, the Blencathra, the Heythrop and the East Essex and, most numerously, by the David Davies. Individuals whose terriers are not only bred for work but whose livelihoods depend on their ability to work were strongly represented. While this strong link exists there can be no question but that the breed will retain its essential working ability.

There were also a number of owners who are members of the Kennel Club, again just as would have been the case during the Parson's day. Most, however, were owners whose admiration for the breed and whose determination that it should reflect all that Parson Jack Russell regarded as important in a terrier it would be unjust to question. They and their terriers had provided the Parson with a living memorial of which he would have been proud.

8

Purpose

The Parson bred his terriers to run with foxhounds and work to fox. They were 'fox terriers' in the truest sense. Other British terrier breeds have also been produced for precisely the same purpose. The Border Terrier is one, the Lakeland Terrier another, both are 'fox terriers', bred to run with hounds over demanding country. The as yet unrecognized Fell or Patterdale Terrier must also be included in the list; so, of course, must both the Smooth and the Wire Fox Terrier. The Border, the Lakeland and the Fell Terriers still run with hounds. The way in which foxhunting developed in the shires, allied to the way in which Fox Terriers have developed, now means that only rarely, if at all, are Fox Terriers employed in this way. Parson and Jack Russell Terriers have now almost entirely taken over the Fox Terriers' original mantle. However, Parson and Jack Russell Terriers, though still in close touch with work, are nowadays seldom employed in precisely the manner the Parson favoured and his hunting country demanded.

The service fox terriers provide differs according to whether they are working as part of a hunt establishment or in some other way, and within hunts it differs according to the particular needs of the hunt. The only constant is that the principal quarry, the only one which, in terms of the development of these breeds, really matters, is the fox.

This imposes a controlling influence far more stringent than any breed standard could ever achieve. If a terrier is unwilling by inclination or unable by physique to work to fox he must forfeit any claim to be regarded as a fox terrier. He certainly cannot be regarded as a working terrier. Breeders and judges may argue interminably about the precise meaning of each and every clause in the standard and about the relative importance of this or that characteristic. Many of these arguments are silenced when terriers are tested against the job for which they were bred. That is why breed club standards emphasize the importance of work and why there is reason to regret the Kennel Club's failure to stress its importance in their Interim Breed Standard for the Parson Jack Russell Terrier.

When the Parson was active the rural population far outnumbered those who were obliged to live in towns. The vast majority of the population were in daily contact with rural activities and rural priorities. The fox population, compared with what it is today, was sparse. Even so the fox was regarded by the majority of the rural population as a pest to be killed by any means and at any time. The Parson, no less than all his hunting colleagues, had to argue the case for conserving rather than slaughtering foxes. This he did by threatening with physical violence his parishioners who shot foxes but even at the end of his life his correspondence records his sadness that foxes were still being poisoned, trapped and shot.

Few among the Parson's friends lived exclusively in towns. Fewer still would be totally divorced from field sports. Those who were deeply involved in foxhunting were the people who were breeding fox terriers. Nowadays very few breeders can be involved in the activities which gave rise to their breeds, and even fewer choose to be involved. They do not work their dogs and, worse still, make little or no effort to understand the demands which work makes or the way in which it influences the make and shape of terriers.

The simple fact is that fox terriers came into being for a particular purpose. Whatever the rights or wrongs of that purpose the fact remains that if the relationship between any breed and its purpose is not fully understood by breeders the way is open for change which will make the breed less suitable for that purpose. Change that is not allied to function will eventually destroy the breed's ability to work. Both Parson and Jack Russell Terriers retain that ability. Their breeders are adamant that, come what may, changing fashions, growing popularity or ambitions for show ring success will not be allowed to take the breeds away from their origins.

Only in England, Wales, Ireland and part of Scotland is it nowadays possible to gain experience of a working fox terrier's purpose in life. It never has been possible overseas. If foxhunting is banned in Britain, as seems increasingly probable, it will not be possible anywhere in the world. Any breed which becomes divorced from the demands and constraints imposed by its original purpose in life, from its original environment and from its root stock, has a tendency to change. Blame for the change may be placed at any one of several doors but in truth without conscious and determined efforts to prevent it change is virtually inevitable.

Show and working spaniels are now as different from one another as chalk and cheese. Both are also very different from the spaniels which existed 100 years ago. They have both changed; so, to a greater or lesser extent, has every other gundog breed. Bulldogs began to change towards the end of the eighteenth century when the small dog shows which then took place could exert no influence over their development. At that time bull- and bear-baiting were becoming unpopular and were banned in 1835. Bulldogs could no longer be tested against the purpose for which they had originally been bred. It was this which changed the Bulldog, not dog shows. By the middle of the nineteenth century Bulldogs had arrived at their present form but it was still over ten years before national dog shows began to take place and nearly twenty-five before the Kennel Club would be founded.

The Irish Wolfhound suffered even more drastically than did the Bulldog. The breed has had an international reputation since Roman times for its size and hunting ability. After wolves became extinct in Ireland the breed began to degenerate and very nearly followed its quarry into extinction. It was saved only because a new career in the show ring became available. For some British breeds dog shows arrived too late to save them from extinction. The Blue Paul, the Old English White Terrier, the Black and Tan Terrier, the Drover's dog and a number of localized breeds all reached the point of no return before dog shows could offer them an alternative career. Surely it cannot be argued that a career in the show ring is an unacceptable alternative to extinction.

In order to protect breeds from thoughtless change it is necessary to know about their original purpose in life. So what is known about the way in which the Parson worked his terriers? Davies's reliable, if limited, evidence is available.

There are also a number of reliable accounts of foxhunting during the middle years of the nineteenth century which help to complete the picture.

What Davies has to tell us varies from general comments, such as that 'on every hunting day a terrier or two invariably accompanied him to the field; and certainly no general ever depended with more trust on the services of an *aide-de-camp* than he on those of his terriers', to more specific references which tell us something about individual terriers.

Tip scarcely ever missed a day for several seasons, and never appeared fatigued, though he occasionally went from fifteen to twenty miles to cover. He died at last from asthma in the Chorley earths, Russell having dug up to him and the fox in half an hour; but, to his master's great grief, the poor old dog was quite dead.

Nettle, too, a prodigy of courage and sagacity, would follow no one but her master; and not even him, except the hounds were at his heels; knowing full well that her services were only required in connection with the hunting-field.

Heinemann, who knew Devon as well as anyone, wrote profusely about hunting in that county. His descriptions are graphic and, though they date from fifty or so years after the Parson's heyday, still offer a glimpse of the unchanged country over which the Parson hunted and, to a lesser extent, the way he hunted it.

Perhaps the prettiest part of moorland fox-hunting is to see hounds drag up to their fox through heather or sedge, or rush on some open plateau along the steep hill-side of some Devonshire combe.

Disturbed frequently by harriers and stag-hounds, and collie-dogs, these moorland foxes lie tightly, and seldom wait to be found, stealing away at the first strange sound, so that when drawing in the open the huntsman of a moorland pack must have his hounds handy as ladies' maids, ready to spread out and draw at a wave from his hand, or come across some valley quickly to his low whistle, of 'Leu, leu,' or 'Tsst, tsst.' No chattering should there be among the little ladies of the field, whose shrill voices carry far in the rarefied air of the moorland, and no blowing of the fragrant weed on the part of the male members of the hunt, if one would find a moorland fox handsomely in the open.

Between hounds and the field lies the great gulf of an impassable combe, which has to be coasted, and by the time that has been done hounds have gained such a start as may not soon be overtaken. Surely, it is true that a fox well found is a fox half killed; yet how many huntsmen one sees drawing some thick gorse like men in a dream, their hounds following the line of least resistance at their horses' heels. There is, indeed, a time for everything; and just as there is a time to practise the silent system, so equally is there a time when voice and horn should galvanize into life both hound and horse and fox. Digging foxes is, perhaps, the dullest part of moorland foxhunting, where earth-stopping is seldom practised or practicable, but it is a necessary evil if one would ask the rather bloodthirsty hill-farmers to preserve foxes for the hunt.

Yet even on Exmoor some system of putting-to main-earths might well be devised with but little expenditure. Terriers are, of course, a necessary adjunct of moorland packs, and it is wonderful how they soon contrive to turn up when hounds have earthed their fox. I remember running a fox to ground once in Curr Cleave, which one of my terriers had bolted an hour before, and, as no terrier turned up, we began to dig. But when we reached our fox, there was the same terrier in grips with him, and I only just saw his hind pad in time to save him from the pack, which I had let in to draw what was apparently their fox. Another day, a bad-scenting one, I saw another of mine – Toby by name – leading the pack all along the fringe of the big Horner woodlands, throwing his shrill treble tongue with the best of them. But wet and weather play sad havoc with terriers, who fare but ill on kennel-food, and it is best to station them in charge of a runner or second horseman at various likely farmhouses in the day's draw.

Dartmoor foxes and Exmoor foxes are stout and strong, and fleet of foot, having long distances to go for food or fellowship, and being real creatures of the wild.

So the native Devon foxes as well as the Devonshire countryside provided a stern test for both hounds and the terriers which ran with them. For a description of the terriers themselves, and especially of the Parson's terriers we must rely on Davies.

> Entered early, and only to fox, Russell's terriers were as steady from riot as the staunchest of his hounds; so that, running together with them, and never passing over an earth without drawing it, they gave a fox, whether above ground or below it, but a poor chance of not being found, either by one or the other. A squeak from a terrier was the sure signal of a find, and there was not a hound in the pack that would not fly to it, as eagerly as to Russell's horn, or his own wild and marvellous scream.
>
> This steadiness from riot was, of course, the result of early education on one object – the fox; nor did Russell consider it needful to train his terriers by progressive steps, according to the plan adopted by Dandie Dinmont.

Comparison between how the very real Parson and a fictional character in a Sir Walter Scott novel trained their terriers cannot be taken too far. Even if it is supposed that Dandie Dinmont's progression from 'rottens' to 'stots or weasels' and finally to 'tods and brocks' is based on a practical method it must be remembered that these terriers were not being educated to work to fox, still less to run with hounds. Perhaps it is best not to inquire too deeply into precisely what Dandie Dinmont or the Border gentry who provided Scott with the model for that character got up to with their terriers.

The fact is that a fox terrier which fails to discriminate between its legitimate quarry and rats, rabbits, stoats, weasels or badgers will be all too likely to lead hounds astray. It will waste time and effort and will have a very limited value as a working fox terrier. In order to avoid any fear of confusion Russell's terriers were, very sensibly, 'entered only to fox'.

Russell's hounds and their followers were able to rely absolutely that a 'squeak from a terrier was the sure signal of a find, and there was not a hound in the pack that would not fly to it, as eagerly as to Russell's horn, or his own wild and marvellous scream'. Terriers which drew hounds to something other than fox would not have lasted long in Russell's kennel. He was ruthless with hounds which displeased him. 'Will, that hound eats no more of my food,' was the euphemism which signalled the end of any hound which failed to meet his exacting standards. Doubtless he was equally ruthless with recalcitrant terriers.

That Russell's terriers were 'entered early' suggests that they were every bit as precocious and eager to begin work as are their modern counterparts. Parson and Jack Russell terriers often show an interest in work long before other breeds show the slightest inclination. They may even show every sign of being keen to work long before they are physically mature enough to face a fox. It is a tendency which, all too often, results in immature terriers being subjected to needless punishment. This is more likely to turn them into hard and punishing workers, not usually welcome with hounds, than it is to break their resilient spirit.

'Russell's terriers were as steady from riot as the staunchest of his hounds' is another statement which tells us more about the Parson's priorities. Riot, in this case, meant an inability to discriminate between fox and other quarry but it also meant that Russell's terriers could be trusted to run with hounds without fear that they would take an unwelcome interest in farm livestock. No terrier could possibly be allowed to run with hounds which was not absolutely trustworthy among all forms of livestock. A terrier must studiously ignore cattle, sheep or poultry no matter what temptation they might offer as they scatter when hounds run through them.

Hunts are quite happy to use their poultry fund to make good the depredations of the foxes they seek to preserve. They are not keen to dissipate limited funds in making good the losses caused by riotous hounds or terriers.

People who have never hunted may be surprised and even incredulous that 14 inch terriers are expected to run with 23 inch hounds, and the Parson was one of those who favoured large hounds. They cannot understand how a small terrier can possibly keep pace with hounds racing on a screaming scent. The simple explanation is that they can't and aren't expected to. Terriers running with hounds not only cut corners but often develop an almost uncanny ability to anticipate the direction the chase is likely to take.

'If in chase,' says Davies, 'they could not always live with the pack, still they stuck to the line, and were sure to be there or thereabouts when they were wanted, if the hounds threw up even for a minute.' Davies provides an example of the way in which a good terrier will not only stay with hounds but, by ingenuity and intelligence, will sometimes even contrive to be ahead of them.

The Parson's hounds had been drawing a deep combe near Lidcote Hall. It was a place where foxes were often found and having been found would, almost as often, make haste to reach an ancient, cavernous badger sett called, appropriately enough, Gray's Holts. Once below ground in that massive and labyrinthine retreat Charley had a very good chance of being safe from even the most determined terrier.

On one particular day a fox left the combe with hounds close to his tail but Tip, one of the Parson's favourite terriers, was seen to be running in quite another direction. It took some time before it was realized that he was making directly for Gray's Holts. The fox, having taken a less direct route, arrived to find his way to safety barred by an agitated and determined terrier. He turned again and put his head to the open moorland to give the hounds a fine run.

To those who have no experience of working terriers, and even to those whose experience has been gained with terriers not called upon to run with hounds, the story may sound somewhat unlikely. In fact there is nothing unlikely about it. Wild animals must learn from their hunting experience to identify places where their quarry is most likely to be found and to anticipate in which direction it is most likely to run. Knowledge increases the chances of success and the chances of survival.

Anyone who has walked the hedgerows with a good terrier will have realized how quickly a store of useful information is gathered and how long it may be retained. A terrier will pay particular attention to places which have proved fruitful in the past. Possible escape routes will be approached cautiously. Tip, who 'scarcely ever missed a day for several seasons', would have had just this sort of knowledge. It is neither strange nor surprising that he anticipated the fox's next port of call. What is surprising is that, apparently, the Parson himself did not anticipate it and send reinforcements to help Tip protect the entrance to the Gray's Holts. Perhaps he knew that Tip could do the job unaided.

Davies offers another example of Tip's ability to put two and two together. 'On a hunting morning,' he says, 'no man on earth could catch him, after he had once seen Russell with his top-boots on.' We have had similar experience. Experienced terriers would take only a polite interest in preparations which might just as well indicate an early start in the vegetable garden as a day with hounds but should a particular spade be taken from the rack they knew precisely what was afoot and would give voice to suggestions as to who should be chosen for the day's sport. Even old-age pensioners whose physical abilities have declined beyond the point at which it would be fair to expect them to face fox are eager to volunteer their services. The flesh may become weak but the spirit remains strong.

' "I like them to throw their tongue freely when face to face with their enemy," said Russell one day, as he stood listening to his famous dog Tip, marking energetically in a long drain some six feet below the surface; "you know then where they are, and what they're about." '

The Parson relied on his terriers telling him where they were when underground. Tip is described as 'dancing about on Gray's Holts, throwing his tongue frantically, and doing his utmost, by noise and gesture, to scare the fox from approaching the earths'. Doubtless the Parson, who, unlike many Masters, appears to have known how to use a spade and was not too grand to do so, would also know from the messages his terriers gave him whether they were on to one or more foxes and whether a badger was sharing the lodgings. His experienced ear would tell him how deep they were, which direction they were moving in and even what sort of ground they were in. By interpreting what his terrier told him he could make plans to act accordingly. A terrier that would speak to his fox provided essential help to diggers. A mute terrier was, until comparatively recently, little better than useless.

Nowadays a small radio transmitter attached to a terrier's collar enables even a mute terrier to be tracked underground. The information provided by transmitter and receiver is far more accurate than is provided by even the most educated ear alone. Anyone who can twiddle a knob can track a terrier below ground. Experience and judgement are not required. Even in the absence of Luddite attitudes towards the use of technology in hunting, it is not unreasonable to wonder what effect such aids might have, not just on terriers but on the age-old relationship between terrier and owner. Transmitters are most often used when people are moving foxes or badgers for some good or, far too frequently, nefarious purpose. They seem to have little application in any truly sporting context. What next? Foxes equipped with transmitters in order to overcome the problems encountered during a poor day for scent?

Some day, perhaps, transmitters will be able to provide the whole range of information a good terrier provides to an experienced ear but that day is probably a long way off. What the use of transmitters already does is avoid the need for a terrier to speak. Transmitters transform that formerly most useless of creatures the mute terrier into something which is, after a fashion, serviceable. Will they mean that in future breeders need not select against mute terriers and so lead to the loss of a formerly vital characteristic? Transmitters also avoid the need for terrier owners to learn by experience, to think and assess. They turn a joint co-operative venture into little more than a mere exercise in excavation.

One of Davies's anecdotes tells us something of the value of an intelligent and experienced terrier. It concerns

> the one-eyed Nelson, a genius in his way; and in point of valour, a worthy namesake of England's immortal hero. Russell had run a fox to ground near Tetcott, the seat of Sir William Molesworth; but tiers of passages, one under the other, rendered the earth so perfect a honeycombe that the terriers were soon puzzled, nor did the diggers know what line to follow; there was scent everywhere. Nelson at length came out, and at some distance off commenced digging eagerly at the greensward; 'Here's the fox,' said Russell, 'under Nelson's nose, or I'll forefeit my head.' The dog went in again, and marking hard and sharp, under that very spot, the men broke ground and speedily came upon the fox. Russell then, with his arm bared, drew him forth.

> In order to retrieve the fox and set him on his legs the Parson

would have had to get at least his arm and upper body into the
excavation. That would have required a hole of generous
proportions. The deeper it was the greater the need for space
into which a man might crawl. Having got himself up to the fox
his precarious position would give him plenty to occupy his
mind. Any distraction which would be caused if his terrier was
not absolutely trustworthy would be most unwelcome. It would
not have even crossed the Parson's mind or the minds of anyone
else who might have been in his position that they might be
bitten by the terrier. Only in the show ring and by people who
know nothing about working terriers is a suspect temperament
ever forgiven. Indeed in the show ring displays of unprovoked
aggression may sometimes be excused as the product of 'terrier
spirit'. This term is used by those who know little about terriers
and nothing about work to excuse a pathological and cowardly
temperament.

Of the Parson's terriers Davies also tells us, 'Tartars they
were, and ever have been, beyond all doubt, going up to their
fox in any earth, facing him alternately with hard words and
harder nips, until at length he is forced to quit his stronghold,
and trust to the open for better security.' Their job was to evict
their fox as quickly as possible and with the minimum of force.
They were not expected to half murder him.

The Parson and all his hunting cronies were interested in
sport, not in exterminating foxes. Indeed the fox population
was, in those days, so sparse that some hunts, such as George
Templer's, kept captive foxes which could be released in order
to provide sport. Others actually bought foxes. The most
famous source was centred around Leadenhall Market in
London. One of the tales told by Davies makes it apparent that
the Parson was not unfamiliar with the trade but he was
probably not a customer. He and Harris had devised another
and far more preferable way of ensuring sport.

A great many foxes were imported from France, where deer
held more interest for sportsmen. They were brought over in
such large numbers that many, against all the odds, survived
and bred. This may go some way towards accounting for the
increase in the fox population during the last hundred years.
Perhaps it also explains the difference between the native,
leggy, grey foxes which still inhabit the British uplands, and the

smaller, darker foxes which inhabit the more fashionable hunting countries, where imported foxes may have had the greatest influence on the native breed.

The number of foxes killed in a season by Russell's hounds was very small indeed when compared with modern tallies. It is not surprising that he took great and sometimes violent exception to those of his parishioners who regarded foxes as vermin to be killed by any means and at any time. Nor is it surprising that they did not readily accept his desire to preserve an animal they regarded as a threat to their livestock. Those whose living was earned from the land were often eager to exterminate foxes by any means. The Parson was equally anxious to preserve them while using hounds to protect stock from their depredations.

9

Evolution and Interpretation of the Breed Standard

What can be regarded as the first standard for the breed was produced by the Parson himself in 1871. It is short and to the point. It omits nothing which might be regarded as essential. Over 100 years later it remains a perfectly adequate guide to what the Parson regarded as the ideal terrier.

The Parson's 1871 Standard

A small energetic terrier of from 14/16 lbs in weight, standing about 14 inches at the withers, legs straight as arrows; a thick skin, a good rough weather-resisting coat, thick, close; and a trifle wiry, well calculated to protect the body from cold and wet, but with no affinity to the wiry jacket of a Scotch Terrier. It is certain that a good horse or dog cannot be a bad colour, but I prefer a white dog. The bitch 'Trump' was a white with just a patch of dark over each eye and ear, with a similar dot not larger than a penny-piece at the root of the tail. Feet should be perfect, the loins and conformation of the whole frame indicative of hardihood and endurance. The size and height of the animal may be compared to a fully grown vixen. Every inch a sportsman, the dog must not be quarrelsome. As regards height, some people prefer them to be rather more on the leg if they are to run with the hounds all day.

It is reasonable to assume that the Parson included in his

description all those things which he regarded as important and omitted those which he regarded as of less importance. Size, overall conformation, temperament, coat and colour weighed far more heavily than did the properties of the head or tail.

The next attempt at producing a breed standard was made by Arthur Heinemann in 1904. It is significant, and not untypical of the man, that, having continually voiced criticism of the Kennel Club and all its works, he should choose to make use of the Kennel Club's basic format.

Arthur Heinemann's 1904 Standard

HEAD: The skull should be flat, moderately broad, gradually decreasing to the eyes. Little stop should be apparent. The cheeks must not be full. Ears V-shaped and small, of moderate thickness and dropping forward close to the cheek, not by the side. Upper and lower jaws strong and muscular and of fair punishing strength. Not much falling away below the eyes. The nose should be black. The eyes dark, small, and deep-set, full of fire, life and intelligence, and circular in shape. Teeth level, i.e. upper on the outside of the lower.

NECK: Clean and muscular of fair length gradually widening to shoulders.

SHOULDERS: Long and sloping, well laid-back, at points, clearly cut at the withers.

CHEST: Deep but not broad.

BACK: Straight and strong with no appearance of slackness.

LOINS: Powerful, very slightly arched, fore ribs moderately arched, back ribs deep. The terrier should be well ribbed-up.

HINDQUARTERS: Strong and muscular, full from droop, thighs long and powerful, hocks near the ground, dog standing well up on them. Not straight in the stifle.

STERN: Set on high, carried gaily but never over back or curled. Of good strength and length. A 'pipe cleaning' tail or too short is most objectionable.

LEGS: Perfectly straight showing no ankle in front. Strong in bone throughout, short and straight to the pastern. Fore and back legs carried straight forward when travelling, stifles not turned outward. Elbows should hang perpendicular to the body, working free to the side.

FEET: Round, compact, not large, soles hard and tough, toes moderately arched, turned neither in nor out.

COAT: Dense, a trifle wiry, abundant. Belly and undersides not bare.

COLOUR: White, with acceptable tan, grey or black at head and foot of tail. Red brindle or liver marks are objectionable.

SYMMETRY, SIZE AND CHARACTER: Terrier must present a gay, lively and active appearance. Bone and strength in a small compass are essentials, but not cloggy or coarse. Speed and endurance must be apparent. Not too short or too long in leg. Fourteen inches to withers the ideal for a dog, 13 for a bitch. Weight when in working condition about 14 lb but a pound more or less entirely acceptable. Conformation that of an adult vixen.

DISQUALIFYING POINTS: Too short, too leggy, legs not straight, nose white, cherry, or spotted considerably with these colours. Ears prick or rose. Mouth under or over shot. Excessively nervous or savage.

Heinemann's standard differs considerably from that produced by the Parson. It describes the properties of the head and the tail in some detail. It appears preoccupied with colour, though not the sort of all-white colour for which the Parson expressed a preference. The standard also seems to call for more bone than an adult vixen would carry, though weight remains set at 14 lbs. The need for speed is also new and perhaps at odds with the undoubted need for stamina and endurance.

Also in 1904 Alys Serrell published a description of what she regarded as her ideal and which has every right to be regarded as an early standard for the breed.

Serrell's 1904 Standard

A dog that should give the best results to the care bestowed upon him should not be much over 14 inches or weigh more than 18lb. A size even smaller than this is better, but on no account must he be light and weedy, or in any degree toyish-looking in appearance. On the other hand, there is no reason why a working terrier should not be as good-looking as he is useful, for with a little care in breeding, a smart, handsome, and intelligent-looking little fellow can soon be arrived at.

A terrier's head should be of medium length, with plenty of room for brains, or he will fail to respond to his training. He should have a strong square jaw, with good big teeth, black nose, small drop ears, and dark eyes. These last should not be too prominent, but should have plenty of fire, and have a keen intelligent look. A deep chest, not too narrow, with a neck of fair length, nice sloping shoulders, and strong quarters, with plenty of propelling power, are desirable points. Then, too, he should be well ribbed-up, and his stern should be carried up, though not too high; his legs must be short and straight, with plenty of bone, and the feet compact, with a good hard pad, of which, however, there should not be too much. His toes must be not only of fair length, but armed with strong nails, as these are of the greatest assistance to him in digging. When in working condition, too, the dog should have plenty of hard, well-defined muscle.

A leggy dog is of little or no use for underground work, as, though he may manage to crawl into the earth or drain, he will speedily become so cramped that he can do nothing, and I have seen more than one terrier dug out quite unable to stand. I like a terrier to be straight in the back, a dip in the shoulders being, to my eyes, a serious blemish. In coat the smooth dog cannot be too thick and dense, the slightest appearance of softness being against him, and both smooth and rough should have a good undergrowth, the outer growth of the latter being crisp and hard. Without the undergrowth the terrier will soon become chilled and wet, as the water will run through his coat and interfere seriously with his power of work.

A good terrier, like a good horse, cannot be of a bad colour, but blue on a rough dog generally means a long silky coat, the mark being derived originally from the blue shag sheep-dog, an animal very common in the counties of both Dorset and Devon.

What might be regarded as the three seminal breed standards
become even more interesting when produced in the same
format and directly compared. That produced by the Parson
himself, though less complete than those which followed is, of
course, of the greatest importance, but that in no way
denigrates Heinemann's standard or that produced by Alys
Serrell. Together the three provide a source from which any
breed which makes use of the Parson's name should not depart
without very good reason.

	Parson Jack Russell 1871	Arthur Heinemann 1904	Alys Serrell 1904
GENERAL APPEARANCE	A small energetic terrier, frame indicative of hardihood and endurance.	Bone and strength in a small compass are essentials but not cloggy or coarse.	A smart, handsome, and intelligent-looking little fellow.
CHARACTERISTICS	Every inch a sportsman.	Must present a gay, lively and active appearance.	Plenty of hard, well-defined muscle.
TEMPERAMENT	The dog must not be quarrelsome.		
HEAD AND SKULL	The skull should be flat, moderately broad, gradually decreasing to the eyes. Little stop should be apparent. The cheeks must not be full. Upper and lower jaws strong and muscular and of fair punishing strength. Not much falling away below the eyes. The nose should be black.	Of medium length, with plenty of room for brains. Strong, square jaw. Black nose.	
EYES	The eyes dark, small, and deep-set, full of fire, life and intelligence, and circular in shape.	Dark, not too prominent but should have plenty of fire and a keen intelligent look.	
EARS	Ears V-shaped and small, of moderate thickness and dropping forward close to the cheek, not by the side.	Small, drop.	
MOUTH	Teeth level, i.e. upper on the outside of the lower.	Good big teeth.	

NECK	Clean and muscular, of fair length gradually widening to shoulders.	Of fair length.	
FOREQUARTERS	Legs straight as arrows.	Legs perfectly straight showing no ankle in front. Not too short or too long in leg. Strong in bone throughout, short and straight to the pastern. Shoulders long and sloping well laid-back, at points, clearly cut at the withers.	Nice sloping shoulders. Legs short and straight with plenty of bone.
BODY	The whole frame indicative of hardihood and endurance. Chest, deep but not broad. Back, straight and strong with no appearance of slackness. Loins, powerful, very slightly arched. Fore ribs moderately arched, back ribs deep. Should be well ribbed-up.	Deep chest, not too narrow, well ribbed-up. Straight in the back.	
HINDQUARTERS	The loins, indicative of hardihood and endurance.	Strong and muscular, free from droop, thighs long and powerful, hocks near the ground, dog standing well up on them, not straight in stifle. Loins, powerful, very slightly arched.	Strong quarters, with plenty of propelling power.
FEET	Should be perfect.	Round, compact, not large, soles hard and tough, toes moderately arched, turned neither in nor out.	Compact, with a good hard pad, of which, however, there should not be too much. Toes of fair strength, armed with strong nails.
GAIT/MOVEMENT	Able to run with the hounds all day.	Fore and back legs carried straight forward when travelling, stifles not turned outward. Elbows should hang perpendicular to the body, working free to the side.	

TAIL	Set on high, carried gaily but never over back or curled. Of good strength and length. A 'pipe cleaning' tail or too short is most objectionable.	His stern should be carried up, though not too high.	
COAT	A thick skin, a good rough weather-resisting coat, thick, close, and a trifle wiry, well-calculated to protect the body from cold and wet, but with no affinity to the wiry jacket of a Scotch Terrier.	Dense, a trifle wiry, abundant. Belly and undersides not bare.	In coat the smooth dog cannot be too thick and dense, the slightest appearance of softness being against him. Both smooth and rough should have a good undergrowth, the outer coat of the latter being crisp and hard.
COLOUR	It is certain that a good horse or dog cannot be a bad colour, but I prefer a white dog. The bitch 'Trump' was white with just a patch of dark over each eye and ear, with a similar dot not larger than a penny-piece at the root of the tail.	White, with acceptable tan, grey or black at head and foot of tail. Red brindle or liver marks are objectionable.	A good terrier, like a good horse, cannot be a bad colour.
SIZE	Standing about 14 inches at the withers the height of the animal may be compared to a fully grown vixen, some people prefer them to be rather more on the leg if they are to run with the hounds all day.	Fourteen inches to withers the ideal for a dog, 13 for a bitch. Weight when in working condition about 14 lb but a pound more or less entirely acceptable. Conformation that of an adult vixen.	Should not be much over 14 inches or weigh more than 18 lb. A size smaller than this is better, but on no account must he be light or weedy, or in any degree toyish-looking.
FAULTS	Must not be quarrelsome.	Too short, too leggy, legs not straight, nose white, cherry, or spotted with three colours. Ears prick or rose. Mouth under- or over-shot. Excessively nervous or savage.	A dip in the shoulders being a serious blemish, absence of undergrowth. Long silky coat.

If the three standards were to be arranged in order of authority they would appear in the order in which they are arranged above. Quite obviously what the Parson had to say about the terriers which bear his name must take precedence over any other authority. Heinemann for his part has every right to be regarded as the man who put the Jack Russell Terrier firmly on the map as a breed in its own right. The influence of Alys Serrell derives from what she had to say in two chapters of a single book.

During the early 1980s several breed standards, each produced by a different breed club, were in use. None diverged significantly from the others but each had its peculiarities and foibles. The breed standard produced by the Jack Russell Terrier Club of Great Britain could, perhaps, lay claim to being the one with the widest influence.

Breed Standard

CHARACTERISTICS: The terrier must present a lively, active and alert appearance. It should impress with its fearless and happy disposition. It should be remembered that the Jack Russell is a working terrier and should retain these instincts. Nervousness, cowardice or over-aggression should be discouraged and it should always appear confident.

GENERAL APPEARANCE: A sturdy, tough terrier, very much on its toes all the time, measuring between 9 inches and 15 inches at the withers. The body length must be in proportion to the height and it should present a compact, balanced image, always being in a solid, hard condition.

HEAD: Should be well-balanced and in proportion to the body. The skull should be flat, of moderate width at the ears, narrowing to the eyes. There should be a defined stop but not over-pronounced. The length of muzzle from the nose to the stop should be slightly shorter than the distance from the stop to the occiput. The nose should be black. The jaw should be powerful and well-boned with strongly muscled cheeks.

EYES: Should be almond shaped, dark in colour and full of life and intelligence.

EARS: Small V-shaped drop ears carried forward close to head and of moderate thickness.

MOUTH: Strong teeth with the top slightly overlapping the lower.

NECK: Clean and muscular, of good length, gradually widening at the shoulders.

FOREQUARTERS: The shoulders should be sloping and well laid-back, fine at points and clearly cut at the withers. Forelegs should be strong and straight-boned with joints in correct alignment. Elbows hanging perpendicular to the body and working free of the sides.

BODY: The chest should be shallow, narrow, and the front legs set not too widely apart, giving an athletic, rather than a heavily chested, appearance. As a guide only, the chest should be small enough to be easily spanned behind the shoulders by average-size hands when the terrier is in a fit working condition. The back should be strong, straight and, in comparison to the height of the terrier, give a balanced image. The loin should be slightly arched.

HINDQUARTERS: Should be strong and muscular, well put together with good angulation and bend of stifle, giving plenty of drive and propulsion. Looking from behind the hocks must be straight.

FEET: Round, hard-padded, of cat-like appearance, neither turning in nor out.

TAIL: Should be set rather high, carried gaily and in proportion to body length, usually about 4 inches long, providing a good hand-hold.

COAT: Smooth, without being so sparse as not to provide a certain amount of protection from the elements and undergrowth. Rough or broken-coated, without being woolly.

COLOUR: White should predominate with tan, black or brown markings.

GAIT: Movement should be free, lively, well co-ordinated with straight action in front and behind.

NOTE: For showing purposes terriers are classified in two groups: 9–12 inches; over 12 inches and up to 15 inches.

Old scars or injuries, the result of work or accident, should not be allowed to prejudice a terrier's chance in the show ring unless they interfere with its movement or with its utility for work or stud.

A Jack Russell Terrier should not show any strong characteristics of another breed.

By accepting what had by that time become the most popular type of Jack Russell, the short-legged variety, the Club of Great Britain had done no more than swim with the prevailing tide. They accepted that terriers might measure anything between 9 inches and 15 inches at the withers. Such a variation in size was far greater than is to be found in the standard of any other breed. Short legs have a tendency to be bowed. It is an undeniable fact that many of the short-legged terriers of this period were bowed to and even beyond the point of deformity. Even so the standard insisted that 'forelegs should be strong and straight-boned'. By accepting short-legged Jack Russells the Club introduced a major departure from what both the Parson and Heinemann had regarded as acceptable.

The Club also explored other changes. They expanded the description of the head and its properties in a way which might have seemed to over-estimate its importance in a working terrier. They wanted a shallow chest, surely at odds with any idea of stamina or endurance. The description of the coat was changed in a way which seemed to set a low priority on its weather-resisting properties.

Where the Club of Great Britain had accepted a wide range of size, the South East Jack Russell Club sought to define two separate sizes. The South East Club's standard said that 'two heights were recognized, 9 inches up to 11 inches (miniature) and over 11 inches up to 13 inches (standard) measured at the shoulder. 'Forelegs,' it said, 'should be straight-boned with joints in correct alignment.' The South East Club's standard set a maximum height which was a full 2 inches less than that allowed by the Club of Great Britain. It also introduced the word 'miniature'. It is a strange word to apply to any working terrier.

Another feature of the South East Club's standard was a list of disqualifying points.

DISQUALIFICATIONS: Any Jack Russell Terrier showing any of the following hereditary objections shall not be placed in the show class, nor be eligible for the advanced register.

1. Signs of out-crossing or any recognizable characteristics of another breed.

2. Badly crooked legs, due either to the main bone-shafts being bent, or the joints being out of alignment.

3. Under-shot or over-shot jaws, or skew mouths.

DEFECTS: The following should be avoided and bred out of the Jack Russell Terrier as being undesirable characteristics.

1. Pricked ears.
2. Unpigmented eye rims and nose.
3. Roach or wheel back.
4. Cow hocks.
5. Curly tails.
6. Cowardly and nervous temperament.
7. Over-long and over-short legs. (In proportion to body.)

NOTE: Type more important than colour/markings.

The emphasis which the South East Club placed on what they referred to as 'out-crossing' gave tacit recognition to the dangers of what, by then, had become commonplace. Any small, terrier-like dog, preferably, but not necessarily, predominantly white might be described as a Jack Russell. The absence of a reliable registration system made it impossible to authenticate many pedigrees.

The Scottish Jack Russell Terrier Club's standard took another slightly different view of height. 'Two heights,' it said, 'are allowed, 9–12 inches and 12–15 inches, measured at the withers. Maximum height 15 inches. Minimum height 9 inches.' The forelegs were described as 'of round and straight bone, the elbows hanging perpendicular to the body'.

The Scottish Club also took the opportunity to introduce its own points of emphasis. Brindle was 'disallowed'. Again, this was a response to the prevalence of crosses with other breeds. Brindle markings are usually an indication of foreign, probably Staffordshire or Bull Terrier, blood.

In view of the brief popularity bow-fronted, so-called Jack Russell Terriers achieved and the way their image seems to have permeated the public mind it should be emphasized that never, in any British breed standard, has there been an acceptance of terriers with other than straight fronts. The nearest that any standard came to accepting bowed fronts was the South Eastern Club's rather half-hearted reference to 'badly crooked legs, due either to the main bone-shafts being bent' as a disqualifying feature. The clause could have been framed, as are similar clauses in all other standards, in far stronger terms.

Anyone who owns a bow-fronted 'Jack Russell' either hasn't got a Jack Russell Terrier at all or has got an exceptionally poor and deformed specimen of the breed.

A further step in the development of the breed standard was made when, in the March 1990 issue of the *Kennel Gazette*, it was announced that 'the General Committee of the Kennel Club has recognised for registration the Parson Jack Russell Terrier'.

Recognition had been based on a breed Standard drawn up by the Parson Jack Russell Terrier Club, to which the Kennel Club made a few, minor alterations. The standard drawn up by the breed club was:

Parson Jack Russell Terrier

Interim Breed Standard

GENERAL APPEARANCE: Workmanlike, active and agile; built for speed and endurance. Scars and injuries resulting from work or accident are acceptable unless working ability is impaired.

CHARACTERISTICS: Essentially a working terrier with ability and conformation to go to ground and run with hounds.

TEMPERAMENT: Bold and friendly.

HEAD AND SKULL: Flat, moderately broad, gradually narrowing to the eyes. Shallow stop. Length from nose to stop slightly shorter than from stop to occiput. Nose black.

EYES: Almond-shaped, fairly deep-set, dark, keen expression.

EARS: Small, V-shaped, dropping forward, carried close to head and fold not to appear above top of skull.

MOUTH: Jaws strong, muscular. Teeth with a perfect, regular and complete scissor bite, i.e. upper teeth closely overlapping the lower teeth and set square to the jaws.

NECK: Clean, muscular, of good length, gradually widening to shoulders.

FOREQUARTERS: Shoulders long and sloping, well laid-back, cleanly cut at withers. Legs strong, must be straight with joints turning neither in nor out. Elbows close to body, working free of the sides.

BODY: Chest of moderate depth, capable of being spanned behind the shoulders by average-sized hands. Back strong and straight. The loin slightly arched. Well-balanced, length of back from withers to root of tail to be equal to height from withers to ground.

HINDQUARTERS: Strong, muscular with good angulation and bend of stifle. Hocks short and parallel giving plenty of drive.

FEET: Compact with firm pads, turning neither in nor out.

TAIL: Strong, straight, set high. Customarily docked with length complimenting the body while providing a good handhold.

GAIT/MOVEMENT: Free, lively, well co-ordinated, straight action front and behind.

COAT: Naturally harsh, close and dense, whether rough or smooth. Belly and undersides coated. Skin must be thick and close.

COLOUR: Entirely white or with tan, lemon or black markings, preferably confined to the head and/or root of tail.

SIZE: Height ideally 35–36 cm (14 inches) at withers for dogs and 33 cm (13 inches) for bitches, but none should deviate more than 1 inch from these heights.

FAULTS: Any departure from the foregoing points should be considered a fault and the seriousness with which the fault should be regarded should be in exact proportion to its degree.

NOTE: Male animals should have two apparently normal testicles fully descended into the scrotum.

The Kennel Club was adamant that the clause which defined size must underline the importance of a minimum acceptable height. They were anxious that no short-legged Jack Russells should, almost literally, creep under the wire to recognition. By doing so they reflected the views of the vast majority of British Parson and Jack Russell Terrier breeders. It was even proposed that judges should submit Parson Jack Russell Terriers to the indignity, suffered by no other sporting breed, of being measured at shows. Fortunately wiser counsel prevailed. The deviation of 1 inch from 14 inches for dogs and 13 inches for bitches was changed by the Kennel Club to a minimum of 13 inches for dogs and 12 inches for bitches. No upper height limit was specified.

The Kennel Club also chose to omit the phrase, to which all breeders attached considerable importance, 'Scars and injuries resulting from work or accident are acceptable unless working ability is impaired' from the first clause of the Breed Standard. In addition the Kennel Club refused to add to the final clause a phrase which was already part of the Border Terrier Breed Standard. This was intended to underline the importance of working qualities. The faults clause would then have read:

> FAULTS: Any departure from the foregoing points should be considered a fault and the seriousness with which the fault should be regarded should be in exact proportion to its degree and its effect on the terrier's ability to work.

The refusal to allow any reference to working ability did much to reinforce the fears of those who believed that the Kennel Club had little or no concern for function. An opportunity to refute firmly held prejudices had been lost. The wishes of the breed's supporters had been ignored. A standard had been produced which ignored a most important, indeed a vital, feature of the breed.

The Kennel Club Secretary had expressed the view that the additional phrase in the Border Terrier standard was nothing more than an unacceptable tautology. Those who finally approved the standard may have taken a similar view. They may not have recognized the value of repetition to achieve emphasis. Maybe the Kennel Club had simply failed to appreciate the importance Parson Jack Russell Terrier as well as Border Terrier enthusiasts attached to working qualities.

What the Kennel Club referred to as its copyright Interim Standard was, almost word for word, that which had previously been published by the Parson Jack Russell Terrier Club.

For a number of years the Kennel Club had been encouraging owners to have dogs not required for breeding surgically neutered. At the same time they had made it difficult for neutered dogs to be shown. Towards the end of 1990 the Kennel Club decided to rectify this anomaly. They did so by allowing all dogs which had been surgically neutered to be shown without prior permission. Unfortunately this had the effect of making a nonsense of the final clause in all Breed Standards. This requires that all dogs should have two apparently normal testicles fully descended into the scrotum. It is impossible for judges to differentiate between castrated dogs and bilateral cryptorchids. Both of them would be given an advantage in the ring over unilateral cryptorchids by the new dispensation.

Many overseas kennel clubs not only refuse to allow cryptorchids to be shown but they will not register puppies unless their sire is known to be fully entire. The new dispensation threatened to complicate this situation in a way that would adversely affect British breeders.

What had become the official standard of the Parson Jack Russell Terrier would form the basis on which, following overseas recognition, the breed would be judged all over the world. It had rectified some of the weaknesses in earlier standards but it had also introduced new weaknesses as a result of the Kennel Club's apparent disdain for working qualities. Even so it had, while covering aspects the Parson had ignored, remained remarkably faithful to both the Parson's own description of the breed and to what was known about the sort of terriers he bred and favoured.

By the time Kennel Club recognition had been achieved the breed's short-lived acceptance of short-legged terriers had passed. The type had disappeared from the hunt and working terrier show rings in Britain. None of the breed clubs gave their support to short-legged terriers. The type still existed in large numbers and remained popular as a companion, often of dubious ancestry. Outside Britain, and particularly in Australia, the situation was somewhat different. Short-legged Jack Russells were still shown and remained the most popular type.

The Jack Russell Terrier Club of Australia had been founded in 1972. It aimed to promote and protect the breed, and to assist with this aim a breed standard was drawn up and finalized in 1983. This standard promoted a terrier between 10 inches and 12 inches in height and weighing between 11 and 12 lb, far smaller than the 14 inch and 14 lb classic touchstone.

The 1990 Australian Jack Russell Terrier Breed Standard

GENERAL APPEARANCE: A strong, active, well-built working terrier of great character with flexible body of medium length. His smart movement matches his keen expression. Tail docking is optional and the coat may be smooth, rough, or broken.

CHARACTERISTICS: A lively, alert and active terrier with a keen, intelligent expression.

HEAD AND SKULL: The skull should be flat and of moderate width, gradually decreasing in width to the eyes and tapering to a wide muzzle with strong jaws. There should be a well-defined stop but not over-pronounced. The length from the stop to the nose should be slightly shorter than from the stop to the occiput with the cheek muscles well-developed. The nose should be black.

EYES: Small, dark and with keen expression. *Must* not be prominent and eyelids should fit closely. The eyelid rims should be pigmented black.

EARS: Button or dropped of good texture and great mobility.

MOUTH: Deep, wide and powerful jaws with tight-fitting pigmented lips and strong teeth closing to a scissor bite.

NECK: Strong and clean allowing head carried with poise.

FOREQUARTERS: Shoulders well sloped back and not heavily loaded with muscle. Forelegs straight in bone from the shoulder to toe whether viewed from the front or the side and with sufficient length of upper arm to ensure elbows are set under the body, with sternum clearly in front of shoulder blades.

BODY: Chest deep rather than wide, with good clearance and the brisket located at the right height mid-way between the ground and the withers. The body should be proportioned marginally longer than tall, measuring slightly longer from withers to the root of the tail, than from withers to the ground. Back level. Ribs should be well sprung from the spine, flattening on the sides so that the girth behind the elbows can be spanned by two hands – 40–43 cm. The loins should be short, strong, and deeply muscled.

HINDQUARTERS: Strong and muscular, balanced in proportion to the shoulder; hind legs parallel when viewed from behind while in free-standing position. Stifles well-angulated and hocks low set.

FEET: Round, hard, padded, not large, toes moderately arched, turned neither in nor out.

TAIL: May droop at rest. When moving should be erect and if docked the tip should be on the same level as ears.

GAIT/MOVEMENT: True, free and springy with the fore and hind legs carried straight forward and parallel.

COAT: May be smooth, broken or rough. Must be weatherproof.

COLOUR: White *must* predominate with black, tan or brown markings.

SIZE: Ideal is 25–30 cm (10–12 inches) in height with the weight in kgs being equivalent to 1 kg to each 5 cm in height, i.e. a 25 cm high dog should weigh approximately 5 kg and a 30 cm dog should weigh 6 kg.

FAULTS: Any departure from the foregoing should be considered a fault and the seriousness with which the fault should be regarded should be in exact proportion to its degree. However, the following weaknesses should be particularly penalized:

(a) Lack of true Terrier characteristics.

(b) Lack of balance i.e. over-exaggeration of any points.

(c) Sluggish or unsound movement.

(d) Faulty mouth.

NOTE: Male animals should have two apparently normal testicles descended into the scrotum.

The standard accepted by the ANKC significantly differs in two respects from that put forward by the Australian Jack Russell Terrier Club in 1983. The size of the dog is brought within narrower limits and no effort is made to describe the quality of the various coat types. In 1983 the standard said that 'for working purposes the height may range from 23 cm to 34 cm (9 inches to 13½ inches)'. The standard which follows recognition therefore moves the maximum allowable height further away from what would be regarded as acceptable in Britain.

In some respects the Australian standard reflects what British breeders regard as important. It also requires characteristics which British breeders ignore or regard as faults.

There is an emphasis on the need to have black pigmented eyelids and lips, which has never appeared in any standard produced in Britain. Of more significance than this cosmetic aspect is the requirement that Australian Jack Russells should be short in loin. This would produce a terrier which is inflexible underground and which would be less able than a longer loined dog to gallop freely across country. The requirement is, therefore, one which detracts from the breed's value as a working terrier.

The Australian standard differs significantly from all others used for Parson or Jack Russell Terriers in respect of size. It asks for a dog only slightly longer than it is tall and suggests a minimum height for working dogs of 10 inches (25 cm). Such a dog might weigh no more than 5 kg (about 11 lb). A dog of this size could not be expected to carry out the sort of work the Parson required of his terriers. Most of the breeds in the toy group may be bigger than the minimum size accepted by the Australian standard for a terrier intended to run with hounds and face a fox.

In America the Jack Russell Terrier Breeders' Association 'was established in 1985 . . . in response to a growing consensus that the Jack Russell Terrier was being misrepresented as a short-legged terrier with a long back whose basic proportions resembled that of a Corgi, rather than a terrier with the symmetry of a foxhound'. The Association promoted the cause of the 14 inch terrier but recognized the popularity of the short-legged type.

The purpose of the Breeders' Association is the preservation and continuance of the original historical Parson Jack

Russell terrier. Throughout history breeds have been changed by breeders to suit current trends, altering the original appearance and abilities of the dog and leaving any connections to its past behind. We see this happening with the Jack Russell. A new interest in a Toy Terrier; one bred only to hunt woodchucks in the US, has many breeders committed to breeding an under 12½ inch terrier, in short an American Jack Russell Hunt terrier.

The diagnosis was accurate, though precisely the same accusations might well have been made about the Parson himself. He too changed his terriers to suit his needs. It is not a process which calls for inevitable censure. The American Association's standard suggests that a 'height that gives overall balance is usually between 12 and 14 inches at the withers. (The ideal height of a mature dog is 14 inches at the withers and bitches is 13 inches at the withers.)' Nothing here differs radically from what was officially accepted in Britain.

The standard adopted by the Jack Russell Terrier Club of America was largely identical with that of the Jack Russell Club of Great Britain. It was produced in close collaboration with the Club of Great Britain's officials. Differences, however, are not without significance. Whereas the Club of Great Britain had at one time set the minimum height at 9 inches, the American standard had a minimum of 10 inches. Instead of splitting the two types at 12 inches they were split at 12½ inches. In addition the phrase 'level bite is acceptable for registration' concluded the mouth clause. The colour clause, doubtless as a result of the bitter experience of some American enthusiasts, made it clear that 'brindle markings are unacceptable'. Finally a catalogue of faults reinforced the positive points required by the standard:

Shyness. Disinterest. Overly aggressive. Defects in bit. Weak jaws. Fleshy ears. Down at shoulder. Barrel ribs. Out at elbow. Narrow hips. Straight stifles. Weak feet. Sluggish or unsound movement. Dishing. Plaiting. Toeing. Silky or woolly coats. Shrill or weak voice. Lack of muscle or skin tone. Lack of stamina or lung reserve. Evidence of foreign blood.

Surprisingly the Parson Jack Russell Terrier Club's standard appears to have been the first to recognize that bitches might be slightly smaller than dogs. What is of more significance is the way in which the minimum height and the point at which the line was drawn between Jack Russell and Parson Jack Russell Terriers has varied. By the early 1980s 9 inches was regarded as an acceptable minimum height. The three British clubs put the split at either 11 or 12 inches. The only other club to accept the small type was the Club of America which set a 10 inch minimum and the split at 12½ inches. What various kennel clubs later chose to regard as a major source of difference simply did not exist. The smaller type of terrier existed and was enormously popular. The consensus of opinion was that it should be identical to its leggier cousin except that its height should be between 9 and 12 inches. It is difficult to see why this should ever have been seen as the source of intractable problems.

The idea that it should be possible to compile a list, in order of importance, of all the faults which may occur in Parson or Jack Russell Terriers or, indeed, in any breed might be seen, initially at least, as a very attractive one. Such a list might be regarded as being of immense potential use as a guide to breeders, to exhibitors and, of course, to judges. The idea, however, appears to stand all which we would regard as important about breeding and assessing pedigree dogs on its head. It suggests that quality is nothing more than the absence of faults rather than the sum of virtues. It seems to emphasize the importance of faults while totally ignoring virtues. It stresses the negative and ignores the positive. It might be no more than a different emphasis but there are important differences between a breeder who tries to avoid faults and one who tries to produce virtues, and between judges who penalize faults and those who reward virtues. A good Parson or Jack Russell Terrier is not the one with the least significant faults but the one with the most outstanding virtues. Those whose judgement is based on a comparison of faults are doing little more than looking for the lowest common denominator rather than for the outstanding product of virtues.

On this basis compiling a hierarchical list of faults would not only be immensely difficult but would, by giving faults greater emphasis than virtues, be very dangerous.

It would be difficult because the list would have to be an enormously long one if it was to cover every possible virtue and fault that are likely to occur and would be of very limited value if it failed to do so. It also seems inevitable that, among the very many virtues and faults which might occur, there will be some which have equal importance or whose importance may vary according to the situation in which they occur and the opinion of the assessor. A complete order of precedence probably doesn't exist and even an incomplete one is likely to vary according to different situations.

The Parson or Jack Russell Terrier has not yet been born which has just one virtue and none have just one fault. Virtues and faults occur in an infinite variety of combinations and it is the overall combination which is important.

The list would not only have to include every possible characteristic, good and bad, and take account of the degree to which each might occur, but would also have to take account of the almost infinite variety of combinations. So what seemed like a good idea is shown to be, after only a little thought, impossible. This is not to say that it is impossible to propose a hierarchy consisting of broad bands, each including a particular category of virtues and faults and with divisions between the bands blurred by the degree and combinations in which virtues and faults occur.

Surely the first and most important quality a Parson or Jack Russell Terrier must have is to look like a Parson or Jack Russell Terrier and the most serious fault it can have is to look like another breed. Type must be the most important virtue of all and any loss of type must be the most serious fault. If type is not important there is no point in trying to breed Parson or Jack Russell Terriers. Anything which will do the job for which the breeds are intended could then be regarded as satisfactory. This is precisely the attitude propounded by some who have only a narrow interest in work. The Parson would not have agreed with them. Such a blinkered attitude would have been anathema to him.

The Kennel Club Breed Standard says that a Parson Jack Russell Terrier is *essentially* a working terrier. It follows then that qualities which enable a Parson terrier to do the job for which it is intended are more important than those of a more cosmetic nature. Equally, faults that prevent a Parson or Jack Russell Terrier from doing the work for which the breeds were intended are more serious than those which do not. This is not a matter of opinion. It is something that is unequivocally stated and stressed in the Breed Standard. The breed was developed for a very special type of work in a particular part of the country and they must be assessed against the demands which are imposed both by the work and by the country.

So, if only by implication, we arrive at a third category of virtues and faults that contains all those which do not affect the ability to work. These should not be dismissed as unimportant. Individually and collectively they make an important contribution to type. Their collective contribution to type and the primary importance of type may go some way towards providing support for a suggestion that cosmetic attributes are every bit as important as any other.

There is also another category of virtues and faults which are of a temporary nature, the product of the way the dog is being cared for or some other changeable factor. The category is one which judges, in particular, would be wise to approach with proper caution. They must not be led into basing decisions on what they saw before the day, on past knowledge or on what they think might, or might not, happen in the future. Nevertheless this category exerts considerable influence over which dogs earn consistently high regard and which are consistently disregarded.

We should not ignore the likelihood that virtues and faults which may be transient can affect both type and ability to work. Perhaps for these reasons they deserve to be placed higher in the hierarchy.

Even now, with a mere four, enormously broad categories a very complex situation has been created that demands something akin to the judgement of Solomon if the infinite combinations and degrees of virtues and faults which not only can but do occur in Parson or Jack Russell Terriers are to be properly assessed. One thing is certain. The process of assessing an individual dog or of comparing one dog with another should never be reduced to lists or rules to be learned and applied by rote. It is a process which can only be satisfactorily accomplished by those who have a deep knowledge of and a genuine interest in the breed.

10

Buying and Selling

It has been said that it is generally impossible for one person to select a spouse for another. While good sense and careful consideration should, perhaps, decide the choice the heart will often rule the head. So it is with choosing a particular breed of dog. Some people are attracted to a dog with a lot of hair which requires constant and expert attention, others prefer a smooth-coated dog. Some people like brachycephalic breeds, others prefer a dog with a long nose. Some like big dogs, others prefer small ones. History and tradition also exert their own attractions. The different tasks breeds have been produced to carry out add yet another dimension. The variations are endless. They make total nonsense of proposals which surface from time to time that it would be possible to run all the qualities required in the ideal companion dog through a computer and then breed just such a dog to suit every possible taste.

However, though personal likes and dislikes are of great importance they should never override the need to take the dog's welfare into account. If someone is of a sedentary nature and intends to remain so it would be unwise to acquire an energetic breed such as a Parson or Jack Russell Terrier. Similarly someone who wanted a quiescent toy or was looking for glamour would be well-advised to avoid these breeds. Both are robust, workaday breeds, brimming with energy and enthusiasm. They have independent attitudes and are sometimes reluctant to accept orders. They are built for a demanding, outdoor sporting life. Some people might regard their most outstanding characteristics as serious drawbacks. Others would be inclined to excuse their failings.

Owning a dog has other parallels with marriage. The assiciation is, or is intended to be, for life, in sickness and in health, for better or for worse. It is a sad reflection on the scruples of our own species that the contract is so often broken by people and seldom by the dog. Those who are unable or unwilling to give a dog all the daily attention it will need throughout what is usually a long life should not get a dog at all.

Those who are prepared to accept all the responsibilities implicit in dog ownership and to carry them out to the best of their ability can hardly do better than become the owner of a Parson or Jack Russell Terrier.

Breeding, rearing, selling and buying dogs are all part and parcel of the same thing. Breeders, caring breeders that is, sell only to individual buyers who can offer good, permanent homes to the puppies they have bred and reared with such care. Sensible buyers buy only direct from breeders.

Dog or bitch?

The most obvious difference between the sexes is that dogs are sexually active throughout the year and bitches only when they are in season. At these times they will need to be closely confined unless the owner is to run the risk of joining the ranks of those who breed unregistered and unregisterable 'Jack Russells' of doubtful parentage. Dogs which are properly supervised and, when necessary, kept in close confinement do not produce unwanted puppies. Confinement is by far the best method of contraception for both sexes though others are also available.

Among other safeguards is surgical neutering. This is the method most favoured by welfare organizations and by the veterinary profession. They claim several incidental advantages which surgery produces. These include the prevention of pyometra and a reduction in the chance of mammary tumours in bitches. It is also claimed that neutered dogs are often less aggressive, more friendly and less frustrated. These claims are sometimes disputed.

The major disadvantage of surgical neutering is that it is irreversible but there are other drawbacks. Major surgery can never be 100 per cent safe. Spaying bitches can lead to vaginal dermatitis and urinary incontinence. Hormonal changes may result in a softer, more woolly coat than is desirable for the breed. Occasionally there may be significant hair loss. The absence of sexual drive may produce a far more placid companion than the owners of Parson and Jack Russell Terriers expect.

Perfectly safe non-surgical means of terminating an unwanted pregnancy are readily available. There are also hormone injections which will postpone the onset of seasons if these occur inconveniently. These do not lead to permanent infertility.

Proper care is by far the best method of contraception.

Puppy or older dog?

If a terrier is required for show or work an older dog that has already begun its career may offer some advantages over a puppy. The prospective owner will thus avoid some of the uncertainties inherent in puppy development. These uncertainties will, however, only be avoided at a price, perhaps a high price. Promising show stock and proven workers do not tend to come cheap, and when they do there may be good reason to doubt their qualities.

A puppy will probably be initially cheaper than an older dog but will demand more attention and training while it is growing, and as an adult it may not fulfil the owner's every hope. By the time it is adult it is likely to have cost far more than it would have done to buy a young adult. On the other hand much of the fun of owning a dog begins with watching a puppy grow and develop and in the pride when it matures into a sensible, well-trained companion, a top-quality show dog or an outstanding worker.

As far as new owners are concerned it is best to acquire a puppy when it is seven or eight weeks old. At this age puppies are not only fully independent of their dams but are at an age when they are best able to assimilate new experiences and to accept a new home. Caring breeders are, however, often reluctant to part with puppies until they are ten or twelve weeks old. They may want to wait until protective vaccinations have been given, or prefer to wait until puppies are bigger and sturdier before sending them to homes which may have no prior experience of dogs and in which they may well have to endure the incessant attention of young children or thoughtless adults. Resolution of this problem is a matter for the puchaser and the breeder. Fortunately Parson and Jack Russell Terriers, of any age, usually adapt to new homes and new conditions without any apparent trauma. A few weeks' difference in age will seldom produce any great problems.

Sources

Breeders

Puppies should only be bought from the person who bred them. Only in the case of older dogs may there be some slight room for discretion. The reasons are simple. If puppies are to grow and thrive they require, during the first vulnerable weeks of their life, the attention of a well-kept mother and a devoted and caring breeder.

Of course there are good breeders and there are breeders whose standards do not bear close examination. Good breeders generate good reputations. Their satisfied customers are their best recommendation.

The best breeders will do their utmost to ensure that puppies go only to suitable homes. They will offer help and advice after the sale has been made and will often encourage the new owner to become involved in the range of activities which increases the fun to be had from owning a dog.

Buy only from a breeder.

Dealers

Puppies bred to ill-nourished bitches in dark sheds and reared by callous breeders cannot be said to have a satisfactory start in life. If they are then shipped in wholesale, indiscriminately mixed consignments to dealers' kennels, where they are mixed with puppies from other, equally dubious sources and subjected to an unfamiliar regime, their welfare will be at even greater risk. Such puppies do not enjoy the sort of care necessary to produce a healthy, temperamentally well-adjusted adult.

Pet Shops

Pet shops are dealers. Wise buyers will avoid them.

Shows

Puppies as well as adults are sometimes offered for sale at hunt and working terrier shows, as well as at other events. Any such source should be avoided. No breeder with any spark of concern for the health and well-being of young puppies would ever consider exposing them to the upset and risk of infection which is part and parcel of a visit to any such event.

Moreover the offer of puppies for sale at a show not only puts the vendor but also the show organizer on the wrong side of the law. Taking part in an illegal transaction is not the best way of embarking on life as a terrier owner, though it may be educational and probably expensive and heartbreaking as well.

Anyone found offering dogs for sale at Kennel Club licensed events will be subject to disciplinary procedures and can expect to be banned from attending shows.

Rescue

The idea of giving a good home to a dog which, through no fault of its own, has fallen on to hard times and is in the care of a welfare or rescue organization is often an attractive one. The idea may derive from the best of motives or simply from a desire to acquire a dog cheaply. However rescue kennels should be approached just as cautiously as any other source.

Even some of the major rescue organizations seem to be as ready as the worst dealers to describe any small mongrel as a Jack Russell Terrier. They may have little or no knowledge of the dog's background and only a very sketchy idea of its temperament.

For anyone who intends to breed or to show, rescue will not

provide what is needed. If a working terrier is required there is no way of knowing whether the dog is likely to be suitable.

Agencies

Beware also of agencies which exist to put potential buyers in touch with breeders who have puppies available and take a fee for the service. Not all these firms are selective about what sort of breeders they have on their books. Some may be puppy farmers of the worst kind who, unwilling to advertise openly, make use of the anonymity provided by these middlemen. Even those which are selective tend to lead to puppies which are appreciably more expensive because of the need to carry a middleman's profits and overheads.

Advertising

Prospective owners must overcome the problem of finding a source from which they can acquire their new dog. They may do so through advertisements.

The best possible advert any breeder can have is a good reputation based on the testimony of satisfied customers. Breeders with such a reputation seldom need any other sort of advert. They will have a queue of people waiting, with varying degrees of patience, for puppies.

Most terrier owners will be only too happy to tell others where a similar dog may be acquired. Probably the best place to find owners in numbers is at shows and these also offer the advantage that there will also be breeders present who may have stock available for sale. Shows are advertised, some weeks prior to the event, in canine newspapers.

If any other form of advert is thought to be necessary a breeder should take care that the advert is not placed in a publication which might damage a growing reputation. An advert placed between one for 'Pit Bull pups from game parents' and another for 'Cross-bred puppies, free to good homes' is unlikely to enhance any breeder's reputation. The specialist canine papers do not accept such adverts. Specialist periodicals have the additional advantage that they reach a readership which has a particular interest in dogs. Another form of advertising, though less immediate than is provided by the commercial specialist press, is available in newsletters and yearbooks produced by breed clubs. These not only reach readers with an interest in dogs but readers with an interest in a particular breed.

Selling

The wisdom of buying only from the breeder is reflected by the wisdom of selling only to people who have every intention of giving a permanent and caring home to the dog. Caring and responsible breeders never sell to dealers.

Those who sell puppies have a number of responsibilities. Many of them are legally enforceable. These may vary from country to country depending on the precise nature of consumer protection legislation. Others are morally obligatory and universal. Not all these responsibilities may be immediately apparent but the prudent breeder will take steps to ensure that all have been met before any dog is sold.

Breeders should ensure that the puppies they offer for sale are in good health and that they are fully weaned and have been well-reared and properly socialized. They should make certain that the buyer has every intention of providing the puppy with a permanent home and should seek assurance that it will receive proper care throughout its life. The breeder should ensure that the buyer has thought carefully about the consequences of buying a dog and that all responsible members of the family are in agreement with the decision. The breeder should ensure that the buyer fully understands what demands ownership of a vigorous terrier is likely to make, what sort of care it will need and what facilities will be required in order to provide this care.

The breeder should carefully guard against making any exaggerated claims for the breed or for the particular puppy and the buyer should be very suspicious of any claim which seems to be exaggerated. It is all too easy for a proud and enthusiastic breeder, even without wishing to deceive, to make claims about the potential of a particular puppy they may have reason to regret when a disappointed purchaser contests the claims before the courts.

It is not unknown for breeders who have themselves achieved little or no success in the show ring to claim that their puppies will become champions. Some, less scrupulous than most, may seek to suggest that an unusually coloured puppy is a rare and, therefore, desirable specimen whereas it may, in fact, be badly mismarked and unsuitable for either show or breeding.

The buyer should be provided with written details of the puppy's diet, and with enough food to ensure that, for a few days at least, it will not have to adjust to a new diet as well as a new home. Written details of the worming régime which has been carried out and of any vaccinations or other veterinary treatment the puppy may have had should also be given to the new owner. An accurate pedigree should be provided as well as evidence of registration.

Buying

Caveat emptor, 'Let the buyer beware', is a common enough phrase which warns any buyer to approach the transaction with care and caution.

The prime requirements of any companion are that it should have a reliable temperament and be in good health. Prejudice might suggest that the show dogs are all highly strung, neurotic and unhealthy creatures. Nothing could be further from the truth. Show dogs must enjoy shows if they are to achieve success. They will have their normal routine disturbed to be taken to shows where they will be expected to accept strange conditions with complete equanimity, be subjected to a detailed examination by a judge and throughout a long day, under continual scrutiny, behave with unfailing good humour towards man and dog alike.

A similar prejudice might operate against terriers with a working background. These are often seen as pathologically. aggressive and uncontrollable. Once more the truth is very different. A working terrier, particularly one which runs with hounds, must have an absolutely reliable temperament as well as being physically sound.

Dogs bred from genuine show and working parents are likely to be far better than those bred purely to satisfy a largely indiscriminate demand for pets.

Once what might be a suitable dog has been located the prospective purchaser must make arrangements to see it. Wise buyers never buy dogs unseen just as wise breeders never sell them to people who have not inspected their purchase.

Inspection should be thorough and, preferably, expert. Those who have no knowledge of dogs should proceed with caution. Never buy dogs which have been housed in conditions which are other than spotless. Never buy dogs which are not themselves clean and in apparent good health and whose kennel mates are also in the same state. Never buy dogs which are either nervous or aggressive or whose parents are nervous or aggressive. Always insist on seeing the dam and, if possible, the sire.

If there is even the slightest room for doubt it is far better not to proceed with the purchase than to make a decision which will subsequently be regretted. Once the decision has been made the dog should be bought outright. Arrangements, often referred to as breeding terms, which offer a reduced initial price in exchange for puppies or stud work in the future invariably result in an expensive purchase and not unusually in problems. Such arrangements should be avoided.

Registration

Do not buy any dog, described as a Parson or Jack Russell Terrier, which is not registered either with a bona fide breed club or with a kennel club.

Registration is intended as a means to help verify pedigrees. No system is totally incorruptible but all are far better than nothing and as time passes and new techniques become available all, especially the best, are becoming increasingly trustworthy. The value of registration depends entirely on the honesty of breeders who supply details which, with some checks, must be taken on trust. Perhaps the first step towards increased registration reliability came about when registers were first stored on computers. That made it necessary for dishonest breeders to outwit the checks and screens, a number of which are not apparent and may be unsuspected, which could be embodied into a computer program, and as time has passed these checks have become progressively more sophisticated. It could be argued that one of the major benefits of official recognition for any breed is that it gives access to established and well-tried registration systems which not only have considerable computer power available to them but also have the authority to discipline those who provide false information.

All worthwhile registers require that the owner of the stud dog verifies that his dog mated the bitch on a particular day. They require that the full breeding and date of birth are provided and they have the authority to extract a heavy penalty from a dishonest breeder should these subsequently be shown to be false.

As a means to protect bitches against the sort of abuse that puppy farmers perpetrate a number of registration systems now impose limits on the number of registered puppies a bitch is allowed to produce. Some record details of hereditary diseases and cosmetic operations. Most kennel clubs publish details of every registration, which not only provides an additional check on accuracy but also offers breeders a source of very valuable information.

Identification

A growing number of registers require that all breeding stock as well as puppies should be tattooed, or otherwise individually identified, so that individuals can be positively identified, but even without this the availability of tissue and blood sampling now makes it possible for the parents of any dog, or indeed any animal, to be identified with total accuracy. The checks on misrepresentation are becoming better all the time but are unlikely ever to replace totally those imposed by personal integrity.

Documents

It is for the breeder to register puppies and to hand over all the requisite registration documents at the time of sale. However, not all registration systems are equally efficient and, even though the breeder may have made applications when the puppies were no more than a week or two old, he may not have completed the process of registration by the time they are ready to go to their new homes.

Furthermore, though registration documents provide new owners with protection against dishonest breeders, the breeder too sometimes has a need for protection against dishonest purchasers. This can, to some degree, be achieved by holding on to registration documents until cheques have been cleared. If registration documents are posted to the new owner the breeder has an address to which subsequent correspondence can be directed.

Veterinary inspection

Many breeders have puppies checked by a veterinary surgeon before they go to their new homes. This does not mean that they fear that something may be wrong with their puppies, rather that they want to ensure that they are healthy. The check offers protection to the breeder as well as to the buyer. Not all buyers have the knowledge to assess the health of a puppy, though the warning signs are not difficult to see, and many welcome an independent professional opinion. Breeders will be anxious not to part with puppies which harbour some problem which is not apparent. Equally a certificate of health offers breeders protection against complaints should a puppy contract an illness after it has left the breeder.

Buyers too may seek the reassurance which a veterinary inspection provides. If any problems which existed but were not apparent at the time of the purchase are revealed redress may be possible.

Right: A smart and successful brace of smooth Jack Russells, winners at the Morpeth Hunt Show in 1983, and owned by the Morpeth Whip *Photo: Jean Jackson*

Below: A very smart and typical Jack Russell Terrier at the Morpeth Hunt Terrier Show in 1983 *Photo: Jean Jackson*

Ruth Wilford's home-bred Hannah of Clystlands won her first Jack Russell championship at the Blackmore Vale Hunt Terrier Show at 11 months of age. She was best Rough Jack Russell bitch, out of a class of 55, at the 1985 Great Yorkshire Show. At a show which commemorated the centenary of the Parson's death she was adjudged the terrier most like Trump *Photo: Anne Roslin Williams*

George Simpson typey brace of Jack Russells, Kim and Rats, c hunting in 1987

Lucy of Clystlands a typical Parson Jack Russell Terrier bitch owned and bred by Ruth Wilford *Photo: Anne Roslin Williams*

After winning 14 BIS awards at Jack Russell Terrier Club shows, Malung Jim Beam, owned by P. J. 'Curly' Sullivan, became the first Australian Jack Russell Champion just two months after recognition of the breed *Photo: courtesy of National Dog*

Best Puppy in Show at the first Australian Jack Russell Terrier Club Show run under AKCC jurisdiction *Photo: courtesy of National Dog*

Tailor, the top winning Jack Russell Terrier stud dog in America, owned by Briarpatch Kennels. He won BIS at the Jack Russell Terrier Club of America's show on six occasions. In 1990 he received the JRTC of America's bronze medallion for special merit *Photo: courtesy of National Dog Review*

Eddie Chapman's Jack Russell Terrier bitch, Sally, which won the championship at the prestigious Lowther Show in 1990 *Photo: Jason Revell*

Above: Parson Jack Russell Terriers made their debut at the Crufts Centenary Show in 1991. Over 80 years previously Arthur Heinemann had judged classes for Working Terriers at the same show
Photo: Sally Anne Thompson

Right centre: Here Pauline Hancock's Ragford Rascal is being examined by Andrew Small at Crufts 1991
Photo: Sally Anne Thompson

Right below: George Simpson's Groundhill Butch stands smartly before the judge at Crufts 1991
Photo: Sally Anne Thompson

Tithebarn Tally was among the winners at Crufts in 1991 and has been a prolific winner at hunt and working terrier shows for his owner John Mackereth *Photo: Malcolm Baird*

Lionel Hamilton Renwick, seen here with Red Rum, is one of the world's leading all rounder judges. He was the Crufts 1989 Best in Show judge and has close connections with coursing, hunting and with working terriers

Blencathra Badger and
Blencathra Nettle,
owned and bred by Paul
Ross, helped to establish
the Parson's type in
America before moving
to Britain where both
achieved considerable
success in Jack Russell
classes. After recognition
their success continued
in Parson Jack Russell
classes at KC shows
Photo: Malcolm Baird

Clifford Hubbard's
excellent *Dogs in Britain*,
written in 1946, contains
this picture of a Parson
Jack Russell Terrier.
The photo was taken by
Mrs Jim Harris, née
Annie Rawle. It shows
just how well the
Parson's type had been
protected up to the late
1940s and how well it
has since been protected
in Britain

David and Margaret
Graham's home-bred
Millbank Glen is by
Eskdale Mick out of
Millbank Tess and is a
consistent winner at
both Kennel Club and
working terrier shows
Photo: Malcolm Baird

Malcolm and Gillian Turnbull's promising puppy, Glenholm Hector, by Barry Jones' Heliwar Ben out of Ridley Reckless of Glenholm, bred by Anne Milne *Photo: Malcolm Baird*

John Mackereth's home-bred Tithebarn Cap, by Richmonds Brock out of Tithebarn Jan, made a successful debut at the Falstone Hunt Terrier Show *Photo: Malcolm Baird*

11

Breeding

There are a number of aspects of breeding that arouse strong feelings which are not always based on objective assessment of the facts, and tend to have a moral basis. For instance, the age at which bitches are first mated, the frequency with which they are subsequently bred from and the length of their breeding career are three such aspects. Inbreeding is another matter which gives rise to an unusual degree of controversy and comment.

In every wild species females are mated as soon as they are sufficiently mature to conceive. Many are mated again within hours of giving birth. This pattern will continue until old age makes them infertile. Many females are, quite literally, pregnant throughout their entire adult lives.

Species which live in herds, flocks or packs are often closely inbred, far more closely and for generation after generation, than most dog breeders would ever contemplate. A dominant male will monopolize a number of females, and some are likely to be his own sisters and daughters. He will eventually be replaced by another, younger, dominant male, probably one of his own sons. He will mate his mother, his sisters and, in the course of time, his own daughters. Precisely the same breeding pattern is to be found among mongrels which are allowed to wander the streets.

Maximizing the breeding output of individuals is necessary to the survival of wild species. Close inbreeding is necessary in order to ensure that the qualities of the most successful animals are transmitted to the next generation. In the face of this natural order it is prudent to weigh the real reasons for suspicions about breeding from bitches at successive seasons, breeding from young and elderly bitches and the use of close inbreeding.

There is no evidence that the physiological welfare of a well cared-for bitch is necessarily at risk if she is bred from at a young age, frequently or into old age. There are, however, many ill cared-for bitches which are subjected to an uncaring régime by callous commercial breeders. The majority of these bitches are of poor quality. No breeder with a conscience would wish to add to the unhappy population of poorly kept, mediocre dogs. They want only to breed good, and hopefully outstandingly good, dogs and to place them in homes where their welfare will be well-protected.

Even the best breeders won't always succeed in producing outstandingly good dogs, of course. Indeed they may seldom succeed but the production of top-quality dogs remains their primary objective, and they are most likely to succeed by breeding selectively only from healthy, vigorous, top-quality dogs.

In order to come close to success they will need knowledge and a large slice of good fortune. These must be allied to a resilient spirit of optimism supported by unremitting attention to detail. Breeding good dogs is not easy. It is probable that the difficulties and challenges entailed provide an important part of the attraction to the best breeders.

Out of concern for the welfare of dogs a number of kennel clubs throughout the world have imposed limits on the lower and upper ages of breeding bitches and on the number of registered puppies or litters they may have. These limits are also often reinforced by the standards which breed clubs impose on their members. The imposition of these limits is a response to concern about the large number of ill-bred, badly reared puppies being produced by breeders who make use of registration to give their products an often spurious stamp of quality. The limits are primarily concerned with population control and general welfare considerations. As such they are welcomed by all caring breeders.

Perhaps the usual point of embarkation on a career as a breeder is reached when the idea occurs that the qualities of a much-loved family pet might be passed on to another generation. Sometimes less laudable motives are evident. The desire to recoup the cost of the bitch, a desire to profit from the sale of puppies, a practical sex lesson for children and even a belief, to which, even today, some vets still subscribe, that every bitch deserves the supposed fulfilment of having a litter might all be advanced as reasons for breeding. None are adequate reasons. The only reason must be a desire to produce top-quality dogs.

Brood bitches

Any bitch from which it is intended to breed must be well-bred. She must be healthy. She must have no glaring faults. She must show no sign of hereditary disease and be unlikely to carry any hidden defects. Any bitch that has any serious temperamental or physical defects or is in any way untypical of the breed should not be bred from.

Once a bitch has reached about eighteen months of age she can then be mated to the most suitable and best available dog. Her first litter might be delayed for another year or even longer without untoward effects. It should not be delayed until advancing age begins to erode her health and vigour.

The decision to breed should be anticipated. Care should be taken when buying a female puppy that she is likely to grow into a bitch fit to be bred from. This means buying a well-bred, well-reared, sound and healthy puppy which is the product of parents with similar qualities.

Variation

Dogs, of course, vary in almost every possible respect. Breeders have made use of this variation to create some hundreds of breeds, each designed for a particular purpose. Breed standards represent an attempt to describe perfection. Perfection is not subject to variation. It is absolute. The aim of all good breeders is to edge ever closer to an unattainable perfection; even so variation exists at all levels. The degree of variation within a breed is, of course, very much smaller than within dogs as a whole but variation, within the tolerance allowed by functional or other demands, still exists. Within a good kennel, variation is even further reduced but is still by no means eliminated.

The curve of normal distribution defines the parameters within which variation exists and within which breeders operate. It demonstrates that, in any given population, there will be a few individuals much better than the rest, far more which are only slightly better than the rest, an awful lot of average specimens, a lot which are slightly worse and a few which are truly awful.

The normal curve for a kennel is contained within that for the breed as a whole. The aim of every good breeder is to ensure that the curve which represents the quality of their kennel is at the quality end of the curve for the breed as a whole.

Some kennels, even quite successful ones, never achieve this. They rely on producing an excellent puppy among a great many of variable quality. If enough puppies are produced they may succeed. They rely on chance, though they might be reluctant to admit the fact. By the same token if an infinite number of monkeys were seated at typewriters one of them would eventually write *Macbeth*. The same monkey wouldn't go on to write *Hamlet* or anything else of any value. Chance would give that honour to another monkey.

The aim of good breeders then is to produce good dogs of a consistent type and ever-improving quality.

Environment

Inherited characteristics are referred to as the genotype. Those which are the product of environmental influence are called the phenotype. The compounded effect of the two offers problems which all breeders must face.

Suppose that a dog is admired for some particular quality. How is a breeder to know whether this quality is inherited, and so is likely to be transmitted to his offspring, or whether it is the product of environmental factors, and so cannot be transmitted to another generation? In the past it was believed that environmental conditions could influence such things as coat colour. The influence was thought to be exerted by something called telegony. That idea has long been discredited but the way in which a puppy is reared and subsequently cared for undoubtedly has a profound effect on its temperamental and physical characteristics.

To complicate things even further, litter size, birth weight, growth rate, mature weight, temperament, coat and skin condition, musculature, skeleton construction, life span and many more qualities are affected by both inherited and environmental conditions.

Line-breeding and in-breeding

The two terms 'line-breeding' and 'in-breeding' are not scientific terms with precise definitions. They are terms sometimes used, in an Alice-in-Wonderlandish sort of way, to carry a variety of meanings.

The term 'in-breeding' will here be used to imply that a close relationship exists between a mated pair. Line-breeding will be used to imply a more distant relationship. Imprecise though they are and though they fail to identify the point at which in-breeding becomes line-breeding, these definitions will be adequate for the present purpose.

Future generations of registered Parson Jack Russell Terriers will be descended from fewer than 500 individuals. Some of these are closely related. All are already line-bred and some are closely inbred. Breeders of Parson Jack Russell Terriers cannot avoid some degree of in-breeding or line-breeding. The same is true of Australian Jack Russell Terriers. It is also true, though perhaps to a slightly lesser extent, of genuine Jack Russell Terriers.

The degree to which the Parson's own terriers and those of his hunting cronies were inbred can be seen from the pedigrees which appear elsewhere in this book. Charlie Littleworth, a Devonian huntsman, condemned in-breeding but was lavish in his praise of Old Foiler.

Old Foiler was born in 1871. He was by Grip, or Old Grip, who was bred by the Parson. He was out of Juddy, again bred by the Parson. As far as we know Juddy never left the Parson's ownership. It seems likely, therefore, that the Parson bred Old Foiler. If he did so he certainly didn't subscribe to fears about close in-breeding. Henry Gibson gave George Whitemore, the

Pedigree of Old Foiler

Parents	Grandparents	GG-parents	GGG-parents
		Grove Tartar	Unknown
			Unknown
	Grove Willie	Grove Nettle	Grove Tartar
			Sting
Sire Old Grip		Grove Tartar	Unknown
			Unknown
	Vixen	Grove Nettle	Grove Tartar
			Sting
		Grove Tartar	Unknown
			Unknown
	Grove Willie	Grove Nettle	Grove Tartar
			Sting
Dam Juddy		Grove Tartar	Unknown
			Unknown
	Vixen	Grove Nettle	Grove Tartar
			Sting

Grove's huntsman, £100 for Old Foiler after seeing him at the 1872 Birmingham Show.

The old breeders whose aim was to produce sound, tough and sensible working terriers made use of the advantages which in-breeding offers. They avoided its perils by their ability to identify outstanding stock and by a rigorous process of selection. This is the point at which modern breeders so often fail. They ignore the faults in a top winning dog or in their own stock. When these faults are multiplied by in-breeding they lay the blame not on their own inability to select breeding stock but on in-breeding itself.

Having selected a suitable animal to which it is intended to inbreed it is then useful to have some means by which the degree of in-breeding can be measured and, thus, controlled.

All animals inherit half of their genes from each parent, thus they get 25 per cent from each grandparent and 12½ per cent from each great-grandparent. So a dog which is the product of a parent/grandparent mating is 25 per cent to the common ancestor. However relationships become much more complex when an ancestor reappears several times in different generations of a pedigree. Wright's Coefficient of In-breeding provides a means by which the degree of in-breeding to a particular individual can be calculated but it involves some rather tedious calculations. We have reduced these calculations to tabular form so that it is possible, by reference to the table, to see precisely what degree of in-breeding exists with any four-generation pedigree.

Why inbreed at all? There are two reasons for in-breeding. The first is quite simply that in a numerically small population it is impossible to avoid and the second is that it offers the best means to perpetuate the desirable qualities of a particular specimen.

The Parson created a strain of white terriers with little, if any, body colour. He did so by selecting white or nearly white terriers and by line-breeding or in-breeding to them. Close breeding could, if docking were to be banned, offer the means to breed terriers with naturally short tails so that the appearance that is now created by docking would be maintained.

In-breeding does not introduce characteristics which the breeding stock does not carry, though the characteristics may not always be apparent. For this reason a thorough knowledge of pedigrees is essential to successful in-breeding. In-breeding cannot itself discriminate between desirable and undesirable characteristics. This is the breeder's task. The breeder who is blind to faults in his own stock or to qualities in other stock may well find that in-breeding not only offers little of value but may be a rapid road to ruin.

The table provides a means to establish the in-breeding to any individual in a four-generation pedigree. It shows that father to daughter, mother to son, full brother and sister matings all produce a 25 per cent degree of in-breeding. Half-brother to sister, uncle to niece, aunt to nephew, grandparent to grandchild, double first cousins and quadruple first cousins all produce a 12.5 per cent degree. As generations pass and

Coefficient of in-breeding, expressed as a percentage, to any individual for every possible combination within a four generation pedigree

Female side	Male side	Position and frequency of progenitor within pedigree					
	1	*2, 3 & 4*	*2 & 3* *2, 4 & 4* *3, 3, 4 & 4*	*2 & 4* *3, 3 & 4* *3, 4, 4 & 4*	*2* *3 & 3* *3, 4 & 4* *4, 4, 4 & 4*	*3 & 4* *4, 4 & 4*	*3* *4 & 4*
1	*	43.7	37.5	31.2	25.0	18.7	12.5
2, 3 & 4	43.7	38.3	32.8	27.3	21.9	16.4	10.9
2 & 3 *2, 4 & 4* *3, 3, 4 & 4*	37.5	32.8	28.1	23.4	18.7	14.0	9.4
2 & 4 *3, 3 & 4* *3, 4, 4, & 4*	31.2	27.3	23.4	19.5	15.6	11.7	7.8
2 *3 & 3* *3, 4 & 4* *4, 4, 4 & 4*	25.0	21.9	18.7	15.6	12.5	9.4	6.2
3 & 4 *4, 4 & 4*	18.7	16.4	14.0	11.7	9.4	7.8	4.7
3 *4 & 4*	12.5	10.9	9.4	7.8	6.2	4.7	3.1
4	6.2	5.5	4.7	3.9	3.1	2.3	1.6

relationships become more complex the labels which suffice for human relationships become less meaningful. It is necessary to look at the place and frequency with which a progenitor appears in the pedigree.

Use of the table shows that Old Foiler was 28.1 per cent inbred to Grove Tartar. It shows in a very graphic manner that a dog's parents have the greatest effect on what it inherits and that the effect declines very rapidly as the particular dog recedes further down the pedigree. A grandparent contributes only half as much as a parent, a great-grandparent only one-quarter as much. It takes four appearances in the fourth generation to carry as much influence as one in the second. So a dog which has the same individual as parent and grandparent is inbred to the extent of 25 per cent whereas parent and great-great-grandparent produces only 6.2 per cent.

The closest form of in-breeding which is possible, 43.7 per cent, occurs when a parent appears in every other generation of the pedigree. In practice any mating which produces a closer relationship than that between parent and offspring should be entered into only after much thought and with considerable caution.

Colour

One of the very few characteristics controlled entirely by inheritance, and not at all by environment, is colour. For Parson Jack Russell Terrier breeders this represents a particular problem.

Colour is of little or no practical consequence as far as working terriers are concerned. Nevertheless it is something about which the Parson expressed strong opinions. His preference was for white terriers. He produced a strain of terriers that were entirely white or had tan markings confined to the head and the root of the tail. Heinemann was less concerned about colour. His terriers were usually predominantly white but some were more heavily marked. Alys Serrell was unconcerned about colour, though the terriers about which she enthused most were not heavily marked. The breed standards of both Smooth and Wire Fox Terriers insist that 'white should predominate'. It is not uncommon to see winning specimens of both breeds in which white does not predominate.

If the Parson preferred white terriers those who now profess to breed terriers which would have been accepted in his kennels must reflect his preference. A cursory examination of the foundation stock of Parson Jack Russell Terrier as registered by the Kennel Club shows that this is not always the case. Very few Parson Jack Russell Terriers on the Kennel Club's foundation register are white. The majority are black and white or tri-coloured.

During 1990 the Kennel Club accepted registrations for 336 terriers which had previously been registered with the Parson Jack Russell Terrier Club. Of these 47 per cent were tan and white, 38 per cent tricolour, 9.8 per cent black and white, 3.6 per cent white and 1.5 per cent were brown and white.

Of the 130 puppies bred from dogs on the foundation register and registered with the Kennel Club during 1990 61.5 per cent were tricolour, 25.5 per cent were tan and white, 11.5 per cent were brown and white and only 1.5 per cent were white. Somewhat surprisingly, no black and white puppies were registered. If what took place in the first year of recognition is repeated in successive years it will not be long before tricolours totally dominate the breed while the colours which the Parson preferred will have been lost. If breeders are to remain faithful to their claim to be preserving the sort of terrier which the Parson bred they must have some regard to his preferences as regards colour and must place a greater emphasis on breeding for the colours which he favoured.

Selection

Selection is inevitable. That only about 10 per cent of all registered dogs ever produce registered offpsring provides evidence of a stringent process of selection. Selection of the parents most likely to produce quality offspring is obviously important to any breed's future. The process of selection may lead to change or can be used to protect against change. Breeders must select in order to preserve desirable characteristics and to eliminate or reduce the incidence of undesirable characteristics.

In this post-Darwin era we all know about selection – survival of the fittest and all that. The phrases have even become part of political rhetoric. We bandy them about with little thought for their origins or their meaning.

Not since the relationship between man and dog was first formed over 10,000 years ago has natural selection meant anything very significant in terms of domestic dogs. Man, not nature, has done the selecting. As time has passed and the criteria on which selection is based have changed so too have the products of selection.

Originally selection would be based on little more than toleration of man's company. Whether man or wolf was responsible for the selection is debatable. As domesticated wolves began to take part in hunting expeditions those which would respond to commands or which were fastest or had the best noses or the keenest eyesight would have been selected. As time passed and the business of keeping body and soul together did not entirely preoccupy man he began to select dogs because their appearance pleased him. Functional requirements would still have been uppermost in his mind.

At this stage if man had wanted to breed dogs with enormous heads or with very short, crooked legs or some other unusual feature he could have done so. The extent of these unnatural attributes would have been kept in firm check by nature itself. Dogs which could not be conceived, be born and live naturally would die. Nature still had the upper hand.

The next stage is not yet complete. New veterinary skills enabled dogs to be conceived, be born and to live to reproduce their kind which would previously have died. The veterinary profession opened a Pandora's Box containing all sorts of exaggerated features which, hitherto, could not have been produced. Some breeders took full advantage of this new freedom to produce dogs with physical and temperamental deformities which they regarded as desirable.

Working terriers were protected from exaggerations by the demands of the tasks they were expected to undertake. These demands cannot be corrupted by fashion or by any other transient factor. A terrier bred to run with hounds, go to ground to fox and persuade that fox to move can either do so or not. Nothing can gainsay performance in the field. That particular process of selection is no longer available. It must be replaced by less positive methods which rely on breeder's preferences.

Inherited disease

About two hundred inherited diseases have been identified in dogs. About three thousand have been identified in our own species. Inherited disease exists in every species, wild as well as domestic. The total elimination of hereditary disease is practically impossible but dog breeders must do their utmost to reduce its incidence as much as possible.

Official recognition has made a number of schemes intended to control hip and eye disease available. It has also reduced the size of the available gene pool. The immediate post-recognition years will be a time when breeders must exert extra vigilance.

A number of hereditary diseases have been identified in what were described as Jack Russell Terriers. These diseases include ataxia, a muscular or nervous condition which produces unco-ordinated movement. Here inheritance may be by a simple recessive gene. Legg-Calve-Perthes disease results in the partial disintegration of the femoral head and results in lameness, especially of puppies. The mode of inheritance is uncertain but Robinson has suggested a mode which mimics monogenic heredity. Patella luxation results in a dislocated hind kneecap and a characteristic three-legged hopping action especially at speed or under testing conditions. The mode of inheritance is uncertain but does not seem to rely on a single gene. *Myasthenia gravis* affects motor nerves to produce the appearance of weakness in the hindquarters and swaying or staggering movement. Inheritance may be through a simple recessive gene.

Lens luxation may in dogs, as with people involved in violent sport, be caused by a blow or blows to the head. It may also be the product of an inherited predisposition. The mode of inheritance may vary from breed to breed.

Achondroplasia is the condition which produces dwarfism and was, during the 1950s and 1960s, widespread among what were described as Jack Russell Terriers. Selection has almost entirely eliminated the disease from pure-bred Parson and Jack Russell Terriers. It is invariably associated with short-legged breeds and probably has a polygenetic mode of inheritance.

As time passes and veterinary skills improve, more diseases, which may be inherited, are likely to be discovered. Their existence need cause neither alarm nor shame. The knowledge and the means exist to control all hereditary diseases. The only cause for shame would be if this knowledge and these means were ignored.

12

Mating to Birth

Bitches are able to conceive only at a particular time during their periodic seasons. Dogs are fertile at any time. Effecting a mating between the two and the timing of the birth of puppies are, therefore, dependent on when the bitch is in season.

Oestrus

Oestrus, the bitch's season, is cyclical. It may be triggered by the presence of other bitches in season, what breeders often refer to as the 'me too syndrome'. It is also influenced by subtle seasonal changes in the quality of daylight.

Wild dogs come into season once a year, usually in spring. Some domestic dogs come into season three times a year, though frequent or irregular seasons are often associated with infertility. Twice a year is regarded as usual. Some variation must be expected and need not be a cause for alarm.

Bitches are fertile only for a few days, sometimes only for a few hours, when they are in season. If they are to conceive they must be mated during this short period. This means a breeder must be able to recognize the subtle signs which indicate when the time is right.

A season may last as long as four weeks, though three is regarded as normal. It consists of two distinct phases. The first, pro-oestrus, being the period when the signs which a breeder must recognize first show themselves. Initially some slight change in the bitch's behaviour might be observed. A tendency to territorial marking, even in the house, by means of small drops of urine may be seen. She may become quieter than usual. She may be less inclined to take exercise. She may also become quarrelsome – bitchy. Other dogs and even bitches are likely to take unusual interest in her rear end. This may be resented. As the days pass her vulva will become swollen and blood-suffused discharge will usually appear. Some bitches, however, keep themselves scrupulously clean. Only the constant licking may indicate that there is a discharge.

After nine or ten days pro-oestrus gives way to oestrus. Typically this lasts for about the same length of time. Oestrus is characterized by further swelling and softening of the vulva. There may be a clear discharge and, she may become restless. She will become very attractive to dogs.

A bitch accustomed to the company of other dogs may become playfully skittish, running and turning before arching her back, curling her tail to one side and presenting her vulva to her intended suitor. Bitches which have, since puppyhood, lived a life isolated from other dogs may fail to show this behaviour. In extreme cases they may have become so imprinted on their owners that they will be very difficult to mate. The normal signs usually occur two or three days after the onset of oestrus, about twelve to fourteen days from the start of pro-oestrus. They usually coincide with her ovulation. It is then that the bitch must be mated. Mating her before the signs appear or after they have passed in order to suit her owner's convenience is not fair on the bitch, her chosen mate nor its owner.

There is little a stud dog owner appreciates less than trying to persuade an experienced stud dog to mate a bitch who is either not ready or which has passed the optimum time for mating.

Mating is followed by a pregnancy lasting about sixty-three days. In an unmated bitch or one who has failed to conceive it is followed by met-oestrus. This lasts about as long as a pregnancy. During this time an unmated bitch will either slowly return to her customary state or will show the preliminary indications of a false pregnancy. Pyometra seems to be more likely during met-oestrus. Met-oestrus gives way to an-oestrus which lasts until the next onset of pro-oestrus begins yet another cycle.

Ovulation

The inexorable advance of science now offers breeders positive and reliable indications of the precise time of ovulation. It thus enables them to arrange to have bitches mated at the optimum time.

Studies of bitch fertility have shown that, in almost 90 per cent of the cases in which bitches failed to conceive, mating them at the wrong time during their season was the cause of the unsatisfactory mating. The remaining 10 per cent were the product of male infertility, nutritional factors, genetic abnormalities or infectious disease in the reproductive tract.

The study showed that bitches might remain fertile from the third day of their season until about the twenty-sixth. In one case a bitch was fertile on the thirty-eighth day of an exceptionally long season. The norm, however, was from about the thirteenth to the fifteenth day. In the wild the chances of conception would be optimised by a bitch being mated several times during her season. This is not always possible, or even desirable, with domestic dogs. The traditional method of mating the bitch when her vaginal discharge ceases to show colour or when she shows, by her behaviour, that she is receptive will doubtless remain the staple means of deciding when the dog and bitch should be brought together but there are now more certain methods.

For some time it has been possible to identify the precise time of ovulation by analysing cells taken from the vaginal wall. This method has now been replaced by analysis, carried out within a few hours where facilities exist, of a small sample of the bitch's blood. This method assays progesterone levels in the blood. These reach a peak about twenty-four hours prior to ovulation. The ovum then matures in the reproductive tract for about seventy-two hours. The bitch should be mated as soon as possible after this period has passed if maximum fertility is to be achieved.

The precise timing becomes even more critical if one or other has a reduced level of fertility. It is also critical if artificial insemination, particularly using chilled or stored semen, is contemplated.

Wild bitches invariably come into season in spring. Their puppies are then born when there is likely to be a plentiful supply of food. Seasons of domestic bitches peak during spring and autumn but may occur at any time of year. A season may interfere with a show programme or with work. It is possible to avoid this by means of an injection which will delay the season until some more convenient time. These injections have been available for some time. They are most unlikely to interfere with subsequent fertility.

Induced seasons

A reliable method of inducing a fertile season by means of a hormone implant is also available. A season will commence about seven days after the implant. The bitch will be fertile about five to seven days later. The new technique will make it possible for breeders to plan litters at the most convenient time. It also holds out the prospect that techniques of embryo transfer, commonly used in many other forms of livestock, may become available to dog-breeders. In the past these have been frustrated by the problems of co-ordinating the infrequent seasons of donor and receptor bitches. Oestrus induction, by facilitating co-ordinated seasons, now offers the possibility of avoiding these difficulties.

Stud dogs

The Parson went to considerable lengths to ensure that his bitches were mated to the dogs he most admired. He brought Old Jock and Tartar from their home in Nottingham so that they could mate his bitches. Perhaps there were also times when his bitches travelled to particular dogs, though it may well have been far wiser, with travel still in a relatively primitive stage, to bring the dogs to his bitches rather than, as is now customary, to take an in-season bitch to a distant stud dog.

A young, healthy and virile stud dog is capable of mating forty or fifty bitches a year without any reduction in his fertility. Over-use will reduce his level of fertility. The use of artificial insemination, especially using stored or dilute semen, could easily multiply the number of bitches which can be mated by a factor of ten or more. During the course of his career at stud a dog might produce some hundreds of puppies. Even the most fecund bitch is unlikely to produce many more than twenty. The numbers give some indication of the relative importance, in breeding terms, of dogs and bitches.

It is of the utmost importance that every dog offered at stud or, more importantly, used at stud is of the highest possible quality, free from major physical or temperamental faults and hereditary disease. Second best is never good enough.

The best stud dogs have the ability to produce puppies of a consistent type to bitches of very different types and breeding. The ability is referred to as prepotency and most often arises in dogs which have been systematically bred and are not the fortunate result of some haphazard mating.

It follows, therefore, that stud dogs should be chosen on their ability to produce the type of puppies a breeder wants to breed. Too often the demand for winning dogs will be in spite of rather than because of their record as stud dogs. A dog which has produced four champions from a hundred pups is probably not nearly so good as one which has produced two from twenty, though the ability of stud dog owners to select bitches likely to suit their particular dog must be taken into account.

There is no point in making anything other than outstandingly good dogs available at public stud and there is usually little point even then unless the dog has demonstrated his worth in ring or field.

The management of a stud dog is not an easy matter. Some dogs need to be trained with some care if they are to be expected to mate assorted bitches virtually on demand. A mating to a compliant and experienced bitch when the dog is nearing twelve months old will introduce him to his tasks but he should not be expected to mate bitches regularly until he is fully mature. Until he is experienced and his libido can be assessed bitches should be selected with care to avoid any which are likely to be difficult. The stud dog owner should be capable of assessing the reason for any of the many problems a reluctant bitch may present and will be able to take appropriate action.

The dog chosen as a mate should be of the highest quality. Second-rate dogs make second-rate sires and produce second-rate puppies or worse. Ideally he should be a proven sire who has already produced top-quality puppies out of bitches closely related to your own. One advantage which recognition offers is a published record of all registered puppies and their breeding. It is possible to discover precisely what every dog has produced. The information will help in the selection of the best dog.

You will, of course, need to discover whether or not your chosen dog is available to mate your bitch. Dogs are not machines and top-quality dogs, even in the prime of life, may have to have the number of bitches they mate limited, especially during the spring months when most bitches tend to come into season and when breeders most often choose to mate them. It is possible also that the dog's owner may, for a variety of reasons, not wish to make him available to mate your bitch.

Stud fees

In Britain it is customary for a stud fee to be payable in its entirety when the mating takes place. The fee is for the services of the dog and the assistance of its owner and is not dependent on the birth of puppies. Some stud dog owners will offer another service if no puppies are born but are under no obligation to do so. They cannot be expected to carry responsibility for any problems associated with the bitch.

The only exception to this rule may occur with dogs which have not previously mated a bitch. For these 'unproven' dogs it is customary for payment of the stud fee to be dependent on the birth of puppies. Unproven dogs, however, are seldom offered at public stud. In most cases, the owner is likely to begin the career of a tyro by mating him to a quiet and experienced kennel companion.

Some will also provide two matings, usually on successive days, for the same fee. Again they are under no obligation to do so. If the initial mating has been successfully accomplished there is little advantage to be achieved by a second mating. Indeed the owner of a dog for whose services there is considerable demand may reasonably be very reluctant to provide a second unnecessary service for any one bitch.

Breeders should avoid any arrangements which involve paying the stud dog's fee, in part or whole, with the promise of puppies. There is reason for suspicion about any stud dog owner who suggests anything other than a straightforward arrangement.

The size of the fee may vary depending on the quality of the dog or rather on its owner's assessment of its quality. It is usually about half the cost of a puppy.

It is the stud dog owner's responsibility to make a healthy, fertile dog available and to make whatever arrangements are necessary to achieve a successful mating. It is the bitch owner's responsibility to take a healthy bitch to the dog at the optimum time in her season.

Infertility

The causes of infertility are many and varied. The most common is the insistence on taking the bitch to the dog when it is convenient for the owner and not at the optimum time during her season. Subjecting the bitch to unusual stress soon after the mating leading to foetal absorption is probably a major cause of infertility. Embryos may also be absorbed for other and often unknown reasons.

Illness, infection, poor condition and extreme age will also produce infertility. Some commonly used tranquillizers have been found to induce infertility in horses and may well have a similar effect on dogs.

There is little point in considering a mating if the fertility of either partner is suspect and unless the bitch, after mating, is kept in a manner which does not threaten the well-being of her puppies.

Mating

Most in-season bitches are likely to be fertile. The first season may occur when a puppy is still under six months old. Seasons may still occur in very old bitches. There seems to be no such thing as a canine menopause. There is no evidence which shows that being mated and enduring the subsequent pregnancy and nursing is harmful to any well-grown and healthy bitch whatever her age. Even so the majority of breeders prefer to wait until a bitch is fifteen to eighteen months old before they mate her and they will not mate a bitch after she has become a veteran.

In the final analysis, however, it is and should be for the breeder to decide when a bitch should be bred from. No fixed rules, no matter how well-intentioned, can possibly take account of all the many and complicated factors involved in the decision.

The Parson was able to bring the best dogs in the country to his kennel in order to mate his bitches. Nowadays it is customary to take the bitch to the dog.

Some stud dogs are creatures of habit which expect adherence to a particular routine before they will mate a bitch. Others will make a valiant effort to mate any bitch at any time and in any circumstances. The usual procedure is for the owner of the bitch, having arrived at the appointed time, to allow her to accustom herself to the surroundings in which the mating is to take place. It is best if this is in a secure, fenced or indoor area. An experienced dog will recognize what is afoot and will go through his customary, almost stereotyped, routine. He will probably examine the bitch before inspecting and marking the boundaries of his territory. He may affect indifference and expect the bitch to signal her readiness. It is usually best if the two are given an opportunity to become acquainted and to indulge in foreplay which gives rise to mutual arousal.

After a while the dog will attempt to mount the bitch. At this stage it is usual for the bitch to be held in order to ease the dog's task. Penetration may follow quickly or may require several attempts. As the dog's penis achieves full erection within the bitch she may feel some pain and struggle. If she is not firmly held she could damage both herself and the dog. Eventually she will become quiet and the dog will usually attempt to turn into the classic 'tie' position. This can only be achieved through co-operation between dog and bitch. The tie is not necessary to a successful mating. It might continue for no more than a minute or two or may last for an hour or even longer. The length of the tie seems to vary inversely with the degree of comfort available to all involved.

Sperm is contained in the first ejaculate and is followed by what is, in effect, a lubricant. The length of the mating does not provide a reliable guide to its likely success.

Eventually the two will part naturally. The dog should then be returned to his kennel and the bitch to her travelling box.

The owner of the stud dog will provide a written verification that the mating has taken place, a pedigree of the dog and confirmation of any arrangements which have been entered into. The bitch's owner will pay the stud fee and await developments with all the patience they can muster.

Artificial insemination

Kennel clubs in various parts of the world take different attitudes towards the use of artificial insemination (AI). Some attempt to control, even to prevent, its use. Others accept that the techniques involved are so simple that they can have no realistic expectation of achieving effective control. Some accept the use of chilled and frozen semen, others ban their use. Chilled semen can be stored and transported and will remain fertile for a period of 3–4 days. Frozen semen, in theory, has an unlimited life in storage. If the technique had been available during the last century puppies might still be being sired by dogs bred by Parson Russell. There is a real likelihood that dogs alive now will still be siring puppies in another 100 years.

As far as dog breeders are concerned the use of these facilities is still in its infancy. The advantages they offer and their inherent drawbacks have not yet been fully explored.

AI could be used to avoid the effect of inherited disabilities or temperamental faults which would prevent the dogs from breeding naturally. Such a use must be strongly deprecated. The possibility also exists that the use of stored semen could enable one dog to mate virtually every bitch in a particular breed. The result would be a diminution of the breed's gene pool. If the dog was subsequently found to carry some hereditary defect the result could be disastrous. In other forms of livestock in which the use of AI is commonplace problems are avoided by the use of systems for evaluating potential sires and their offspring both prior to and during their use as AI donors. No such systems are available to dog breeders. It is, therefore, prudent to limit the use of AI and particularly that of stored semen.

Embryo transplants

Oestrus induction could make a bitch ovulate at three-monthly intervals. She could be fertilized by natural means or artificially and her embryos transferred to another bitch. Because she does not undergo a pregnancy of normal duration or rear her litter the strain on her would be much reduced. She could, therefore, continue to produce puppies for as long as she remains fertile. Embryos taken from one bitch could be transported across the world before being implanted in another bitch. They don't even have to be implanted into a bitch of the same breed.

For many years it has been customary to implant cow embryos into female rabbits in order to transport them to distant countries where they are then implanted into the cow that will carry them through the remainder of their term of pre-natal development. Whether such techniques will ever become popular with dog breeders is doubtful but they are already available.

Pregnancy diagnosis

In the past breeders have had to exercise patience before the birth of a litter provided the only irrefutable proof that a bitch was indeed pregnant. Skilled palpation, when the embryos were about three weeks old and had grown to about the size of a pea, might show that embryos were present but failure to find any did not mean that the bitch was not pregnant. Equally the presence of developing embryos at this stage did not mean that they would reach full term.

Reliance on observed signs of pregnancy could be confused by pseudo-pregnancies which mimic the real thing very accurately and are capable of misleading even the most confident expert. The use of X-rays could detect pregnancy at forty-two days but could be expensive and might have untoward side-effects on developing puppies.

Ultrasonic instruments offer a safe and convenient means of detecting the presence of puppies twenty-four days after conception. Ultrasonic methods of pregnancy diagnosis are likely to be replaced by blood tests, which, as they become more sophisticated, should be capable of detecting pregnancy at ever earlier stages.

For practical purposes palpation and the exercise of patience until physical signs, swollen vulva, enlarged mammary glands and growing corpulence emerge, will, for some time, remain the methods most commonly used by breeders.

Pregnancy

A normal pregnancy lasts for sixty-three days.

Once a bitch has been mated she must be kept away from all dogs and they away from her. Parson and Jack Russell Terriers are unusually adept at escaping from even the most stringent forms of security. The ability of a bitch to avoid even the tightest security in her desire to find a mate is matched only by the ability of wandering dogs to find a way to reach her.

As soon as possible, however, the bitch should be returned to her customary régime. The comfort and lack of stress associated with familiarity are important during the early stages of a pregnancy when tiny embryos must firmly implant on the walls of the uterus if they are to develop into healthy puppies.

After four days the fertilized ovum divides into two cells, into four after five days, into eight after six days and so on, until after eight days, it has become a multi-cellular mass known as a morula. The morula then makes its way down the uterine tube and into the uterus where it develops into a complex blastocyst. A placenta develops which, about 20–21 days after fertilization, attaches to the wall of the uterus. Until this process is complete the developing puppies are at their most vulnerable.

During the next three weeks the development of the puppies will slowly enlarge the bitch's abdomen but it is not until towards the end of the sixth week that they begin to increase rapidly in size. Only when this stage is reached will the bitch require increased nutriment. This is best provided through several small meals consisting of more than usually nutritious food.

As pregnancy develops the bitch should slowly be withdrawn from hard exercise, though her exercise régime should be sufficient to keep her fit. She should be prevented from getting

into fights, withdrawn from work and should not be taken to
shows. Shows produce excitement and stress but, perhaps,
more importantly are a major source of infection. In any case
an in whelp bitch is not at her best and is not likely to do herself
justice in the ring. She has more important things to do and so
has the breeder.

About fifty-eight days after fertilization the puppies will have
developed to the stage at which they could sustain independent
life, though the closer birth is to the 63-day normal full term the
more likely they are to survive.

Abortion

Bitches sometimes abort as a result of stress, a fight, being
required to work or even the excitement of a show. Unless the
abortion takes place in the later stages of pregnancy even the
most observant owner may see no evidence of the event. He
may assume, when the bitch fails to give birth, that she did not
conceive.

Bitches which are subjected to unacceptable stress may also
reabsorb foetuses during the early stages of pregnancy. The
evidence for this is provided by uterine scars in bitches which
have never produced puppies but which have been mated.

Abortion may also be deliberately induced after a mis-
alliance by an injection of stilboestrol or oestradiol up to
twenty-four hours after the mating has taken place. Experimental evidence now suggests that an injection of prostaglandin
up to 30–34 days after mating will also make the bitch abort or
absorb the puppies without any unwanted side-effects. The
availability of these forms of non-surgical treatment raises
doubts about the validity of neutering as a means to eliminate
the production of unwanted puppies. Neutering involves major
surgery. It is accompanied by risks and the possibility of
unwanted side-effects.

Feeding during pregnancy

The better manufacturers of proprietary food offer a range of
products appropriate to different stages in a dog's life. They

will offer one suitable for pregnant and nursing bitches. She should be introduced to this about halfway through her pregnancy and kept on it until she has fully recovered from the strain of nursing her litter. These specialist diets contain all the additional nutrients the circumstances they cater for demand.

The way in which various supplements are advertised sometimes seems calculated to give the impression that breeders are in some way neglecting their duty unless they give their bitches a liberal supply of these nostrums. In fact a healthy bitch which enjoys a well-balanced diet is unlikely to need any supplements at all. Indeed an excess of some can lead to disorders in both bitch and puppies.

The development of modern wormers makes it possible for some to be given to pregnant bitches. This ensures that puppies are not born with an infestation of parasites which will retard their development.

Only during the later stages of pregnancy is it necessary to make any great adjustment to a bitch's diet. She should be put on to an appropriate proprietary food and, as her pregnancy progresses, should have her daily intake split into two or three smaller meals rather than one large one.

Whelping

No matter how experienced a breeder is the time when bitches are giving birth remains one which is imbued with excitement, apprehension and anticipation. As the sixty-third day approaches anticipation mounts. A watchful eye is kept on the bitch to discern any slight changes in her behaviour which might suggest that whelping has begun.

The first stage of whelping is triggered by an involuntary and complex action of the pituitary gland, the ovaries, the suprarenals, the placenta and the uterus. Initially outward signs may consist of nothing more than an unusual restlessness on the part of the bitch, possibly some indication that she is in discomfort. She may wander about seeking, but not finding, ease. She may be easily disturbed, especially by unfamiliar sights or sounds. A phlegmatic or stoic bitch, however, may show no outward sign of her developing condition even to the most practised eye. The only easily measured indication may well be that her temperature will fall from the usual 101.5°F to about 98°F, perhaps in order to help prepare her puppies for the less comfortable world they are about to encounter. The fall in temperature will take place over a matter of days. Until the temperature is below 100°F whelping should not be regarded as imminent.

The bitch may shred her bedding, both in an effort to prepare a nest for her pups and as a means to alleviate her discomfort. This stage may last for no more than a few hours but might last for forty-eight hours without need for alarm. As the first stage progresses the discomfort will subside. The bitch will become more at ease. Towards the end of the stage the vaginal discharge will become more profuse and more viscous, producing strings of mucus hanging from the vulva.

The second stage, during which the cervix becomes fully dilated and the pups begin their long journey down the birth canal, slowly replaces the first stage. The bitch will usually lie quietly, earlier discomfort and agitation gone. She will await the birth with every sign of patience. The breeder must endeavour to do the same.

Although signs of progress are not apparent what takes place during this second stage is vital to the successful conclusion of a natural birth. The foetuses will change their position so that they can move more easily down the birth channel. The cervix will become fully dilated to allow their passage.

Eventually abdominal muscular contractions will show that the birth is proceeding. The bitch is pushing the pups into the outside world. Some, if not all, will have detached from the uterine wall. It is now vital that they are born as quickly as possible.

The first sign that birth is imminent will be the appearance of a dark, fluid-filled bag at the vulva. The bag is the membrane which contains the first puppy. If all goes well the puppy and its placenta will quickly be expelled and will be followed by others at intervals of not more than an hour and usually very much less.

It is at this stage that the breeder is very much alone. If problems occur because the bitch cannot expel her pups there is no time to summon veterinary assistance if they are to be saved.

A large litter might create a traffic jam which cannot be cleared by natural means. A puppy may be laid awkwardly. Exploration may reveal the cause of the problem and by easing the unborn puppy into a better position the situation might be rectified so that normal progress is resumed.

A maiden bitch may be confused by the arrival of her first puppy. Not surprisingly she may not know what is expected of her, though instinct usually directs her. The puppy must be released from its enveloping membrane and dried, both to keep it warm and to stimulate breathing. It must be detached from the placenta, by cutting the cord about half an inch from the puppy's body. When this has been done the puppy should be returned to its mother and encouraged to suck.

The first flow of milk contains an abundance of colostrum, a substance which provides newborn puppies with a degree of immunity to infection during the first few weeks of their lives. Its presence in the milk is stimulated by eating the placentas. It is therefore essential that puppies suck while colostrum is still abundant in the milk.

Usually after the birth of the first puppy the bitch will realize what is expected of her. She will open the membrane, clean, dry and invigorate the puppy by licking it and will bite through the umbilical cord.

Sometimes a surfeit of maternal concern may lead her into too vigorous licking, or to nibble the umbilicus too short. Some bitches may even become confused and nibble at the pups themselves. The breeder needs to be at hand to oversee the entire process if such mishaps are to be prevented. Once the puppies have begun to suck the bitch will curl round her puppies and she and they will rest after their ordeal.

The bitch will appreciate some refreshment, as she will have done throughout the birth. Occasional drinks of water in which some glucose has been dissolved will maintain her stores of energy.

After a few hours' rest she can be given a small light meal and encouraged to relieve herself. Her first motions may be very dark and sticky. This is the result of eating the placentas and need cause no alarm. While she is away from her puppies soiled bedding can be changed.

Puppies

Within the first few hours of their life puppies should be scrupulously checked to ensure that they are in good health. The process of birth and subsequent behaviour of an inexperienced and possibly over-excited bitch may injure a puppy in some way. Check, too, that all the puppies are feeding. A fat, well-rounded and contented puppy is easily distinguished from the thin, unhappy little creature which is not feeding well.

If each has been weighed at the time of birth they can again be checked. Increasing weight is a reliable guide to well-being and, as more evidence is gathered, helps to provide the sort of information a breeder needs in order to predict how big puppies will be at maturity.

Genetic fingerprinting

Very occasionally the birth of puppies may give rise to doubts about their true parentage. Sometimes such doubts have been harboured throughout the bitch's pregnancy.

There have been times in the past when pregnancies have been terminated only because of uncertainty as to the sire's identity. 'Genetic fingerprinting', by analysis of a blood or tissue sample, can verify, with absolute certainty, the parentage of any puppy. Termination because of uncertain parentage is now unnecessary. The technique is being increasingly used to expose cases of fraud.

The thirty-eight pairs of chromosomes normally carried by dogs contain all the information about their genetic constitution. By examining the number, form and size of chromosomes it is possible to detect abnormalities and defects which could lead to the transmission of inherited defects and diseases, sexual abnormalities and other undesirable characteristics. Karotyping has been used to identify problems in a number of breeds and will certainly become ever more widely used by those who wish to reduce the incidence of hereditary defects.

13

Rearing

Rearing a litter of puppies is, at once, the most demanding and most enjoyable aspect of breeding dogs. Depending on how they are reared, carefully bred puppies can be helped to their full potential or they can be ruined. Far too many carefully bred puppies are prevented from realizing their potential by indifferent rearing which either denies them the care they need or which gives them well intentioned but inappropriate care.

Puppies have a wide range of needs which change as they develop and become more independent. Throughout their development the one constant need is the unremitting attention of their breeder. It is often said that puppies are great time-wasters. Certainly good breeders spend a great deal of time watching and playing with their puppies, checking on their progress, ensuring that each is in good health and getting to know each as an individual. None of this is time wasted. Pleasurable contact with people is essential to the proper development of puppies. Constant supervision by a caring breeder will reveal the presence of problems before they become serious.

Puppies are born with nervous systems and senses only partly developed. The ability to feel pain, to see and to hear develop during the first crucial ten days of their life. During this time they should more than double their birth weight. If their development is not to be impeded their needs must be understood and satisfied.

By far the best place to rear a litter of puppies, at least for the first few weeks, is in the house. There they can be under constant supervision, can grow up amid all the sights and sounds of a busy household, are warm and dry and can be constantly enjoyed by a proud breeder.

Warmth

A puppy's first need after it is born is for warmth. It emerges, always with at least some difficulty, from an environment in which the temperature was maintained at a constant 101.5°F and where nutriment was available without effort, into a world in which both warmth and food must be sought.

Most of the heat needed by newly born puppies is derived from their dam, as is all of their nutriment. It follows, therefore, that she must be in good health and content to minister to their needs. Once this has been achieved a great many of the breeder's problems will be reduced.

If the litter has been born in the breeder's home they will, at least, share the same temperature but even this, in some spartan homes, might be insufficient. Supplementary heat can be provided in a number of ways but care should be taken to ensure that the bitch cannot amuse herself by chewing trailing electricity wires and that the heat is neither excessive nor too dry. Young puppies and even their mothers can easily become dehydrated in hot, arid conditions.

Perhaps the best and safest way of providing heat is to conserve that produced by the bitch. The construction of cleverly designed well-insulated whelping boxes will be well within the capabilities of some breeders. Others will make use of temporary insulation material such as fabric blankets or, best of all, foil survival blankets to create the required conditions within the nest.

Accommodation

The box, or its successor, in which the bitch gave birth will provide adequate accommodation for the first two or three weeks but after that the bitch will spend more time away from her puppies, and as they grow and begin to explore their surroundings, more space will be needed. If the whelping box is placed in a larger run or cage, about four feet by two feet is ideal; there will be room for the family to develop as well as security from inquisitive members of the breeder's family.

Once more the choice is between buying a suitable cage or

run or constructing one. The two important criteria are that the cage should be capable of being easily and thoroughly cleaned, which means no absorbent material and no inaccessible corners, and that it should either be indestructible or be capable of being easily repaired. If the box is only going to be infrequently used it also helps if it is collapsible. The choice is between wire mesh cages, and boxes made out of sheets of plywood, sheet plastic or even metal.

Inherited defects

Inherited diseases which are, given the necessary information, to some extent predictable have already been discussed. The line between what we have chosen to refer to as diseases and defects is perhaps not a well-defined one. Perhaps defects are less serious than diseases, though they should not be regarded as trivial. Breeders must make every effort to avoid them.

Neither Parson nor Jack Russell Terriers are prone to inherited problems. The breeds will only be maintained in that happy situation if breeders maintain their vigilance and take whatever steps are appropriate to prevent the proliferation of any inherited defects which might occur.

Those who keep accurate and detailed records will slowly build up a mass of invaluable information. Breeds in which this information is shared and, where possible, recorded within the registration system have the best chance of avoiding the spread of inherited defects.

Of course the mating will have been planned with a view to avoiding any hereditary diseases but even the most careful planning can occasionally result in unpleasant surprises.

The most likely are the followwing:

Cleft palates

These may vary in degree. A slightly cleft palate will result in a milky discharge coming down the nose as milk taken in through the mouth finds its way through the gap in the palate and into the nasal channels. Slight clefts usually clear up spontaneously but more severe cases may require surgery.

Cryptorchidism

A condition in which one or both testicles are retained in the abdomen rather than being descended into the scrotum. Retained testicles are likely to become tumorous and should be surgically removed. Dogs with both testicles retained are infertile but those with one retained and one descended are fertile and can, given the opportunity, pass the condition on to their offspring. Any male puppy which does not have two fully descended testicles by the time it is a few weeks old should be treated with suspicion, as should any normal puppies in the same litter.

Dwarfism

More correctly referred to as achondroplasia, this is more likely to be encountered in puppies bred from short-legged parents. The condition was once common in what were described as Jack Russell Terriers and still occurs far too frequently for comfort.

Heart defects

They occur in all animals, just as they do in our own species. They may result in a puppy's early death or may, if it survives, result in a reduced ability to take vigorous exercise. The condition will be picked up by a veterinary health check prior to puppies going to their new homes.

Jaw faults

These may take the form of an overshot bite, in which the upper jaw protrudes excessively beyond the lower, or an undershot bite in which the lower jaw protrudes beyond the upper. In severe cases the condition may be a product of the actual jaw being deformed; in less severe cases, not always apparent until the second teeth are in place, the jaw deformity may be slight. In both cases the dog's career in the show ring or at work will be adversely affected.

Kinked tails

May result from an accident in the nest, be the product of the way the puppy was laid in the uterus or may be inherited. Since the tail is an extension of the spine any puppy born with a kinked tail should be treated with suspicion.

Swimmers

These are puppies born with a deformity in which the movement of the forelimbs resembles that of a swimmer. The chest tends to become progressively broad and flattened. Mild cases can, sometimes and with difficulty, be cured but for more severe cases the prognosis is poor.

Umbilical hernia

A condition in which internal organs protrude through the stomach wall to form a soft swelling. Small hernias may disappear spontaneously, larger ones will require surgery. There is some evidence that suggests that the tendency to form hernias runs in families.

Waterlogged puppies

They suffer from a condition known as anasarca and are unmistakable because of their bloated, liquid-suffused form. They invariably die and should be humanely destroyed.

Culling

Puppies that are unlikely to grow into healthy specimens of the breed able to live normal lives free from pain or discomfort should be culled as soon as their condition is confirmed. The presence of a congenital defect, damage caused during the birth or subsequently or of obviously substandard puppies should all suggest to the breeder that culling must be considered.

Sometimes, too, a bitch will produce an unusually large litter. Eight or even ten puppies are not unknown. The bitch will have difficulty in rearing such a large litter and the consequence may be that not all will survive and even if they do the struggle will produce some weakly individuals. The choice is between reducing the number to more manageable proportions or augmenting the bitch's efforts.

Hand-rearing

Hand-rearing, no matter how conscientiously carried out, can only be regarded as a very poor second best to the real thing and should be undertaken only when all other possibilities have been considered and when there is every reason to expect that the end result will be a normal and healthy puppy. It may be better to cull weakly puppies and it is certainly better to find a foster-mother for some of a large litter or for orphaned puppies,

A number of commercial substitutes for bitch milk are available. All are better than anything which a breeder can concoct and the prudent breeder will have an emergency supply available as well as a feeding bottle of appropriate size. Both milk substitute and feeding bottles can be obtained from a veterinarian.

Fading puppies

What is commonly referred to as Fading Puppy Syndrome, the canine equivalent of cot deaths, probably encapsulates a number of different conditions each with a different cause. The term is used, often indiscriminately, to describe the unexplained deaths of apparently healthy young puppies.

It is probable that damage caused by a difficult birth, hypothermia, infections resulting from dirty conditions, inadequate nutrition and inherited defects account for many of the deaths ascribed to Fading Puppy Syndrome. Prevention by strict attention to hygiene, adequate warmth allied to careful supervision and prompt remedial action is required.

Other problems

Puppies are at their most vulnerable during the early weeks of their lives. Although they derive some protection from infection from their dam they have little or no protection against imported and unfamiliar infections. Breeders should curb their pride and not expose puppies to being handled by other breeders and should themselves ensure that they do not import infection from other kennels, from shows or, indeed, from anywhere.

Fortunately modern technology has produced a number of disinfectants which assist the breeder to keep infection at bay. Some of these are specific to certain canine infections, parvovirus for example, and all, coupled with scrupulous attention to hygiene, offer valuable general protection.

It is not possible to catalogue all the problems a breeder may encounter and to attempt to do so would create a false impression. Breeders should certainly be prepared for problems, because the more they breed the more likely they are to encounter them, but their efforts should be directed towards avoiding problems by planning mating with care and rearing puppies conscientiously. They can then direct their attention to the demanding task of rearing a trouble-free litter. Once the puppies are well-accommodated and feeding well the breeder must begin to consider the routine matters which will become necessary.

Docking

The surgical removal of a small part of the tail is almost entirely a cosmetic operation, justified as a prophylax against future tail injuries. In May 1991, however, following a long campaign by the Royal College of Veterinary Surgeons, an amendment to the British Veterinary Surgeons Act will make it illegal, after January 1993, for lay persons to dock puppies. Docking had previously been outlawed in parts of Scandinavia and it was already apparent that other parts of the world were moving towards similar restrictions.

As far as Parson and Jack Russell Terriers are concerned the situation has a degree of historical piquancy. Trump was both docked and cropped, as was the fashion for both terriers and foxhounds. Foxhounds are now left with both tails and ears intact. Contemporary sources claimed that the Parson neither cropped nor docked his terriers. However, it seems very unlikely that he would have been content with long-tailed terriers and far more likely that he was able to breed terriers with naturally short tails.

Parson and Jack Russell Terrier breeders in Britain and Scandinavia and eventually, perhaps all over the world, must choose between accepting long tails or breeding for naturally short ones. A number of terrier breeds do have naturally short tails. Some Fox Terriers, some Parson and some Jack Russell Terriers are born with tails from which only a minute part is removed when puppies are docked. It should not be beyond the capabilities of breeders to retain the present appearance of their terriers by breeding for naturally short tails. A ban on docking may encourage a return to a practice which the Parson may have accepted voluntarily.

Dew claws

Surprisingly, perhaps, the removal of dew claws seems to have avoided the debate which has surrounded cropping and docking. All puppies are born with dew claws, the vestigial remains of a fifth toe or thumb, on the forelegs and some are born with dew claws on the hind legs. All are usually removed partly because they are unsightly and partly because they can be a source of trouble in the future. A torn or ingrowing dew claw causes far more pain to an adult dog than does its removal from a puppy.

The operation, if carried out by practised hands and in suitable conditions, is a trivial one that causes only momentary discomfort. However it is not an operation which should be carried out other than by an experienced person or under their direct supervision. For this reason we will not attempt to discuss the methods which can be employed.

If the operation is to be carried out without anaesthetic it must, by law, be performed before the puppies have opened their eyes and thus before their nervous systems are fully developed. Nature protects most young things from what would otherwise be the unbearable pain associated with birth by arranging that senses at that time are not fully acute. If dew claws are removed at this time the discomfort is minimal.

A pair of sharp, well-sterilized scissors, some mild antiseptic and a steady hand and eye are all that is required. Take the bitch out of earshot. Take each puppy in turn and snip the dew claws off close to the leg, apply antiseptic and return the puppy to the nest. Finally check that all the puppies have been treated. It is surprisingly easy to miss one or to miss a dew claw, and allow the bitch back to her brood. She will be solicitous but not unduly disturbed, they will suck immediately and all should be well.

Worming

Improvements in vermicides now make it possible for puppies to be wormed at about fourteen days old. This means that, unlike in the past, they do not have the additional encumbrance of an infestation of worms when they are developing at a prodigious rate. Puppies born to bitches which have been kept free of worms, which are themselves wormed early and are subsequently wormed regularly, will not only develop better but will pose none of the threats the anti-dog lobby associate with every dog.

Worming routines should scrupulously follow the manufacturer's instructions if they are to have maximum effect. It is also a wise precaution to guard against building up a resistance to the customary wormer by periodically changing to a wormer which has a different chemical base than that in customary use.

Periodic thorough 'spring cleaning' with an appropriate disinfectant of kennels, beds and runs will also help to prevent a build-up of parasites, infections and other unwanted guests.

Weaning

The process of weaning puppies used to be a matter of laboriously mixing milk substitutes, not all of which could be regarded as suitable, and teaching puppies to lap. If a bitch is well-fed and in good health her milk supply, though slowly decreasing in quality, will be sufficient to sustain her puppies until they choose to eat independently.

If a dish, suitable for very small puppies, containing a ground-up and fairly sloppy mixture of the food which the bitch is being fed is placed with the puppies while the bitch is being exercised they can be encouraged to take an interest in the food. Some will do so immediately, others will have little or no interest. If this is done three or four times a day and the bitch allowed to clean up the ensuing mess, within a few days the puppies will be eating independently.

Some bitches will regurgitate food for their puppies and a few, if given the opportunity, will continue to do so to the detriment of their own well-being, long after the puppies are independent. Such conscientious bitches can seriously debilitate themselves, and after the fifth or sixth week should be kept well away from their puppies each feeding time until they have digested their food.

Socialization

All puppies go through several critical stages during the course of their development. As they grow the nature of each stage varies and the wise breeder will take steps to ensure that the conditions in which the puppy lives recognize and provide for the puppies' needs at each stage.

During the period from birth to about twenty days the puppies' main needs are for sufficient warmth, food, sleep and massage to ensure survival.

The period from three weeks to about seven weeks is an especially critical one in the development of all puppies. It is during this period when their senses become far more acute and when, as a consequence, they become increasingly aware of their surroundings. The experiences a puppy receives during this period will have a profound effect on its temperament for the rest of its life. Puppies reared in isolation without the benefit of well-controlled outside stimuli, which have been alarmed or frightened or which have been deprived of maternal care for long stretches during this period, especially during the early part of the period, may well have their social attitudes permanently impaired. Work at the Animal Behaviour Division of the Roscoe B. Jackson Memorial Laboratory has shown that puppies weaned before the age of seven weeks are far more likely to become noisy and nervous than are those which are weaned afterwards. Puppies may seem to be independent long before they are seven weeks old. They will eat on their own, may show little interest in taking nourishment from their mother and a degree of intolerance towards litter mates. Nevertheless they are still going through a process of learning both from their dam and from their litter mates. If this process is curtailed their emotional development will be retarded and the result may well be a puppy unable to relate well either to other dogs or to people. This is why, apart from the often very unsatisfactory conditions in which the puppies they offer for sale are reared, it is most unwise to buy any puppy, and especially a very young puppy, from a dealer.

At least from the age of five weeks puppies should be taken from the nest for short periods of affectionate cuddling. This helps to develop an attachment and trust of people as well as to instil a degree of independence from dam and litter mates. Breeders often ignore the fact that puppies are expected to assume an independent life, perhaps devoid of all contact with their own species, when they are no more than eight or nine weeks old and, in some cases, even earlier. Yet in the wild puppies would continue to enjoy their parents' support and to learn from them until they themselves were adult.

From about seven to twelve weeks old the puppy is best able to establish relationships with man. If it is deprived of human contact during this period or has unpleasant experiences in man's hands its ability to establish relationships will be stunted. Every puppy should be carefully protected from unpleasant experiences but be exposed to as many pleasurable ones as possible and have a great deal of individual attention during this period if their social development is to be maximized. There is a growing body of evidence which suggests that at eight weeks of age and for a couple of weeks afterwards puppies are best able to adapt to a new life. From this point of view eight weeks is perhaps the best age for them to go to their new homes but, of course, other factors must also be taken into account.

Vaccination

Routine vaccination is nowadays able to provide protection against a group of diseases which, in the past, breeders had to accept would take a toll of their puppies.

Parvovirus is a disease which first appeared in the late 1970s when there was neither field immunity nor an effective vaccine available to protect puppies. Many died as a result. Now field immunity has built up and a specific vaccine is available. Even so parvovirus remains as the main threat to puppies. It tends to have almost epidemic characteristics, flaring up in a small area before subsiding only to reappear elsewhere. When the disease is rife vaccines should be given as early as possible. When it is quiescent they can be given along with other vaccines.

Before the appearance of parvovirus the main threats to puppy health were distemper, hardpad and the two forms of leptospirosis. A single vaccine, followed within a few weeks by a booster and subsequently at yearly intervals will provide almost 100 per cent protection. The type of vaccine and the precise details of the régime will be entirely dependent on what the veterinary surgeon uses.

14

Activities

For many years only one terrier breed had the opportunity to enjoy the complete range of activities that recognition opened up to Parson Jack Russell Terriers and, in some parts of the world, to Australian Jack Russell Terriers – the Border Terrier. They have been able to be present at all the events run under Kennel Club aegis, at shows, obedience competitions, agility and, more recently, fly-ball competitions since 1920. They have also enjoyed hunt and working terrier shows and the racing which often brings these events to a noisy and frantically enjoyable close. They have been used to assist disabled people and have given comfort and companionship to people who cannot have a dog of their own.

They have continued to be worked and have extended their usefulness into fields for which they were not originally intended. The fears expressed prior to recognition have not been realized, though it is necessary for breeders and exhibitors to be ever alert for the first signs that their breed is beginning to lose meaningful contact with its origins. The dangers exist, just as they exist for any recognized breed, but that is not to say that they need be realized if breeders, exhibitors and judges are aware of them and guard against them.

Working

Parson and Jack Russell Terriers have one and only one source of what can legitimately be regarded as work and that is to fox. Indeed the purist might argue that only when Parson Jack Russell Terriers are running with foxhounds are they being worked in the manner for which the Parson bred them. Few owners nowadays have the opportunity to work their terriers to fox and fewer still the opportunity to run them with hounds. This need not, however, deprive the breed of perfectly acceptable substitutes which will provide sport for them and their owners and, in some cases, make a useful contribution to the control of vermin.

In Britain it is no longer legal in any circumstances to work terriers to badger or to otter. Coypu are now extinct and so the alternatives are rabbits and rats, with rats, according to a former Duke of Beaufort, providing a very good substitute for foxes. Mink provide what is perhaps the nearest thing to real work since they provide an opportunity for terriers to run with hounds and to face a quarry capable of determined retaliation. Overseas the quarry may be more varied and sometimes more demanding.

Well-trained terriers also make efficient beaters for a spot of rough shooting and in Europe may be used to track wounded animals – though working tests, originally designed for Dachshunds, which elevate tracking ability to a primary requirement, should be treated with caution lest they make tracking ability more important than basic terrier work.

Tests which involve terriers venturing down large tunnels to face a caged rat are well-intentioned and may provide fun of a sort. Unfortunately they are based on a false premise and as such cannot be regarded as providing a reasonable test of working ability. If too much reliance is placed on such tests they may even encourage characteristics not wanted in a working terrier.

Showing

In some breeds exhibitors and judges seem to take the view that nothing succeeds like excess. That is not true of either Parson or Jack Russell Terriers. Exaggerated characteristics, a bigger head, a shorter back, heavier bone, more substance, greater or lesser size, or more luxuriant hair are all qualities which, taken to excess, would destroy any dog's ability to do the job for which the breed was intended. They are not qualities that are sought in either Parson or Jack Russell Terriers. In both breeds type, that indefinable but essential quality which separates one breed from another, coupled with the ability to work are of absolute importance.

For anyone who entertains a desire to enter the show ring with a Parson or Jack Russell Terrier the first requirement must be a good specimen of the breed. The key to success in the show ring does not, however, lie only in having a good dog. It is necessary also to get that dog to shows looking its absolute best and to make its quality apparent to the judge. A good dog is, of course, the key to success but before the door can be opened it is necessary to know how to make proper use of the key.

Show dogs must be in good muscular condition, the product of plentiful exercise. All too often a judge's hands and eyes will reveal a lack of condition. The judge will wonder whether the dog ever gets any exericse or whether it lives its life confined in a small box. His experience will tell him that a badly conditioned dog is likely to move far less well than it might if it was well muscled. When the dog moves he will watch for the tell-tale signs and will often find them. As the day progresses dogs which are unfit will quickly lose that spark of enthusiasm which is, in any hotly contested class, often the difference between major and minor places.

Show dogs must, therefore, be fit, though not the rock-hard, pared-to-the-bone fitness a hound or working terrier attains at the end of a long, hard season. In the ring both hounds and terriers will carry a little more condition than when they are working. In this respect Parson, Jack Russell and Border Terriers are different from all other terrier breeds. Some show terriers are shown in a condition which appears to verge on obesity. Most carry far more surplus weight than do these three breeds, which are still expected to be able to work for a living.

It is surprising how often dogs which are not well muscled are not as clean as they might be. From some rises a smell which all but their owners must find offensive and which can do nothing to impress the judge. No judge who finds himself examining a dirty terrier from which rises the stench of an ill-kept kennel and which leaves his hands coated with the greasy accumulations of neglect is likely to want to give the dog a high, or even any award. A clean, well-conditioned terrier will always beat a dirty, ill-conditioned one of similar quality.

Those who harbour a prejudice against the show ring will

often point to the incessant grooming which seems to be necessary in some breeds. They decry shows as 'hair-dressing competitions'. They are right only to the extent that skilful trimming should not be the basis for creating the desired appearance of a Parson or Jack Russell Terrier but they are wrong to suggest that a clean and well-groomed terrier somehow has its ability to work undermined. That is no more true of dogs than it is of racehorses or, indeed, of people.

Condition and cleanliness are important and rightly so. There is another requirement which is perhaps the most important of all. No dog, no matter what its quality, will achieve consistent success in the ring unless it enjoys shows.

A terrier should be confident and interested in the ring. Those which get to the very top exude a quality which is usually referred to as 'presence' and is impossible to define. They are the dogs whose star quality attracts the judge's eye. They have character and personality, perhaps even a degree of arrogance.

Quite often this quality is apparent while the dogs are still in the nest. If they are also top-quality specimens of their breed their owner has reason for optimism. Presence is perhaps as difficult to protect as it is to define. Many a willing and promising pup has been reduced to a bored also-ran long before its show career has had the chance to develop.

Each individual terrier reacts differently to shows. Some can be shown often without them becoming bored, others have a low tolerance of shows and need to have their career planned accordingly. It is all too easy to take a winning pup to show after show without noticing the subtle, tell-tale signs which suggest that shows are becoming less fun, a tedious routine to be endured rather than enjoyed. Failure to notice and to take appropriate action will inevitably result in a terrier which fails to achieve its early promise.

Shows often involve a long journey and considerable disruption of customary routines. They should be approached much as an athlete would approach any major competition. Some days before the event hard training will be replaced by something less demanding, diet will be carefully regulated, travel arrangements will be planned so that unnecessary stress is avoided and everything will be aimed at getting the athlete to the starting line not just at the absolute peak of physical fitness but in the right frame of mind. Exhibitors who approach dog shows with similar care and anticipation are likely to enjoy more success than those who give their terrier hard exercise and a large meal prior to bundling it into a car for a long and probably hot and tiring journey to the show.

Diet should be regulated with care to ensure that the terrier is neither too fat nor too thin when it enters the ring. Some dogs will lose weight during a journey, others will not do so. Their diet should take careful account of individual peculiarities. Demanding exercise, especially any which exposes the terrier to risk of injury, should be curtailed before the show. The terrier should be provided with a clean, comfortable and familiar box or cage in which to travel. Some of his customary food should be packed. A terrier which learns to associate shows with hunger is not likely to retain enthusiasm for the exercise.

Having arrived at the show in good time terriers need time to accustom themselves to the atmosphere much as footballers will stroll out on to the pitch before an important match. They need to relax and familiarize themselves with the surroundings. An unfamiliar cavernous hall, a flapping tent or a crowded ring may be all that is needed to deter a dog from showing to best advantage.

Eventually the time will come for the breed to be judged. If you are not in the first class you will have an opportunity to see what other exhibitors do. If you are in the first class try not to be the first to come under the judge's scrutiny. Watch and learn. No one, however, is going to criticize your novice state. The judge will help, so will most exhibitors. Showing dogs is usually a friendly game in which experienced people are always ready to assist newcomers.

Judging

This is easy until you learn how to do it.

Judging dogs, whether at shows run under Kennel Club rules or at shows for hunt and working terriers, demands the honest, unbiased exercise of judgement based on considerable knowledge accumulated after close contact and detailed study of the particular breed. The best judges are often people who have shared their homes with top-class specimens of the breed. All good judges have a long, practical experience of top-quality dogs of some breed.

Judging is not an exercise intended to settle old scores, to reward friends or to promote one's own kennel. It is a demanding task which should be undertaken only by those who have the necessary experience, knowledge and competence. In most countries judges are required to undergo a course of training and to satisfy examiners of their ability. In Britain, at both working terrier shows and the lower levels of shows run under Kennel Club rules all that is required to begin a judging career is an invitation to do so. It is all too easy for prudence to succumb to ambition and for someone who lacks the necessary qualities to be exposed to a humiliating and damaging experience.

What all judges should realize is that they, perhaps more than the dogs they judge, are not only on display and under the intense scrutiny of exhibitors and ringsiders alike but that the decisions they make and the manner in which they arrive at those decisions will be subjected to close post-mortem examination long after the event has taken place. It is true, of course, that good judges enjoy an enviable status and even importance but it must be realized that bad ones may easily have a hard-won reputation totally destroyed by an inept, eccentric or dishonest performance.

Before anyone accepts an invitation to judge they must have a thorough knowledge of the breed, preferably acquired as a result of long years of breeding, working and exhibiting. They must also be aware of what the process of judging entails whether at working terrier shows or at shows run under Kennel Club rules, the two being different in a number of ways. Only then should anyone even consider accepting an invitation to judge.

Obedience

Neither Parson nor Jack Russell Terriers can be regarded as among the world's most obedient breeds. Their strong streak of independence inclines them to question authority so that instant obedience, of the type required at the highest level of obedience competitions, is seldom attained. Even so both breeds can perform well in obedience and give pride and satisfaction to their owners.

Agility

Any terrier that is expected to work for a living must be agile. Agility competitions, especially now that courses take account of the size of the dogs which compete, are almost tailor-made for terriers trained to a basic standard of obedience. Agility competitions are run over standard courses which test a dog's ability to run, jump, twist and turn and to respond to simple commands. Similar abilities are also demanded of the dog's owners and the end result is a great deal of fun for both dog and owner.

Terrier racing

Terrier racing brings a great many hunt and working terrier shows to a noisy and exciting conclusion. At some shows racing remains what it has always been, a source of fun and excitement, but at others the desire to win large prizes and not insubstantial side bets have imparted a serious edge to competition.

What is required is a terrier which will break quickly from traps similar to those used for greyhound races and chase an artificial lure over a short sprint course. The terrier will have to submit to being loaded into the traps, to the not always friendly attentions of other competitors during the race and to the scrum which ensues when the race is over. Terrier racing is not for the faint-hearted owner or terrier.

Ring training

Strictly speaking ring training is not intended as an activity in its own right. Its purpose is to provide a means whereby puppies and people can prepare for a career in the show ring. Puppies learn to mix amicably with other dogs of all sorts and to go through the routine that will be expected of them in the show ring, and people learn how to show their dogs. Sometimes the process of learning is given an extra edge by means of a monthly competition which, for some exhibitors, may satisfy all their competitive instincts. Others are content to enjoy a weekly opportunity to mix with other dog owners, to share experiences and to exchange information. For many people, however, a weekly trip to the ring training class run by a local canine society represents an opportunity to mix with other dog owners and to enjoy a pleasant social occasion with people who share a common interest in dogs.

Therapy dogs

Doctors have now recognized that contact with some species other than our own can be beneficial to our health and general well-being. Dog owners tend to live longer and recover from illness more quickly than do non dog owners.

These simple and indisputable facts are now being widely used to help people who, for one reason or another, are obliged to live in institutions where they cannot keep a dog of their own. Many hospitals, homes, special schools and prisons now have a dog or two on the staff so that inmates can enjoy contact with another species. The benefits are diverse in the extreme. Heart patients recover more quickly, withdrawn people begin to communicate, non-ambulant patients learn to walk again, violent people become more tractable and all because they have contact with a dog.

Where it is not possible for the institution to have a dog or two on staff, arrangements are often made for suitable dogs and their equally suitable owners to pay regular visits so that patients and inmates can benefit from contact with a sociable dog. Many countries run schemes to provide this service and it is certainly one a socially minded owner would want to consider.

Junior handling

For teenagers and even for people who have not yet reached such an advanced age junior handling competitions offer an opportunity to compete with others of like age. Judges, unfortunately themselves not always good or even competent handlers, assess the competitors against their ability to present their dogs to the judge to the best possible advantage. The competitions at their best provide harmless fun which encourages the interest and enthusiasm of youngsters. At their worst they embody all the cut-throat elements which competitions with massive rewards seem inevitably to attract. They compound this by encouraging some parents to pressurize reluctant children to take part in competitions in which they have little real interest.

The range of activities that ownership of a dog opens up is almost endless. Success at the highest competitive level can open the door to invitations to travel the world as a judge. At another level ownership of a smart, well-trained dog will attract admiring attention which often leads to worthwhile social contact between people with similar interests. Nor should we dismiss the value of the companionship, pride and security which dog ownership provides.

15

On-going Care

Towards the end of the nineteenth century about half the homes in Britain contained at least one dog. There were about one million dogs in Britain. The Dogs' Home, Battersea, received about 20,000 strays each year. A hundred years later only about one in four homes contain a dog, though, of course, there are far more homes and far more dogs, something over seven million. In spite of the massive increase in numbers the Dogs' Home, Battersea, still receives about 20,000 strays a year. The vast majority of dogs are far better cared for than was the case a hundred years ago.

Ever since the reign of King Canute laws have been enacted in Britain which were intended to enforce what the ruling authority regarded as a responsible attitude towards dog ownership. Most often these laws were punitive in their attitude. They were intended either to protect the interests of an elite minority or to collect revenue for some cause totally unconnected with dogs. All failed to exert effective control over dog ownership, they produced little or no revenue and neither did they inculcate a more responsible attitude towards dog ownership.

The responsibilities which all dog owners have are to the welfare of their dog and to the welfare of the society in which they live. Neither are matters which can ever be entirely addressed by legislation, though legislation aimed at those who ignore their responsibilities is an obvious necessity.

All dogs have a right to expect adequate standards of care from their owners. Indeed they have a right to expect that, even before their birth, their breeders would have had a care for their future well-being and would not knowingly have produced puppies which could not be expected to have a reasonable expectation of a long, active and healthy life. Their breeders will have done their utmost to ensure that puppies are placed in permanent, caring homes. Their new owners will do all in their power to discharge their responsibilities both to their dog and to society.

Dogs bred and reared with care and which are, subsequently, well looked after are far less likely to become ill than are the unhappy creatures which live throughout on the very edge of survival. Having a healthy dog is largely a matter of acquiring a healthy dog and then doing all that is necessary to keep it in good health.

Experimental evidence exists to show that badly reared animals are more likely to produce sickly offspring than are those that have been well-reared. The same evidence also shows that well-reared animals, barring ill-fortune, are likely to live longer and healthier lives than are those that are less well-reared. Giving a dog proper care is not simply a matter of common humanity it is also a matter of sound economic good sense.

Names

The need to provide every registered terrier with an individual and unique name necessarily means that, except as kennel names, the days have gone when simple names such as those favoured by the Parson, Tip, Nettle, Nelson, Juddy, could be chosen. Nowadays most dogs will have two register names, the first indicating the kennel in which it was born and the second an individual name.

Names should, surely, be appropriate to the breed. Chippendale would hardly be appropriate to a dog which is supposed to have straight legs. Thistledown would not fit a dog with a hard coat. Curlew would be inappropriate for a dog with a strong muzzle. Various books on hunting, including Beckford himself, offer lists of names which are appropriate to hounds. These are equally suitable for terriers. Usually these are two, or more rarely three, syllable words.

The old adage 'give a dog a bad name and hang him' expresses an extreme point of view. But the value of a suitable name which is catchy and memorable without being silly should not be underestimated.

Veterinary care

Well before a puppy is acquired it is wise to establish contact with a good, local veterinary surgeon. Ask around local dog owners, especially those who have several dogs, to discover which of the vets in the area they have greatest confidence in and offers the best service. Vets, like their patients, vary in quality and cost. It pays to shop around. A good vet is a pearl beyond price.

Vaccination

There are a number of diseases, some life-threatening and others likely to leave permanent damage, to which dogs are prone and against which vaccines offer almost complete protection. Puppies may be vaccinated when they are no more than a few weeks old and the protection subsequently reinforced annually. Distemper, hardpad, leptospirosis, parvovirus and, where it cannot be kept at bay by the enforcement of stringent quarantine laws, rabies are the principal diseases against which vaccines provide effective protection.

Feeding

Dogs are carnivores, which does not mean that they eat meat, at least not what we usually regard as meat. Carnivores eat other animals.

The American National Research Council has published guidelines for optimal ranges of protein, fat and carbohydrates in canine diets. Three ranges are identified. The lowest is for maintenance, that is adult dogs in good health and not subject to hard work or exercise. The second is for growing puppies and pregnant or lactating bitches. The third is for dogs under stress, which is to say recovering from injury or illness, or undergoing hard work.

Nutriment guidelines

	Metabolic energy (%)		
	Protein	*Fat*	*Carbohydrates*
Maintenance	15–65	5–65	5–65
Growth and breeding	25–50	25–45	5–45
Stress	30–40	45–55	5–25

The table not only serves to illustrate just how difficult it is for any dog owner to formulate a well-balanced diet but also provides a good guide by which the quality of commercially produced dog foods can be assessed. No food which provides less than 15 per cent protein, 5 per cent fat and 5 per cent carbohydrate can be regarded as adequate for any dog. The other major component of any diet is water. What are termed dry foods tend to contain about 11 per cent moisture. If fed dry foods in this state the dog must have constant access to a liberal supply of clean drinking water. Canned foods, on the other hand, consist largely of water. Some canned foods may contain as much as 82 per cent water. There is nothing sinister in this because meat itself is about 70 per cent water. Untreated tripe, a favourite traditional food offers 12 per cent protein, 11 per cent fat and over 76 per cent water. Fed with biscuits, which tend to offer about 12 per cent protein, 15 per cent fat and about 70 per cent carbohydrate, tripe would offer a diet deficient in protein.

It has been shown that two of the principal causes of ill-health in dogs are, as with our own species, the wrong diet and too little exercise. If dogs were fed more wisely and exercised more assiduously they would have less need of the services of veterinary surgeons.

Nowadays there is absolutely no excuse for feeding a dog badly. Feeding it well is not only easier but is also far cheaper than feeding it badly. There are a large, and constantly increasing, number of products on the market, manufactured by reputable firms who spend the ransom of several kings to ensure that their products are of the best possible quality. The best market a variety of carefully balanced diets suitable for puppies, pregnant and nursing mothers, convalescent dogs, aged dogs, working dogs, sedentary dogs, even obese dogs. Every conceivable condition is catered for. All the dog owner needs to do is buy the appropriate food and follow the instructions on the label.

Many dog owners, however, seem reluctant to follow any instructions. They will buy a carefully formulated, balanced diet and then unbalance it by adding a little of this and a handful of that. By doing so they undo much of the value of the food itself. By adding supplements to a well-balanced diet they may even create a diet which endangers their dog's health.

Comfort

It is sometimes assumed that because Parson and Jack Russell Terriers are hardy breeds they require little more than the minimum of care. Hardiness must never be used as an excuse to deprive any animal from enjoying the best possible standards of care and even a few luxuries. Take a good look round any good kennel of Foxhounds and you will see cleanliness almost to hospital standards. Hounds will rest in deep, clean bedding and their coats will gleam with cleanliness, health and vitality. Compare that picture with what is too often seen at hunt terrier shows where dirty and underfed terriers will be decanted from a scruffy and malodorous box by an owner proud to own a real working terrier.

Housing

Davies tells us that 'Russell looked upon his terriers as his fireside friends – the *penates* of his home; nor was he ever happier than when to some congenial spirit he was recording the service they had done him in bygone days.'

There is no reason to doubt that the Parson's terriers lived in his home, shared his fireside and were his constant companions, though visitors, Old Jock and Tartar among them, were bedded in warm loose boxes. Indeed when the Parson moved to Black Torrington his first task was to build new stables for his horses and kennelling for his terriers. Sadly these were destroyed by fire soon afterwards and never replaced. For the Parson a terrier was not to be stuck away in a kennel and taken out only when it was needed, and he clearly didn't subscribe to the belief that terriers whch enjoy the luxury of their owner's fireside become too soft for work.

In our experience terriers involved in either work or show face all sorts of stresses and strains of which their owners are not always aware. When a terrier returns from work carrying an injury the fact is apparent to all but the most feckless owner, but a day with hounds, even if no injuries are incurred, is hard work. Terriers, like their owners, return home tired and in need of sustenance and rest. Some owners feel they have earned a hot bath, a good meal, a glass of whisky and the opportunity to relax but their terriers, which have faced all the risks and done the lion's share of the work, are often pushed back into their spartan kennels and given no more than their customary meagre fare.

It says a lot for the spirit and courage of terriers that even though they live in less than ideal conditions they will often acquit themselves well in the field; but why should they be expected to live a hard life both at home and at work?

Bedding

The best possible bedding for a Parson or Jack Russell Terrier is another Parson or Jack Russell Terrier. Failing that owners must resort to a variety of substitutes. Synthetic fur fabrics marketed specifically as dog bedding offer a touch of luxury, are long lasting and easily washed. Pillows and cushions are less robust and also harder to keep clean.

Kennel dogs may use the same bedding as those which live indoors. They may also use wood chips, though it is important to use only whitewood if the dog's coat is not to be discoloured and to ensure that it is neither damp nor contaminated. Hay and straw are traditional forms of bedding. Both may harbour pests and both may discolour coats. Newsprint should also be avoided unless one has no objection to owning a grey terrier.

Printers may sometimes be able to supply unprinted paper from roll ends and this makes excellent bedding especially for young puppies.

Toys

As with bedding the best toy a Parson or Jack Russell Terrier can have is another of the same sort. Failing that a game with another dog or with its owner will suffice.

Retrieving an object provides fun and exercise as well as a basic lesson in obedience and a source of some pride for the owner. Sticks or balls are ideal providing that they are clean and cannot be swallowed. Avoid golf balls, and also plastic or rawhide toys intended to relieve a dog's boredom by providing it with something to chew. Plastic is indigestible and could, if swallowed, obstruct air or digestive passages. So too might rawhide chews some of which have been found to contain residual poisons and so pose an added threat.

Injuries

Some owners, intent on impressing others with their terrier's working ability, will even go to the despicable extent of deliberately injuring terriers in order to create the impression that they have recently been worked. Terriers do get injured at work, though the better they are the fewer injuries they receive. Injuries may also result from accidents about the home or elsewhere. Terriers which are injured should receive proper and prompt treatment. Injuries, recent or otherwise, should never be paraded as supposed badges of a terrier's courage and ability.

One of the problems associated with any tough and hardy breed is that they will often make light even of quite serious injuries so that an owner who is not acutely observant may fail to notice the tell-tale signs that all is not well.

Stress

Terriers which have had a hard day in the field will often still be eager for their evening exercise and on the following day will show no apparent signs of their hard day's work. On the other hand a terrier that has spent a day at a show and may well have had less than its customary exercise, and not, in usual circumstances, sustained any injury or, for that matter, been called upon to inflict any, may well show every sign of being very tired when he returns home and on the following day may show a preference for rest rather than exercise. Some breeds and some individuals seem to suffer more from stress than do others.

Recognition of the stress involved and a show programme that gives a terrier, particularly a youngster, time to recover physically and mentally is far more likely to produce a dog which achieves success at the highest level than is a programme dictated only by the owner's enthusiasm and, perhaps, greed.

Exercise

A fit, adult Parson or Jack Russell Terrier is capable of walking further and faster than any but the most exceptional owner. A sedate stroll to the end of the road and back hardly qualifies as exercise. What is needed is a vigorous and free gallop to retrieve a ball or in playful pursuit of a kennel mate. Free exercise is far better than a boring and sedate walk on a lead but discretion should be used. Terriers seldom learn the value of moderation, they enter into everything wholeheartedly. Vigorous exercise during the heat of the day will do little good and may do positive harm. Exercise over frozen or sun-baked ground may also result in injury. Youngsters and older dogs should be exercised with care and regard for their particular needs. Just as juvenile athletes can be 'burnt out' by too much exercise so too can puppies while more elderly citizens, while continuing to need and benefit from exercise, may be unable to tolerate its most demanding forms.

During exercise a watchful owner should be in constant

control. Excited terriers tend to have more vigour than sense and a playful scrimmage can quickly become serious; a chase can be diverted to other quarry. Puppies, in whelp bitches and older dogs might become exhausted.

Exercise can be combined with unobtrusive lessons in basic obedience and with early lessons for a prospective working terrier and should, at all times, be under the control and supervision of the owner.

Control

No dog should ever be allowed to stray outside its owner's control. When they are not under constant supervision at home they must be kept within a secure area, inside or out. When away from home they must either be on a lead or subject to their owner's commands. No dog should ever be allowed to wander unaccompanied.

The usual method by which an owner controls a dog is by means of a collar and lead. Terrier owners, borrowing a method frequently used for young hounds also make use of a brace link by which the two terriers, usually an older, sensible one and a youngster, can be fastened together, either to allow free exercise or for exercise on a lead. These well-tried and simple implements have their variants and even alternatives.

In the show ring it is customary to replace a collar and lead with a lightweight show slip which gives the owner control without interfering with the terrier's appearance. Slips come in a range of materials from nylon cord or tape to fine chain and leather.

A light show slip is often the best way of introducing a puppy to this form of control. A few lessons, preferably away from the distractions of home and playfellows, are usually all that is necessary to teach a puppy to walk on a lead and if the penny doesn't drop or if you have an older dog which needs firmer control the traditional method is the choke chain. A sharp jerk on the lead gives an equally sharp reminder to the dog. A better and kinder method is to make use of a *Halti*, a modification of a horse's halter, which gently turns a dog's head to one side when it begins to pull.

Spring-loaded leads which extend up to three metres but which can be reeled in to a normal lead length provide a good means of keeping control while allowing a dog somewhat more freedom than the traditional lead allows.

However no dog should go through life on the end of a lead. The value of free exercise has been stressed. No dog should be allowed to run free until its owner has good reason to be confident that it will return when called and whatever the provocation to do otherwise. Lessons should begin at home with a dog answering to its name and a simple command. Start by calling when the dog is coming to you anyway, continue by calling it when it has nothing much better to do. Squat or kneel so that you offer a less imposing and more inviting outline. Slowly progress until obedience, even when other distractions are considerable, can be relied upon. When the dog obeys offer praise and reward. Don't punish a dog which will not come to call. Punishment will only reinforce the disobedience. Rely on rewarding obedience.

Sometimes rather than have a dog return it is better that it should stay where it is. Teach it to sit by your side by lifting its head and pressing its rear end into a sitting position, at the same time giving the command to sit. When the dog has absorbed the lesson progress to getting it to sit on command at a greater and greater distance from you.

Unless you wish to become involved in higher levels of obedience, perhaps for competition, these two commands, reinforced by understanding of the word 'no' are probably enough to serve basic needs.

Praise and reward are the basis of all effective training. Should punishment ever be necessary it should be inflicted when the dog can associate it with the particular mis-demeanour. Punishment given at an inappropriate time serves only to confuse and frighten a dog and often leads to further misdemeanour.

There is no need to inflict pain in order to punish. To do so may well be counter-productive. With any small breed a good shaking by the scruff of the neck will not only underline displeasure but, by mimicking the action of a pack leader, will reinforce dominance. It does no more than injure dignity and pride.

Identification

There are all sorts of good reasons for having every dog positively identified. An indelible identification mark may act as a deterrent to thieves, will help to trace a dog if it strays and will help to avoid cheating. Tattooing is the only permanent method of identification which can be read without the use of instruments. Micro-chip implants rely on the chip's continued viability and on the availability of equipment capable of reading the information carried by the chip. Collar tags are too easily removed to deter thieves or to provide a reliable reference to identity. Tattooing can be carried out at seven weeks of age, causes only momentary discomfort and may help to avoid problems in the future. Many breeders now routinely have their puppies tattooed before they go to their new homes.

Insurance

In an increasingly litigious age every dog owner should carry third party insurance which is sufficient to cover any accident or damage his dog may cause. The cost of such insurance is minimal and can often be added to normal household insurance, though there are also specialist firms which offer specific cover through breed clubs or to individuals. Some household insurance firms offer reduced premiums to homes which contain a dog because these homes are less likely to be burgled.

Since the early 1980s companies which specialize in canine insurance have made their appearance in most countries. They offer a varied and valuable service that is carefully tailored to the many needs of all sorts of dog owners. Many breeders insure their puppies before they leave the nest, thus providing themselves and the new owner with protection during the most vulnerable time in a puppy's life.

Teething

Adult dogs normally have a total of forty-two teeth consisting of six incisors, a pair of canines, and eight premolars in both the upper and lower jaws; the upper jaw also has four and the lower jaw six molars.

Milk teeth, without a complement of molars, begin to appear when puppies are about two weeks old. This first set are shed progressively from about four months of age and the second set is usually fully in place by the time the puppy is six months old. Sometimes stubborn milk teeth will obstruct and may misplace the second teeth, thus detracting from the dog's subsequent show career. A close watch should, therefore, be kept on a puppy's teeth so that any stubborn milk teeth can be removed before they cause problems.

Dogs have strong teeth. They need them to manage their natural diet, and because they don't normally eat sugar these teeth will normally last for their entire life. Tartar is the biggest threat to tooth health. Some dogs seem to accumulate tartar at an amazing rate, others hardly at all and the rate doesn't seem to be dependant on diet. It is a simple matter to remove tartar with a brush and paste from a compliant dog; those which object will need veterinary attention.

Parasites

Any dog, no matter how well cared-for, may pick up parasites, internal or external, from other animals, usually from another dog. Unpleasant though they undoubtedly are, most are relatively harmless both to the dog and to those who may come into contact with it. Most too are very easily disposed of. A very few, however, can be dangerous to the dog and are not easily treated. Many parasites which infest dogs are also to be found on foxes. It is important, therefore, that a working dog should be regularly examined for parasitic infestation and should be treated with appropriate deterrents.

External parasites consist, in descending order of size, of ticks, lice, fleas and mites. A tick, gorged with the dog's blood on which it feeds, may be the size of a fingernail. It will hang immobile, usually from the dog's head, having become attached as the dog investigated some interesting piece of undergrowth where sheep or hedgehogs have been. A dab with cotton wool soaked in surgical spirit will loosen the tick's grip and allow it to be removed. Dogs that are regularly exercised over land on which sheep graze might benefit from regular deterrent washes, though some of these may discolour the coat.

Fleas are usually acquired from another dog, a cat or from an animal the dog has been hunting. Their presence produces intense itching the site of which, on close inspection, will reveal small black flecks of faecal matter. The fleas themselves are often too active to be easily seen. An armoury of baths, sprays and powders is now available to resist or repel infestation.

Reinfestation can be prevented by the use of deterrent washes or sprays as well as by making absolutely sure that any hospitable surface – furniture, carpeting or bedding – with which the dog may have been in contact is also thoroughly disinfected.

Lice seem to cause more irritation than do fleas. They also move much more slowly and so are more likely to be seen. Their presence is confirmed by the eggs which adhere to the dog's coat, usually round the head and neck. The treatment for fleas is usually also effective against lice.

Mites come in a variety of different types, some of which cause little more than irritation while others can be a source of real problems. Harvest mites, *Trombicula autumnalis*, may be picked up from infested grass or undergrowth. They cause intense itching but are easily treated with a suitable parasiticide. The same is true of the far smaller rabbit fur mite, *Cheyletiella*.

Ear mites, *Otodectes cynotis*, are most often picked up from cats. They cause intense itching, the resultant scratching perhaps causing more harm than the mites themselves. Treatment with a suitable parasiticide will usually solve the problem though the configuration of some dog's ears seems to make total eradication difficult and reinfestation more likely.

Mange mites, *Demodex canis* and *sarcoptes scabei*, are microscopic, live within the hair follicles and produce localized or general dermatitis and hair loss. Generalized *Demodex* is difficult to treat and can be life-threatening. The danger is that because it seems to produce little or no irritation its presence is sometimes ignored until an intractable stage has been reached. Any dog which develops the tell-tale pustules on head, thighs or joints should be examined without delay by a veterinary surgeon. Treatment is difficult and problematical.

Sarcoptic mange produces frantic scratching so intense that the dog may damage itself. It is easily transmitted from one host to another but is readily treated by means of appropriate regular washes.

The regular use of effective vermicides is necessary if puppies are to be well-reared without the debilitating effect of parasitic infestation and if adults are to be maintained in good health. Regular treatment will also ensure that there is no foundation for objection to the presence of dogs on the grounds that they harbour parasites which may harm people.

Most internal parasites are easily eradicated. The two roundworms, *Toxocara canis* and *Toxascaris leonina*, and tapeworms, *Dipylidium caninum*, should be regularly treated with a suitable preparation obtained from a veterinary surgeon. Pills, liquids and pastes are all available. In our experience pastes are the easiest to measure out so that the appropriate dose is given and are also easiest to administer both to puppies and adults.

Other internal parasites include hookworm, *Uncinaria stenocephala*, whipworm, *Trichuris vulpis*, and lungworm, *Filaroides osleri*. Fortunately none are common because all are difficult to treat. Hookworm produces diarrhoea and anaemia, whipworm produces a dark but intermittent diarrhoea and lungworm a harsh cough and loss of condition.

Grooming

Neither Parson nor Jack Russell Terriers require the sort of grooming which demands great skill and expensive implements. A good brush and comb, a pair of scissors and a pair of nail clippers are all that is required. Regular grooming, never less than once a week and preferably for a few minutes each day, is the best way of ensuring that a dog is and remains in good health, free from parasites and looking at its best.

Bathing

Dogs' sweat glands are largely confined to their tongues, that is why they pant when they are hot. It is also why they don't need bathing as often as do their owners. Dogs and their owners do, however, have different ideas about what constitutes an attractive smell. If a dog rolls in some putrefying carrion his owner may not share his enjoyment of the effect which is caused. Equally a white dog looks far better if he is white and not grey or yellow. There are certainly times when a dog needs to be bathed.

By all means use shampoos formulated for human use but remember that these are intended to produce soft hair and that some contain colour enhancers. If you are showing your dog you will want it to have a hard coat and will not want its coat to retain traces of any substances which may lead to disqualification. Better to use a shampoo prepared for dogs and perhaps one which contains ingredients which will kill and deter parasites.

Chalk, talcum or magnesium powder is sometimes used to cleanse a white dog. Whether it actually removes dirt is open to debate but what is certain is that all traces of any such foreign substance must be removed before the dog enters the show ring.

Nails

Dogs which are seldom exercised on hard surfaces may not subject claws to enough wear to keep them short. Cutting them is a simple matter with the right implement – files or clippers. Care should be taken to avoid the quick, which in white-clawed dogs is visible as a pink core to the claw.

Old age

Dogs suffer most of the same problems in old age as we do and, also like us, need and deserve special attention to alleviate the worst effects of advancing age. Joints become less pliable, muscles less robust. In extreme cases they may even become painful. Ears, eyes and digestive systems work less well than they did in youth. The caring owner makes sensible adjustments to the normal routine when appropriate and will seek regular veterinary advice.

Unfortunately dogs do not live as long as we do. Owners must learn to adapt to their old age and their eventual loss.

Euthanasia

One of the services we can offer our dogs when, for whatever reason, life has become a burden to them is to relieve them of all further suffering by having them humanely killed. Dogs which have been very badly injured, old dogs which have some terminal and painful illness and, at times, dogs which have very seriously misbehaved are best relieved of life. The decision is not an easy one for any fond owner to reach but will be assisted by a good vet. A simple injection will cause the heart to stop and the dog will slide peacefully into oblivion. It's a better and kinder way to go than many of us will face.

Ethics

Several kennel and breed clubs have produced codes of ethics with which anyone who makes use of their services must comply. The codes are intended to offer protection to anyone who buys a registered dog and, perhaps more importantly, to the dogs themselves. The Kennel Club's General Code of Ethics is typical of many.

Kennel Club General Code of Ethics

This Code of Ethics applies to everyone who has agreed to be subject to the jurisdiction of the Kennel Club. They, whether owner, keeper or in temporary charge of a dog for any purpose, accept their responsibility in that they will:

1. Properly house, feed, water and exercise all dogs under their care and arrange for appropriate veterinary attention if and when required.

2. Not allow any of their dogs to roam at large or to cause a nuisance to neighbours or those carrying out official duties.

3. When their dogs are away from home, ensure that the

dogs shall wear properly tagged collars and shall be kept fully leashed or under effective control.

4. Acknowledge responsibility to clean up after their dogs in public places or anywhere their dogs are being exhibited.

5. Agree without reservation that any veterinary surgeons operating on any of their dogs in such a way that the operation alters the natural conformation of the dog or any part thereof may report such an operation to the Kennel Club.

6. Not breed from a bitch in any way which is deleterious to the bitch or her breed.

7. Conform with a special code of ethics for the relevant breed in order to produce sound and typical stock.

8. Only sell puppies and older dogs to homes where there is a reasonable expectation of a happy and healthy life and will help with the rehousing of a dog if the initial circumstances change.

9. When placing their dogs in a new home, provide written details of all dietary requirements and supply guidance concerning responsible ownership.

10. That they will not knowingly sell any dog to commercial dog wholesalers, retail pet dealers or directly or indirectly allow dogs to be given as a prize or donation in a contest of any kind.

11. Not knowingly misrepresent the characteristics of the breed nor falsely advertise dogs nor mislead any person regarding the quality of the dog.

12. When selling or transferring a dog to another person, ensure that all relevant Kennel Club documents are provided to the new owner.

In addition the Kennel Club, again as other clubs in other parts of the world, has said that it will not, except in very special circumstances, register puppies from bitches more than eight years old or which have already produced six registered litters.

Anyone who registers or transfers a dog with the Kennel Club must accept the terms on which the service is provided. The Kennel Club has the power to impose penalties on anyone who subsequently fails to abide by its requirements. Punishment might be no more than a warning or a fine but in more serious cases could result in suspension from exhibiting at or taking any part in any activity held under Kennel Club rules and/or withdrawal of registration and other services either for a period of time or for life.

The Code and other conditions, therefore, offer considerable protection both to those who buy Kennel Club registered dogs and to the dogs themselves. For these reasons alone recognition of the Parson Jack Russell Terrier was widely welcomed. Sadly the Jack Russell Terrier and its owners do not receive similar protection.

KENNEL CLUB FOUNDATION REGISTER

The Kennel Club began to accept registrations for Parson Jack Russell Terriers in 1990. Initial registrations were taken from the Parson Jack Russell Terrier Club's existing register. This system remained operative until September 1990. After this date the Kennel Club would only accept registration of Parson Jack Russell Terriers if both parents were already registered with the Kennel Club. Terriers taken from the Parson Jack Russell Terrier Club register and placed on the Kennel Club register form, in effect, the foundation stock from which all Kennel Club registered Parson Jack Russell Terriers throughout the world are drawn.

Key to colours
T = tan
W = white
Br = brown
B = black
Tri = tricolour

Name Year of Birth	S	Col	Sire	Dam	Breeder	Owner
Ardencote Tinker 86	B	Tri	Hill Farm Cracker	Hill Farm Katie	Mrs M. Clarke	Mrs J. Wood
Ashmead Cyd 87	B	B&W	Ridley Red Alert	Bonny of Ashmead	Mrs L. Wilkinson	Miss S. Rayment
Bannerdown 81 Tinker of	B	Tri	Heliwar Duster	Heliwar Patch	B. Jones	J. Creed
Beltane Barra Boy 89	D	Tri	Fife Bristle	Birksburn Angel	I. McBay	Miss S. Harugy
Beltane Firefox 89	D	Tri	Fife Bristle	Birksburn Angel	I. McBay	W. Parsons
Beltane Tote Runner 89	D	T&W	Fife Bristle	Birksburn Angel	I. McBay	W. Davis
Beltane Wanderer 89	D	T&W	Fife Bristle	Birksburn Angel	I. McBay	Mr & Mrs A. Durie
Beltane Zak 89	D	Tri	Fife Bristle	Birksburn Angel	I. McBay	W. Davis
Ben Bow Dollie 86	B	T&W	Turner's Rusty	Cobstone Bramble	R. Gray	Breeder
Ben Bow Dottie 88	B	T&W	Foxwarren Warrior	Ben Bow Dollie	R. Gray	Breeder
Ben Bow Nellie 88	B	T&W	Foxwarren Warrior	Ben Bow Dollie	R. Gray	Breeder
Ben Bow Willie 88	D	T&W	Foxwarren Warrier	Ben Bow Dollie	R. Gray	Breeder
Blencathra Badger 84	D	T&W	Foxwarren Tigger	Blencathra Dorset	P. Ross	Breeder
Blencathra Nettle 84	B	T&W	Foxwarren Tigger	Blencathra Dorset	P. Ross	Breeder
Blencathra Woody of Duxbury 86	D	Tri	Foxwarren Tigger	Blencathra Dorset	P. Ross	Miss M. Benedetto
Bride Valley Bossy 89	D	Tri	Beaver Brooke	Bride Valley Scamp	B. Blake	Breeder
Bride Valley Jack 85	D	Tri	Stromer	Joker	B. Blake	Breeder
Bride Valley Nellie 84	B	Tri	Rebbel	Snoopy	B. Blake	Breeder
Bride Valley Pepper 89	B	Tri	Beaver Brooke	Bride Valley Scamp	B. Blake	Breeder
Bride Valley Scamp 88	B	Tri	Bride Valley Jack	Nellie	B. Blake	Breeder
Buckley Bella 88	B	W	David Jones Scrap	Smart Lady of Clystlands	D. Jones	H. Stanway

Name Year of Birth	S	Col	Sire	Dam	Breeder	Owner
Cassacre Spice 86	B	T&W	Red Hawk at Ridley	Cassacre Skip	Ms C. Samways	Breeder
Cassacre Smudge 86	D	T&W	Red Hawk at Ridley	Cassacre Skip	Ms C. Samways	Breeder
Cassacre Sweenie 86	D	T&W	Red Hawk at Ridley	Cassacre Skip	Ms C. Samways	Breeder
Clardia Abbey 81	B	T&W	Nairn's Danny	Clardia Patches	Mrs P. Haytread	E. Parmenter
Clarendon Flint 85	B	Tri	Red Hawk of Ridley	Cassacre Skip	Ms C. Samways	Breeder
Clarendon Jed 87	D	T&W	Clarendon Pedlar II	Clarendon Scamp	J. Green	Breeder
Clarendon Misty II 87	B	T&W	Eden's Timmy	Clarendon Scamp	J. Green	Breeder
Clarendon Tipper 90	B	T&W	Eden's Timmy	Clarendon Kelly	J. Green	Breeder
Clystlands Abigail 88	B	T&W	Eskdale Beck at Clystlands	Cobstone Lucy at Clystlands	Mrs R. Wilford	Breeder
Clystlands Belinda Ridley 86	B	Tri	Foxwarren Scrumpy	Clystlands Victoria	Mrs R. Wilford	Mrs S. Atter
Clystlands 90 Blazing Star at	B	Tri	David Davies Scrap	David Davies Lucky	D. Jones	Mrs R. Wilford
Clystlands Brush 81	D	T&W	Heliwar Duster	Cracker at Clystlands	Mrs R. Wilford	Breeder
Clystlands Captain of Jalus 81	D	Tri	Brigadier of Clystlands	Betina of Clystlands	J. Luscott	Breeder
Clystlands 87 Chatterbox at	B	Tri	David Davies Chip	Patsy of David Davies	D. Jones	Mrs R. Wilford
Clystlands Charlotte 88	B	T&W	Eskdale Beck at Clystlands	Cobstone Lucy at Clystlands	Mrs R. Wilford	J. Creed
Clystlands Cider of Ragford 83	B	T&W	Foxwarren Scrumpy	Hannah of Clystlands	Mrs R. Wilford	Mrs J. Hancock
Clystlands 87 Dolly of	B	Tri	Tuck's Badger	Tuck's Tandy	Mr & Mrs B. Tuck	Mrs R. Wilford

Name Year of Birth	S	Col	Sire	Dam	Breeder	Owner
Clystlands 80 Hannah of	B	Tri	Bannerdown Benjamin	Galpin's Quaver	B. Galpin	Mrs R. Wilford
Clystlands Major 81	D	T&W	Brigadier Clystlands	Betina of Clystlands	Mrs R. Wilford	Breeder
Clystlands Peppercorn 88	D	B&W	Bower Charlie	Hannah of Clystlands	Mrs R. Wilford	Breeder
Clystlands Rascal 84	D	T&W	Clystlands Oscar	Tarsia Donna at Clystlands	Mrs R. Wilford	Breeder
Clystlands Rebel 84	D	T&W	Clystlands Oscar	Tarsia Donna at Clystlands	Mrs R. Wilford	Breeder
Clystlands Snowball 88	D	W	Eskdale Beck at Clystlands	Cobstone Lucy of Clystlands	J. Creed	Mrs R. Wilford
Clystlands 84 Smart Lady of	B	T&W	Thomas's Polo	David Davies Sally	D. Jones	Mrs R. Wilford
Clystlands 90 Trail Blazer at	D	Tri	David Davies Scrap	David Davies Lucky	D. Jones	Mrs R. Wilford
Clystlands 88 Tobias at	D	Tri	David Davies Scrap	David Davies Spot	D. Jones	Mrs R. Wilford
Clystlands Victoria 83	B	T&W	Clystlands Major	Clystlands Betony	Mrs R. Wilford	Breeder
Cobstone Lucy of Clystlands 85	B	T&W	Clystlands Samuel	Taw Vale Penny	Mr & Mrs R. Harris	Mrs R. Wilford
Coed-Ban 90 Bilberry of	D	Tri	Pete of Coed-Ban	Kim	B. Blyth	Mrs M. Jones
Coed-Ban Catriona 84	B	Tri	Davies Rip	Coed-Ban Coora	Mrs M. Jones	Breeder
Coed-Ban Citrine 86	B	Tri	Coed-Ban Chester	Coed-Ban Catriona	Mrs M. Jones	Breeder
Coed-Ban Connery 89	D	Tri	Coed-Ban Nettle	Coed-Ban Citrine	Mrs M. Jones	Breeder

Name Year of Birth	S	Col	Sire	Dam	Breeder	Owner
Coed-Ban Corrie 89	B	Tri	Coed-Ban Nettle	Coed-Ban Citrine	Mrs M. Jones	Breeder
Coed-Ban Ermine 82	B	T&W	Foxwarren Marcus	Coed-Ban Sabrina	Mrs M. Jones	Breeder
Coed-Ban 86 Jemma of	B	T&W	Kapaldo Spyder	Lewis's Betty	Mrs M. Jones	A. Lewis
Coed-Ban 89 Jess of	B	T&W	Middletin's Rex	Blythe's Bramble	B. Blythe	Mrs M. Jones
Coed-Ban Nettle 88	D	Tri	Coed-Ban Scatter	Coed-Ban Nettie	Mrs M. Jones	Breeder
Coed-Ban 88 Pete of	D	T&W	Twizzle	Simpson's Patch	B. Blythe	Mrs M. Jones
Coed-Ban Samba 86	B	T&W	Coed-Ban Solway	Coed-Ban Ermine	Mrs M. Jones	Breeder
Coed-Ban Savannah 89	B	T&W	Coed-Ban Seamus	Coed-Ban Samba	Mrs M. Jones	Breeder
Coed-Ban Scatter 86	D	T&W	Coed-Ban Chester	Coed-Ban Sadie	Mrs M. Jones	Breeder
Coed-Ban Seamus 88	D	T&W	Coed-Ban Scatter	Coed-Ban Samba	Mrs M. Jones	Breeder
Coed-Ban Spice 88	B	T&W	Coed-Ban Scatter	Coed-Ban Ermine	Mrs M. Jones	Breeder
Coed-Ban Sugar 88	B	T&W	Coed-Ban Scatter	Coed-Ban Ermine	Mrs M. Jones	Breeder
Cotswold Vale Nettle 88	B	B&W	South Dorset Ben	South Dorset Meg	N. Valentine	Breeder
Cotswold Vale Ticket 88	B	B&W	Cotswold Vale Trim	Cotswold Vale Nettle	N. Valentine	Breeder
Cotswold Vale Tilly 88	B	B&W	Cotswold Vale Trim	Cotswold Vale Nettle	N. Valentine	Breeder
Cotswold Vale Trim 86	B	T&W	Foxwarren Bitter	Cotswold Vale Annie	N. Valentine	Breeder
Cotswold Vale Trinket 86	B	T&W	Foxwarren Bitter	Cotswold Vale Annie	N. Valentine	Breeder

Name Year of Birth	S	Col	Sire	Dam	Breeder	Owner
Croxlea Dollar 87	B	Tri	Dixie of Foxwarren	Croxlea Tusk	Miss L. Porter	Breeder
Croxlea Gal 83	B	Tri	Foxwarren Scrumpy	Jaki at Croxlea	Miss L. Porter	Breeder
Croxlea Jon 83	D	Tri	Foxwarren Scrumpy	Jaki at Croxlea	Miss L. Porter	Breeder
Croxlea Spooky 89	B	Tri	Croxlea Jon	Foxwarren Dolly	Miss L. Porter	Breeder
Croxlea Tusk 87	B	Tri	Tuck's Badger	Tuck's Tandy	Mr & Mrs B. Tuck	Mr R. Wilford
David Davies 89 Bryn from	D	Tri	David Davies Scrap	Richard's Trooper	B. Richards	Mrs R. Wilford
Digmoor Daisy 90	B	T&W	Foxwarren Tegwyn at Digmoor	Digmoor Mitzi	M. Regan	Mrs H. Denton
Digmoor Merlin 89	D	T&W	Digmoor Barney	Digmoor Tina	Mr & Mrs M. Regan	Breeders
Digmoor Rose 88	B	Tri	Foxwarren Sam at Digmoor	Digmoor Megan	Mr & Mrs M. Regan	Breeders
Digmoor Scamp 89	B	T&W	Foxwarren Tegwyn at Digmoor	Digmoor Rose	Mr & Mrs M. Regan	Breeders
Digmoor Taffy 90	D	T&W	Foxwarren Tegwyn at Digmoor	Digmoor Mitzi	Mr & Mrs M. Regan	Breeders
Digmoor Tiger 89	D	T&W	Foxwarren Tegwyn at Digmoor	Digmoor Rose	Mr & Mrs M. Regan	Breeders
Digmoor Trixy 88	B	T&W	Hurman	Sindy	Mr & Mrs R. Johns	Mr & Mrs M. Regan
Digmoor Tyke 89	D	Tri	Foxwarren Tegwyn at Digmoor	Digmoor Tag	Mr & Mrs M. Regan	Breeder
Duxbury Jack 88	D	Tri	Blencathra Woody of Duxbury	Weardale Gravity of Duxbury	Miss M. Benedetto	Breeder

Name Year of Birth	S	Col	Sire	Dam	Breeder	Owner
Edgemills Breeze 90	B	T&W	Foxwarren Tegwyn at Digmoor	Misty	S. Dunn	Breeder
Edgemills Misty 86	B	T&W	Foxwarren Scrumpy	Cassie	S. Dunn	Mr & Mrs M. Regan
Emmrill 86 Vicki of	B	Tri	Severn Valley Nip	Thatcher	Mrs H. Sherwood	Mrs M. Huxham
Eskdale Beck at Clystlands 87	B	Tri	Heythrop Tiger	Eskdale Trixie	E. Porter	Mrs R. Wilford
Eskdale Lizzie at Clystlands 87	B	Tri	Heythrop Tiger	Eskdale Trixie	E. Porter	Mrs R. Wilford
Exmoor Adge 89	D	W	Ragford Worzel	West Somerset Vale Poppy	Mrs M. Cutler	Breeder
Exmoor Tag 90	B	T&W	Exmoor Tramp	Exmoor True	Mrs M. Cutler	Breeder
Exmoor Tarn 87	B	T&W	East Devon Tod	Taw Vale Tonto	Mrs M. Cutler	Breeder
Exmoor Trapper 88	D	T&W	Huxtable's Sailor	Exmoor Trim	Mrs M. Cutler	Breeder
Exmoor Trim 87	B	Tri	East Devon Tod	Taw Vale Tonto	Mrs M. Cutler	Breeder
Exmoor True 88	B	Tri	Huxtable's Sailor	Exmoor Trim	Mrs M. Cutler	Breeder
Foxwarren Dolly 89	B	T&W	Bracken of Knightwood	Rarry of Foxwarren	E. Chapman	Mrs L. Timmins
Foxwarren Max 89	D	Tri	Foxwarren Dodger	Foxwarren Jess	E. Chapman	Mrs E. Small
Foxwarren Ricky 88	D	Tri	Foxwarren Dodger	Foxmoor Talent of Foxwarren	E. Chapman	Mrs E. Small
Foxwarren Tegwyn at Digmoor 88	D	W	Foxwarren Dodger	Trasia Weazle	E. Chapman	Mrs & Mrs M. Regan
Galebern Tissy 88	B	T&W	Galebern Badger	Galebern Poppet	Mr & Mrs B. Tuck	Breeders

Name Year of Birth	S	Col	Sire	Dam	Breeder	Owner
Galebern Tola 88	B	W	Galebern Badger	Galebern Poppet	Mr & Mrs B. Tuck	Breeders
Galebern Trisca 88	B	W	Galebern Badger	Galebern Tandy	Mr & Mrs B. Tuck	Breeders
Glenholm Amy 89	B	T&W	Tiverton Buster	Tootsie of Glenholme	Mrs A. Milne	Mrs L. Timmins
Glenholm Blaze 89	D	Tri	Ridley Robber of Belmorr	Heliwar Skat of Glenholm	Mrs A. Milne	Breeder
Glenholm Ohmie 82	B	Tri	Lucky Pepper of Howdenbank	Glenholm Oddie	Mrs A. Milne	Breeder
Glenholm Spot of Treeburn 80	D	Tri	Drumbeg Hamish	Tibshelf Gemma	Mrs A. Milne	J. Gardner
Graylag Gypsy of	B	T&W	Kemmish's Rooster	Kemmish's Susie	Mr Kemmish	M. Gray
Ground Hill Butch 89	D	Tri	Ground Hill Kim	Ground Hill Pip	G. Simpson	Breeder
Ground Hill Kim 87	D	T&W	Ground Hill Badger	Ground Hill Sall	G. Simpson	Breeder
Ground Hill Midge 90	D	B&W	Ground Hill Badger	Ground Hill Sall	G. Simpson	Breeder
Ground Hill Pip 87	D	T&W	Ground Hill Ben	Ground Hill Rats	G. Simpson	Breeder
Ground Hill Sall 83	B	B&W	Brock	Bunty	G. Simpson	Breeder
Ground Hill Topper 90	B	Tri	Kenterfox Flint	Kenterfox Patch	K. Gould	G. Simpson
Ground Hill Twist 89	B	T&W	Ground Hill Kim	Tinker	G. Simpson	Breeder
Harfield Jake 89	D	T&W	Harfield Ted	Harfield Jill	B. Ludlan	A. Jones
Heathland Noble Sam 88	D	Tri	Gentile's Trigger	Gentile's Mindy	A. Gentile	R. Noble
Heliwar Ben 87	D	Tri	Heliwar Nipper	Heliwar Dixie	B. Jones	Breeder
Heliwar Betts 87	B	T&W	Heliwar Butch	Heliwar Judy	B. Jones	Breeder
Heliwar Bow 87	D	Tri	Heliwar Brock	Heliwar Sugar	B. Jones	Breeder

Name Year of Birth	S	Col	Sire	Dam	Breeder	Owner
Heliwar Bron 85	B	T&W	Heliwar Warwick	Heliwar Spud	B. Jones	Breeder
Heliwar Bullett 89	D	B&W	Heliwar Doc	Heliwar Josie	B. Jones	Breeder
Heliwar Conn 84	B	Tri	Heliwar Pro	Heliwar Mitz	B. Jones	Breeder
Heliwar Dela 88	B	T&W	Heliwar Butch	Heliwar Judy	B. Jones	Breeder
Heliwar Doc 87	D	T&W	Heliwar Skipper	Heliwar Bron	B. Jones	Breeder
Heliwar Don 87	D	T&W	Heliwar Skipper	Heliwar Bron	B. Jones	Breeder
Heliwar Flo 88	B	T&W	Davies Gol	Heliwar Boss	B. Jones	Breeder
Heliwar Gill 85	B	T&W	Heliwar Worry	Deliwar Dilly	B. Jones	Breeder
Heliwar Glen 88	D	Tri	Heliwar Nipper	Heliwar Dixie	B. Jones	Breeder
Heliwar Ivy 89	B	T&W	Heliwar Skipper	Heliwar Bron	B. Jones	Breeder
Heliwar Jess 89	B	Tri	Heliwar Sam	Heliwar Viv	B. Jones	Breeder
Heliwar Josie 87	B	B&W	Heliwar Kip	Heliwar Pip	B. Jones	Breeder
Heliwar Mel 89	B	Tri	Heliwar Don	Heliwar Coco	B. Jones	Breeder
Heliwar Midge 86	B	Tri	Heliwar Skipper	Heliwar Conn	B. Jones	Breeder
Heliwar Pinder 88	D	T&W	Heliwar Scoop	Heliwar Kess	B. Jones	Breeder
Heliwar Poll 89	B	B&W	Heliwar Skipper	Heliwar Bron	B. Jones	Breeder
Heliwar Radge 84	B	T&W	Heliwar Warwick	Heliwar Cassie	B. Jones	I. Marfleet
Heliwar Ramp 84	D	Tri	Smith's Duster	Heliwar Kit	B. Jones	Breeder
Heliwar Rocky 88	D	B&W	Heliwar Flint	Heliwar Dipper	B. Jones	Breeder
Heliwar Skat of Glenholm 88	B	Tri	Heliwar Mac	Heliwar Gill	B. Jones	Mrs A. Milne
Heliwar Skipper 83	D	Tri	Heliwar Skipper	Heliwar Needle	B. Jones	Breeder
Heliwar Snowy 88	B	B&W	Heliwar Chaff	Heliwar Coff	B. Jones	Breeder

Name Year of Birth	S	Col	Sire	Dam	Breeder	Owner
Heliwar Spud 83	B	B&W	Heliwar Bryn	Heliwar Min	B. Jones	Breeder
Heliwar Tess 89	B	T&W	Heliwar Glen	Heliwar Gill	B. Jones	Mrs E. Hogg
Heliwar Tiger 88	D	Tri	Heliwar Morgan	Heliwar Trip	B. Jones	Breeder
Heliwar Tissy 88	B	B&W	Heliwar Max	Heliwar Sarn	B. Jones	Breeder
Heliwar Toby 87	D	Tri	Heliwar Nipper	Heliwar Dixie	B. Jones	Breeder
Heliwar Tramp 87	B	Tri	Smith's Duster	Heliwar Kit	B. Jones	Breeder
Heliwar Triker 84	B	T&W	Heliwar Bran	Heliwar Mist	B. Jones	Breeder
Heliwar Ursula 89	B	T&W	Heliwar Skipper	Heliwar Trip	B. Jones	Breeder
Heliwar Vic 89	D	Tri	Heliwar Billy	Heliwar Tramp	B. Jones	Breeder
Heliwar Warwick 82	D	T&W	Heliwar Spike	Heliwar Jade	B. Jones	Breeder
Holmgate 89 Lupin of	B	T&W	Burton's Jack	Burton's Spice	S. Burton	L. Smith
Ibbsparr Pippa-dee 89	D	T&W	Prosper	Spit	Mrs E. Rickard	Mr & Mrs A. Ibbotson
Jalus 86 Joseph of	D	T&W	Clystlands Captain	Tufter Bustle of Jalus	Mrs Green	J. Luscott
Jalus Quincy 89	D	T&W	Joseph of Jalus	Jalus Polly	J. Luscott	Breeder
Kapaldo Bandit 85	D	T&W	Tommy Trouble	Goulding's Yan	Goulding	A. Lewis
Kapaldo Joe 86	D	T&W	Kapaldo Spyder	Kapaldo Sian	A. Lewis	Breeder
Kapaldo Rags 86	B	T&W	Tommy Trouble	Goulding's Yan	Goulding	A. Lewis
Kapaldo Spyder 83	D	T&W	Gould's Tornado	Gould's Jet	K. Gould	A. Lewis
Kapaldo 86 Taff of	D	T&W	David Davies Chip	David Davies Di	D. Jones	A. Lewis

Name Year of Birth	S	Col	Sire	Dam	Breeder	Owner
Kenterfox Bess 89	B	B&W	Kenterfox Flint	Joker	K. Gould	Breeder
Kenterfox Bexx 90	B	W	Kenterfox Flint	Kenterfox Liz	K. Gould	M. Knowles
Kenterfox Bonnie 90	B	T&W	Kenterfox Flint	Kenterfox Patch	K. Gould	Breeder
Kenterfox Cindy 89	B	B&W	Kenterfox Flint II	Kenterfox Vixon	K. Gould	Breeder
Kenterfox Clint 88	D	T&W	Kenterfox Flint	Kenterfox Judy	K. Gould	Breeder
Kenterfox Clyde 90	D	Tri	Kenterfox Flint	Kenterfox Patch	K. Gould	Breeder
Kenterfox Connie 89	B	Tri	Kenterfox Flint	Kenterfox Judy	K. Gould	Breeder
Kenterfox Drizle 89	B	Tri	Kenterfox Flint	Kenterfox Patch	K. Gould	Breeder
Kenterfox Flint 85	D	Tri	Rex	Floss	K. Gould	Breeder
Kenterfox Flint II 86	D	Tri	Kenterfox Flint	Vixon	K. Gould	Breeder
Kenterfox Jack 88	D	T&W	Stormer	Vixon	K. Gould	Breeder
Kenterfox Jay 87	B	T&W	Kenterfox Flint	Joker	K. Gould	Breeder
Kenterfox Jill 83	B	B&W	Nip	Vixon	M. White	K. Gould
Kenterfox Judy I 84	B	T&W	Thunder	Vixon	K. Gould	Breeder
Kenterfox Judy II 85	B	T&W	Thunder	Kenterfox Jill	K. Gould	Breeder
Kenterfox Lady 89	B	B&W	Kenterfox Flint	Joker	K. Gould	Breeder
Kenterfox Mystro 86	D	T&W	Kenterfox Flint	Kenterfox Judy I	K. Gould	Breeder
Kenterfox Pat 84	B	T&W	Thunder	Vixon	K. Gould	Breeder
Kenterfox Patch 88	B	Tri	Stormer	Vixon	K. Gould	Breeder
Kenterfox Prince 89	D	B&W	Kenterfox Flint	Kenterfox Jay	K. Gould	Breeder
Kenterfox Rascal 89	D	B&W	Kenterfox Flint II	Kenterfox Vixon II	K. Gould	Breeder
Kenterfox Rip 87	D	Tri	Kenterfox Flint	Joker	K. Gould	Breeder

Name Year of Birth	S	Col	Sire	Dam	Breeder	Owner
Kenterfox Snowy 89	D	W	Snowy	Kenterfox Judy II	K. Gould	Breeder
Kenterfox Spot 88	B	Tri	Stormer	Vixon	K. Gould	Breeder
Kenterfox Stormer 89	D	B&W	Kenterfox Flint	Kenterfox Patch	K. Gould	Breeder
Kenterfox Tess 86	B	W	Kenterfox Flint	Vixon	K. Gould	Breeder
Kenterfox Tiny 88	B	B&W	Kenterfox Flint	Joker	K. Gould	Breeder
Kildale Marie 83	B	Tri	Kildale Patch	Kildale Breckon II	F. Thompson	Breeder
Lingmoor Wisp 89	B	Tri	Parkin's Russ	Parkin's Candy	S. Parkin	C. Gaskell
Littleheath's Tuff Nutt 89	B	T&W	Jervis' Judge	Jervis Nettle	M. Jervis	Miss J. Yerbury
Lountwood Flixx 90	B	T&W	Lountwood Sam	Lountwood Ace	G. Shaw	M. Knowles
Lountwood Sam 88	D	T&W	Lountwood Jake	Lountwood Peg	G. Shaw	Breeder
Lountwood Vixen 86	B	T&W	Lountwood Jake	Lountwood Bess	G. Shaw	Breeder
Margove Butcher 88	D	T&W	Ground Hill Kim	Ground Hill Rats	G. Simpson	N. Porritt
Mayfleet Floss 89	B	T&W	Foxwarren Jet	Heliwar Radge	I. Marfleet	Breeder
Mayfleet Kit 89	B	T&W	Foxwarren Jet	Heliwar Radge	I. Marfleet	Breeder
Minden Jill at Culrain 86	B	T&W	Bratchie's Jock	Minden Tess	Mrs Murray	Mrs A. Maclaughlin
Minden Sam 86	D	Tri	Bratchie's Jock	Minden Tess	Mrs C. Murray	Mrs L. Miller
Minden Spike 84	D	Tri	Holiday's Todd	Crisp of Minden	Mrs C. Murray	Breeder
Minden Spot 86	D	Tri	Bratchie's Jock	Minden Tess	Mrs C. Murray	Mrs L. Miller
Minden Tess 85	B	Tri	Minden Rascal	Crisp of Minden	Mrs C. Murray	Breeder
Mischief Whitnoles Midge 87	B	T&W	Floyd's Digger	Tufter Sally	A. Floyd	Miss J. Clive

Name Year of Birth	S	Col	Sire	Dam	Breeder	Owner
Modbury Harriers Ben II 89	D	Br&W	Modbury Harriers Ben I	Modbury Harriers Gem	G. Baskerville	Breeder
Modbury Harriers Heidi 86	B	Br&W	Modbury Harriers Mustard II	Modbury Harriers Sugar	G. Baskerville	Breeder
Modbury Harriers Jenna 89	B	Tri	Modbury Harriers George	Modbury Harriers Tiz	G. Baskerville	Breeder
Modbury Harriers Misty II 89	B	T&W	Modbury Harriers Ben II	Modbury Harriers Misty I	G. Baskerville	Breeder
Modbury Harriers Nan 88	B	T&W	Modbury Harriers Luke	Modbury Harriers Nell	G. Baskerville	Breeder
Modbury Harriers Nell 85	B	Br&W	Modbury Harriers Sam	Modbury Harriers Carol	G. Baskerville	Breeder
Modbury Harriers Nougat 89	B	Br&W	Modbury Harriers Luke	Modbury Harriers Nell	G. Baskerville	Breeder
Modbury Harriers Pied Piper 90	D	T&W	Modbury Harriers George	Modbury Harriers Jenna	G. Baskerville	Breeder
Modbury Harriers Tim 89	D	T&W	Modbury Harriers Luke	Modbury Harriers Nell	G. Baskerville	Breeder
Modbury Harriers Trump Card 89	D	T&W	Modbury Harriers George	Modbury Harriers Nan	G. Baskerville	Breeder
Modbury Harriers Weasel 87	B	T&W	Modbury Harriers Luke	Modbury Harriers Tiz	G. Baskerville	Breeder
Moorsview Flash 86	B	Tri	Foxtor Flashman	Foxtor Lucky	A. Perkins	R. Johns
Moorsview Judy 89	B	Tri	Driver	Moorsview Flash	Mr & Mrs R. Johns	Breeder
Moorsview Patches 89	D	Tri	Driver	Moorsview Flash	Mr & Mrs R. Johns	Breeder

Name Year of Birth	S	Col	Sire	Dam	Breeder	Owner
Nordach Gone Away 89	B	Br&W	Somervale Jake	Somervale Patch	Mrs A. Rees	Breeder
Nordach Stirrup Cup 89	B	Tri	Somervale Jake	Somervale Patch	Mrs A. Rees	Breeder
Ottaswell 84 Fudge of	B	T&W	Sayner's Spider	Sayner's Waffle	Mrs B. Sayner	A. Jones
Ottaswell 83 Just Barney of	D	T&W	McWilliam's Tim	Spencer's Bracken	Mr & Mrs M. Spencer	Mr & Mrs D. Hunt
Pebbles Manor 89	B	Tri	Gould's Flint	Gould's Floss II	K. Gould	D. Masters
Pixie Peterose 90	B	T&W	Deakin's Poacher	Deakin's Tic	Mrs W. Deakin	Miss R. Rayner
Polly's Delight 88	B	T&W	Brinkley's Tinker	Dines Penny	Mrs A. Dines	Mrs J. Raymond
Raeburn Suzie 88	B	Tri	Minden Sam	Minden Smudge of Raeburn	Mrs L. Miller	Breeder
Raemill Rosie of Broomloan 90	B	Tri	Minden Spike	Raeburn Suzie	Mrs L. Miller	Breeder
Ragford Bennett 88	D	T&W	David Davies Scrap	Clystlands Cider of Ragford	Mrs P. Hancock	Breeder
Ragford Craftsman at Clystlands 87	D	T&W	Ridley Red Alert	Clystlands Cider of Ragford	Mrs P. Hancock	T. Eggins
Ragford Crofter 87	D	T&W	Ridley Red Alert	Clystlands Cider of Ragford	Mrs P. Hancock	Breeder
Ragford Punch 84	D	Tri	Young Spider	Clystlands Bryony	Mrs P. Hancock	Breeder
Ragford Rascal 88	D	T&W	David Davies Scrap	Clystlands Cider of Ragford	Mrs P. Hancock	Breeder
Ragford Rennet 88	B	Tri	David Davies Scrap	Clystlands Cider of Ragford	Mrs P. Hancock	Breeder
Ragford Soda 90	B	Tri	David Davies Scrap	Clystlands Cider of Ragford	Mrs P. Hancock	Breeder

Name Year of Birth	S	Col	Sire	Dam	Breeder	Owner
Ragford Whiskey 80	B	T&W	Foxwarren Sinbad	Ragford Bramble	Mrs P. Hancock	Breeder
Ragford Wurzel 85	D	Tri	Russue Rapper	Clystlands Bryony	Mrs P. Hancock	Mrs M. Cutler
Ratpack 85 Bullet of the	D	T&W	Mcintyre's Bill	Blythe's Nip	B. Blythe	S. Hutchins
Ratpack 90 Clyde of the	D	Tri	Bullet of the Ratpack	Suzie of the Ratpack	Miss E. Dorling	S. Hutchins
Ratpack 90 Cuddles of the	B	T&W	Bullet of the Ratpack	Coleridge's Suzie	S. Hutchins	J. Mann
Ratpack 89 Lucy of the	B	T&W	Bullet of the Ratpack	Nell of the Ratpack	M. Brinkley	S. Hutchins
Ratpack 85 Nell of the	B	Tri	David Davies Tally	David Davies Trim	S. Hutchins	D. Jones
Ratpack 89 Spike of the	D	T&W	Bullet of the Ratpack	Nell of the Ratpack	M. Brinkley	S. Hutchins
Redwood Captain 90	D	Tri	Ridley Pilot	Hazel of Redwood	Mrs J. Ibbett	Breeder
Redwood 86 Hazel of	B	T&W	Tarsia Splinter	Tarsia Phantom	Mrs Brewer	Mrs J. Ibbett
Redwood Lace of Westbeck 90	B	Tri	Ridley Pilot	Hazel of Redwood	Mrs J. Ibbett	Breeder
Redwood Little Meg 90	B	T&W	Redwood Tyke	Ridley Red Flight	Mrs J. Ibbett	D. Cobourne
Redwood Lucinda 89	B	Tri	Redwood Pilot	Tasha of Redwood	Mrs J. Ibbett	Mr & Mrs I. Sanford
Redwood Meg 88	B	T&W	Tek of Redwood	Hazel of Redwood	Mrs J. Ibbett	Miss T. Barnfather
Redwood Nettle 89	B	W	Redwood Pilot	Tasha of Redwood	Mrs J. Ibbett	Breeder
Redwood Peppers 90	D	T&W	Ridley Pilot	Hazel of Redwood	Mrs J. Ibbett	Miss V. Harper

Name Year of Birth	S	Col	Sire	Dam	Breeder	Owner
Redwood Pilot 87	D	T&W	Oakley Sailor	Ridley Red Flight	Mrs J. Ibbett	Breeder
Redwood Sam 90	D	T&W	Redwood Tyke	Ridley Red Flight	Mrs J. Ibbett	P. Eddery
Redwood Suzy 88	B	T&W	Tek of Redwood	Hazel of Redwood	Mrs J. Ibbett	Breeder
Redwood Tackles Ridley 90	D	T&W	Ridley Pilot	Hazel of Redwood	Mrs J. Ibbett	Mrs S. Atter
Redwood Tyke 88	D	T&W	Tek of Redwood	Garon's Suzy	Mrs J. Ibbett	Mrs Garon
Ridley Reckless of Glenholm 88	B	Tri	Ridley Robber of Belmorr	Clystlands Belinda Ridley	Mrs S. Atter	Mrs A. Milne
Ridley Red Alert 88	D	T&W	Hursley Pilot	Ridley Redwing	Mrs S. Atter	Breeder
Ridley 85 Red Falcon of	D	T&W	Ridley Red Alert	Borthwick Star	Mrs I. Eversett	Mrs. M. Moorey
Ridley Red Flight 84	B	T&W	Hursley Pilot	Ridley Redwing	Mrs S. Atter	Mrs J. Ibbett
Ridley Replica 88	B	Tri	Ridley Robber of Belmorr	Clystlands Belinda Ridley	Mrs S. Atter	Breeder
Ridley Robber of Belmorr 86	D	Tri	Ridley Red Alert	Foxworker Tara	Mrs M. Shannon	Mrs J. Morrison
Ridley Rowena of Reynwood 88	B	Tri	Ridley Robber of Belmorr	Clystlands Belinda Ridley	Mrs S. Atter	Mr & Mrs G. Burton
Ridley Ruffian 88	D	Tri	Ridley Robber of Belmorr	Clystlands Belinda Ridley	Mrs S. Atter	C. Chapman
Ripling Bullett 83	D	Tri	Read's Sam	Read's Hubble	Mr & Mrs Harris	Mr & Mrs S. Collis
Ripling Hermit 89	D	T&W	Ripling Revel	Ripling Hobby	Mr & Mrs S. Collis	Breeders
Ripling Hobby 84	B	T&W	Ripling Bullet	Tarsia Plover	Mr & Mrs S. Collis	Breeders
Ripling Pippet 84	B	T&W	Ripling Bullet	Tarsia Plover	Mr & Mrs S. Collis	Breeders
Ripling Rail 90	B	T&W	Ripling Revel	Ripling Hobby	Mr & Mrs S. Collis	Breeders

Name Year of Birth	S	Col	Sire	Dam	Breeder	Owner
Ripling Revel 87	D	T&W	David Davies Scrap	Ripling Wispa	Mr & Mrs S. Collis	Breeders
Ripling Solar 87	B	T&W	David Davies Scrap	Ripling Wispa	Mr & Mrs S. Collis	Breeders
Romaco Brock 89	D	B&W	David Davies Piper	Sayner's Trixie	Mrs B. Sayner	R. Miles & Miss R. Copping
Romaco Trot Boy 89	D	T&W	Tiger of Romaco	Maud	Mrs A. Titchner	R. Miles & Miss R. Copping
Roncols Hunter 88	D	T&W	Dinlanzet Leo	Dinlanzet Midge	Mrs A. Zetter	R. Crockett
Roncols Lucy of Larrikins 89	B	B&W	Roncols Hunter	Spainshall Jill	R. Crockett	Mrs A. Burgess
Roncols Meg 89	B	B&W	Roncols Hunter	Roncols Jill	R. Crockett	Breeder
Roncols Odie 90	B	B&W	Roncols Hunter	Roncols Sadie	R. Crockett	Breeder
Roncols Ratty 90	B	B&W	Roncols Hunter	Roncols Sadie	R. Crockett	Breeder
Roncols Tug 90	D	B&W	Roncols Hunter	Roncols Sadie	R. Crocket	Breeder
Ryemill Dizzy 83	B	Tri	East Essex Sam	Ryemill Penny	Mr & Mrs P. Edge	Breeder
Ryemill Fudge 81	B	T&W	East Essex Sam	Ryemill Penny	Mr & Mrs P. Edge	Breeders
Ryemill Mighty Mouse 87	B	Tri	Ludlam's Dan	Ryemill Dizzy	Mr & Mrs P. Edge	Breeders
Scarborough 87 Microchip of	D	T&W	Schofield's Pip	Chaloner's Ski	Mr & Mrs Schofield	P. Messruther
Shellfield Pop 89	D	T&W	Ragford Crofter	Shellfield Snap	N. Handy	Breeder
Shotley Worry 88	B	T&W	Hume's Gravel	Weardale Tina	D. Hume	Miss M. Benedetto
Somervale Charlie 84	D	T&W	Somervale Toby	Somervale Jessie	Mr & Mrs E. Rich	Breeders
Somervale Danny 87	D	Tri	Robert's Toby	Somervale Jasmin	Mr & Mrs E. Rich	Breeders
Somervale Jake 85	D	Tri	Kemmish's Rooster	Somervale Jessie	E. Rich	Mrs A. Rees
Somervale Jasmin 85	B	W	Kemmish's Rooster	Somervale Jessie	Mr & Mrs E. Rich	Breeders
Somervale Jessie 81	B	Tri	Kanawha Jasper	Kanawha Bubbles	Mr & Mrs E. Rich	Breeders

Name Year of Birth	S	Col	Sire	Dam	Breeder	Owner
Somervale Katey 88	B	T&W	Somervale Danny	Somervale Jessie	Mr & Mrs E. Rich	Breeders
Somervale Molly 87	B	T&W	Foxwarren Scrumpy	Somervale Jessie	Mr & Mrs E. Rich	Breeders
Somervale Raz of Graylag 86	B	B&W	Somervale George	Somervale Jessie	Mr & Mrs E. Rich	M. Gray
Somervale Rip 85	D	W	Kemmish's Rooster	Somervale Jessie	Mr & Mrs E. Rich	Breeders
South Shropshire Sparkle 84	B	Tri	David Davies Toby	South Shropshire Spice	M. Roeson	S. Dixon
Spademan Judy 88	B	T&W	Kenterfox Flint	Kenterfox Judy I	K. Gould	M. Mann
Spademan Percy 88	B	T&W	Kenterfox Flint	Kenterfox Judy I	K. Gould	M. Mann
Swerbrook Style 82	B	Tri	Heythrop Tinker	Swerbrook Spary	Mrs J. Cox	Breeder
Tarsia Donna at Clystlands 86	B	T&W	Tarsia Splinter	Tarsia Phantom	Mrs A. Brewer	R. Hadley
Tarsia Dicky Bird 85	D	T&W	Tarsia Shrike	Tarsia Cello	J. Mackereth	Mr & Mrs R. Elias
Taw Vale Tonto 83	B	T&W	Taw Vale Boomer	Taw Vale Mischief	J. Coates	Mrs M. Cutler
Tebloclin Tosh 89	D	T&W	Kenterfox Flint	Kenterfox Jay	K. Gould	Mrs L. Colbert
Tithebarn Bracken 89	D	T&W	Blencathra Badger	Tithebarn Jan	J. Mackereth	D. Pearce
Tithebarn Cap 90	D	Tri	Richmond's Brock	Tithebarn Jan	J. Mackereth	Breeder
Tiverton Buster 87	D	Tri	Belmorr Sonny	Tiverton Boo Boo	J. Valentine	Breeder
Tiverton Tike 89	D	Tri	Timberbush Hot	Tiverton Zoey Toddy	J. Valentine	R. Willoy
Tiverton Twist 89	B	T&W	Timberbush Hot	Tiverton Zoey Toddy	J. Valentine	Breeder
Tiverton Zoey 87	B	Tri	Belmorr Sonny	Tiverton Boo Boo	J. Valentine	Breeder
Torrington Stormer 89	D	Tri	David Davies Scrap	David Davies Lucky	D. Jones	Mrs. R. Wilford
Trebloclin Tosh 89	D	T&W	Kenterfox Flint	Kenterfox Jay	J. Valentine	Mrs L. Colbert

Name Year of Birth	S	Col	Sire	Dam	Breeder	Owner
Treeburn Lady Dinky 81	B	T&W	Glenholm Spot of Treeburn	Elsa of Firpark	Mrs O. Gardner	Breeder
Treeburn Rusty Dinky Lad 83	D	T&W	Threehouses Bronco	Treeburn Lady	Mrs O. Gardner	Mr & Mrs Gardner
Trystlands Toska of Kelco 88	B	Tri	Trystlands Oscar	Trystland's Glenburn Jill	J. Fullerton	Miss L. Allan
Tutmur Ashley 87	B	Tri	Somervale Toby	Sprule of Tutmur	Mr & Mrs M. Tuttle	Breeders
Tutmur Maple 89	B	B&W	Eskdale Beck at Clystlands	Tutmur Ashley	Mr & Mrs M. Tuttle	Breeders
Tutmur 88 Solo of	D	Tri	Oliver's Turk	Oliver's Hookey	R. Oliver	Mr & Mrs J. Tuttle
Tutmur 83 Spruce of	B	Tri	Heythrop Timber	Heythrop Thistle	R. Bigland	Mr & Mrs M. Tuttle
Tutmur Sweet Chestnut 89	B	B&W	Eskdale Beck at Clystlands	Tutmur Ashley	Mr & Mrs M. Tuttle	Breeder
Tutmur Topper 86	D	T&W	Tiger of Romaco	Sprule of Tutmur	Mrs J. Tuttle	P. Mayes
Tutmur Willow 89	B	Tri	Eskdale Beck at Clystlands	Tutmur Ashley	Mr & Mrs M. Tuttle	Breeders
Tymarsh Ella 88	B	Tri	Kenterfox Flint	Kenterfox Jill	K. Gould	Mr & Mrs J. Morgan
Tymarsh Erik 89	D	Tri	Kenterfox Flint	Kenterfox Tiny	K. Gould	Mr & Mrs J. Morgan
Warmstone George 89	D	Tri	Warmstone Poacher	Tymarsh Ella	P. Morgan	Mr & Mrs A. Graham
Warmstone Maddie 89	B	Tri	Warmstone Poacher	Tymarsh Ella	P. Morgan	Mr & Mrs A. Graham
Watling Joe 89	D	Tri	Watling Oscar	Watling Trapper	R. Hadley	Breeder
Watling Judy 87	B	Tri	Watling Oscar	Shadow of Watling	R. Hadley	Breeder
Watling Lulu 87	B	Tri	Foxwarren Eddie	Watling Smurf	K. Robinson	R. Hadley
Watling Misty 87	B	T&W	Watling Oscar	Watling Trapper	R. Hadley	Breeder
Watling Toby 84	D	Tri	Stanford's Todd	Shadow of Watling	R. Hadley	M. Forrester

Name Year of Birth	S	Col	Sire	Dam	Breeder	Owner
Weardale Gravity of Duxbury 85	B	T&W	Spoor's Rip	Spoor's Sherry	R. Spoor	Miss M. Benedetto
Westmead Tizzy 86	B	Tri	Beacon Jock of Westmead	Katie of Wwestmead	M. Baker	Mrs J. Stanley
Whitnoles Fizzy 89	B	T&W	Foxwarren Scrumpy	Mischief Whitnoles Midge	Mrs L. Clive	Breeder
Whitnoles Jester 89	D	Tri	Foxwarren Scrumpy	Whitnoles Molly	Mrs L. Clive	Mrs R. Nash
Whitnoles Jolly Swagman	B	T&W	Foxwarren Scrumpy	Mischief Whitnoles Midge	Mrs L. Clive	Breeder
Whitnoles Trooper 89	D	Tri	Foxwarren Scrumpy	Whitnoles Molly	Mrs L. Clive	Mrs R. Nash
Woodlands Dash 85	B	T&W	Tiger of Romaco	Woodlands Pepper	Mrs R. Hopkins	Breeder
Young Toff 83	D	B&W	Tuck's Bunter	Tuck's Poppet	Mr & Mrs B. Tuck	Breeder

BRITISH CHAMPIONSHIP SHOW RESULTS:
1990/91

Parson Jack Russell Terriers made their début in breed classes at a British Championship Show in May 1990. * indicates Best of Breed winner.

Show (No. of dogs/entries) Judge	Owner, Best Dog, DoB, Breeder, Sire – Dam. Owner, Best Bitch, DoB, Breeder, Sire – Dam.
Scottish KC, May (22/39) J. Falconer	Ross's BLENCATHRA BADGER*, 10/2/84, br Exh., Foxwarren Tigger – Blencathra Dorset. Atter's RIDLEY REPLICA, 6/5/88, br Exh., Ridley Robber – Clystlands Belinda Ridley.
South Wales (18/23) Simon Jackson	Wilford's CLYSTLANDS TANGLE*, 21/7/89, br Exh., Clystlands Rebel – Dolly of Clystlands. Samway's RIDLEY REBECCA OF CASSACRE, 21/11/89, br Atter, Ridley Red Alert – Clystlands Belinda Ridley.
Blackpool (18/31) Frank Jones	Hancock's RAGFORD RASCAL*, 25/1/88, br Exh., Scrap – Clystlands Cider at Ragford. Ross's BLENCATHRA NETTLE, 10/2/84, br Exh., Foxwarren Tigger – Blencathra Dorset.
Scottish KC, Aug. (22/32) Barry Jones	Atter's RIDLEY POACHER*, 21/11/89, br Exh., Ridley Red Alert – Clystlands Belinda Ridley. Samway's RIDLEY REBECCA OF CASSACRE, 21/11/89, br Atter, Ridley Red Alert – Clystlands Belinda Ridley.

Darlington (41/50)
Harold Wright

Simpson's GROUND HILL BUTCH, 2/8/89, br Exh., Ground Hill Kim – Ground Hill Pip.
Murray's MINDEN TESS, 28/6/85, br Exh., Minden Rascal – Crisp of Minden.

Ladies KA (31/41)
Peter Thompson

Wilford's TOBIAS AT CLYSTLANDS, 9/7/88, br D. Jones, David Davies Scrap – David Davies Spot.
Simpson's GROUND HILL PIP*, 2/7/87, br Exh., Ground Hill Ben – Ground Hill Rats.

Crufts 1991 (34/37)
Andrew Small

Ross's BLENCATHRA BADGER*, 10/2/84, br Exh., Foxwarren Tigger – Blencathra Dorset.
Atter's RIDLEY REPLICA, 6/5/88, br Exh., Ridley Robber – Clystlands Belinda Ridley.

APPENDIX 3

WHELPING TABLE

Date of service / Date of whelping

Date of service	1	2	3	4	5	6	7	8	9	10	11	12	13	14	15	16	17	18	19	20	21	22	23	24	25	26	27	28	29	30	31
Jan	1	2	3	4	5	6	7	8	9	10	11	12	13	14	15	16	17	18	19	20	21	22	23	24	25	26	27	28	29	30	31
Mar	4	5	6	7	8	9	10	11	12	13	14	15	16	17	18	19	20	21	22	23	24	25	26	27	28	29	30	31	1 Apr	2	3
Feb	1	2	3	4	5	6	7	8	9	10	11	12	13	14	15	16	17	18	19	20	21	22	23	24	25	26	27	28	–	–	–
Apr	4	5	6	7	8	9	10	11	12	13	14	15	16	17	18	19	20	21	22	23	24	25	26	27	28	29	30	1 May	–	–	–
Mar	1	2	3	4	5	6	7	8	9	10	11	12	13	14	15	16	17	18	19	20	21	22	23	24	25	26	27	28	29	30	31
May	2	3	4	5	6	7	8	9	10	11	12	13	14	15	16	17	18	19	20	21	22	23	24	25	26	27	28	29	30	31	1 June
Apr	1	2	3	4	5	6	7	8	9	10	11	12	13	14	15	16	17	18	19	20	21	22	23	24	25	26	27	28	29	30	–
June	2	3	4	5	6	7	8	9	10	11	12	13	14	15	16	17	18	19	20	21	22	23	24	25	26	27	28	29	30	1 July	–
May	1	2	3	4	5	6	7	8	9	10	11	12	13	14	15	16	17	18	19	20	21	22	23	24	25	26	27	28	29	30	31
July	2	3	4	5	6	7	8	9	10	11	12	13	14	15	16	17	18	19	20	21	22	23	24	25	26	27	28	29	30	31	1 Aug
June	1	2	3	4	5	6	7	8	9	10	11	12	13	14	15	16	17	18	19	20	21	22	23	24	25	26	27	28	29	30	–
Aug	2	3	4	5	6	7	8	9	10	11	12	13	14	15	16	17	18	19	20	21	22	23	24	25	26	27	28	29	30	31	–
July	1	2	3	4	5	6	7	8	9	10	11	12	13	14	15	16	17	18	19	20	21	22	23	24	25	26	27	28	29	30	31
Sept	1	2	3	4	5	6	7	8	9	10	11	12	13	14	15	16	17	18	19	20	21	22	23	24	25	26	27	28	29	30	1 Oct
Aug	1	2	3	4	5	6	7	8	9	10	11	12	13	14	15	16	17	18	19	20	21	22	23	24	25	26	27	28	29	30	31
Oct	2	3	4	5	6	7	8	9	10	11	12	13	14	15	16	17	18	19	20	21	22	23	24	25	26	27	28	29	30	31	1 Nov
Sept	1	2	3	4	5	6	7	8	9	10	11	12	13	14	15	16	17	18	19	20	21	22	23	24	25	26	27	28	29	30	–
Nov	2	3	4	5	6	7	8	9	10	11	12	13	14	15	16	17	18	19	20	21	22	23	24	25	26	27	28	29	30	1 Dec	–
Oct	1	2	3	4	5	6	7	8	9	10	11	12	13	14	15	16	17	18	19	20	21	22	23	24	25	26	27	28	29	30	31
Dec	2	3	4	5	6	7	8	9	10	11	12	13	14	15	16	17	18	19	20	21	22	23	24	25	26	27	28	29	30	31	1 Jan
Nov	1	2	3	4	5	6	7	8	9	10	11	12	13	14	15	16	17	18	19	20	21	22	23	24	25	26	27	28	29	30	–
Jan	2	3	4	5	6	7	8	9	10	11	12	13	14	15	16	17	18	19	20	21	22	23	24	25	26	27	28	29	30	31	–
Dec	1	2	3	4	5	6	7	8	9	10	11	12	13	14	15	16	17	18	19	20	21	22	23	24	25	26	27	28	29	30	31
Feb	1	2	3	4	5	6	7	8	9	10	11	12	13	14	15	16	17	18	19	20	21	22	23	24	25	26	27	28	1 Mar	2	3

APPENDIX 4

BIBLIOGRAPHY

Cavill, David, *All About Mating, Whelping and Weaning* (Pelham Books) 1981

Davies, E. M. L., *Memoir of The Rev. John Russell and his outdoor life* (Chatto & Windus) 1878

Edney, Andrew, *Dog and Cat Nutrition* (Pergamon) 1982

Evans, Jim and White, Kay, *The Book of the Bitch* (Henston) 1988

Evans, Jim and White, Kay, *The Doglopaedia* (Update – Siebert Publications) 1987

Fiennes, Richard and Alice, *The Natural History of the Dog* (Weidenfeld and Nicolson) 1968

Hobson, Jeremy, *Working Terriers, Management and Training* (The Crowood Press) 1987

Horner, Tom, *Take them Round, Please* (David and Charles) 1975

Horner, Tom, *Terriers of the World: Their History and Characteristics* (Faber) 1984

Jackson, Jean and Frank, *The Making of the Parson Jack Russell Terrier* (Boydell and Brewer) 1986

Jackson, Jean and Frank, *Parson Jack Russell Terriers* (Crowood Press) 1990

Lucas, Sir Jocelyn, *Hunt and Working Terriers* (Chapman and Hall) 1931

Morris, Desmond, *Dogwatching* (Jonathan Cape) 1986

O'Farrell, Valerie, *Manual of Canine Behaviour* (British Small Animal Veterinary Association) 1976

Plummer, Brian, *The Working Terrier* (Boydell and Brewer) 1978

Robinson, Roy, *Genetics for Dog Breeders* (Pergamon Press) 1982

Sandys-Winsch, Godfrey, *Your Dog and the Law* (Shaw and Sons) 1978

Serpell, James, *In the Company of Animals* (Blackwood) 1986

Silvernail, Evelyn L. *The New Complete Fox Terrier* (Howell) 1976

Sutton, Catherine, *Dog Shows and Show Dogs* (K & R Books) 1980

Turner, Trevor, *Veterinary Notes for Dog Owners* (Popular Dogs) 1990

Williams, Elsie, *Fox Terrier* (Popular Dogs) 1965

INDEX